Look What You Can Make With
BOXES

Over 90 Pictured Crafts and Dozens of Other Ideas

Edited by Lorianne Siomades

Look What You Can Make With

Boxes

Edited and designed by Lorianne Siomades
Photographs by Hank Schneider

Boyds Mills Press

Designer:

Lorianne Siomades

Production:

Rachel Bakota

Craftmakers:

Yvette Boucher

Paulette Carlson

Nancy C. Duhaime

Lorianne Siomades

Contributors:

Judy Burke

Jennifer Carling

Diane Cherkerzian

Laurie J. Edwards

Kathy Everett

M. Mable Lunz

Carol McCall

Beth Murray

Wanda Payne

James W. Perrin Jr.

Kathy Ross

Constance Sharp

Lorianne Siomades

Sharon Dunn Umnik

Colleen Van Blaricom

Hilda K. Watkins

D.A. Woodliff

Published by Bell Books
Boyds Mills Press, Inc.
A Highlights Company
815 Church Street
Honesdale, Pennsylvania 18431
Printed in China

Publisher Cataloging-in-Publication Data
Look what you can make with boxes: over 90 pictured crafts and dozens of other ideas /
edited by Lorianne Siomades ; photographs by Hank Schneider.—1st. ed.
[48]p. : Ill. ; cm.
Summary : Toys, games and other ideas all from boxes.
ISBN 1-56397-704-4
1. Handicraft—Juvenile literature. 2. Boxes—Juvenile literature.
[1. Handicraft. 2. Boxes.] I. Siomades, Lorianne. II. Schneider, Hank, ill. III. Title.
745.54—dc21   1998   AC   CIP
Library of Congress Catalog Card Number 97-76815

First edition, 1998
Book designed by Lorianne Siomades
The text of this book is set in 10pt Avante Garde Demi, titles 43pt Gill Sans Extra Bold

10 9 8 7 6

Getting Started

This book is filled with fun, easy-to-make crafts, and each one begins with a box. You'll find a wide variety of things to make, including toys, games, and gifts.

Directions

Before you start each craft, read the directions and look closely at the photograph, but remember—it's up to you to make the crafts your own. If we decorate a craft with markers, but you want to use glitter paint and stickers, go for it. Feel free to stray from our directions and invent new crafts.

Work Area

It's a good idea to keep your work area covered. Old newspapers, brown paper (from grocery bags), or old sheets work well. Also, protect your clothes by wearing a smock. A big, old shirt does the job and gives you room to move. Finally, remember to clean up when you've finished.

Materials

You'll need a lot of boxes, so start saving now. Ask friends and relatives to help. Keep your craft-making supplies together, and before making a craft, check the "You Will Need" list to make sure that you have everything. We often give suggestions for what kind of box works well for each craft. Also, since you'll need scissors and glue, tape, or a stapler for almost every craft, we don't list these supplies. (We do list craft glue—which is tackier than regular glue—when it helps to use it.)

Other Stuff

When we show several similar crafts, we'll often list numbered directions that apply to all of the crafts, then specific directions for each craft.

Free painting tip: Sometimes boxes have a shiny coating, and poster paint won't stick to them. Try mixing liquid soap with the paint. It works for us. You could also use acrylic paints.

That's about all. So, find a bunch of boxes, select a craft that you like, and have some fun. Before you know it, you'll be showing everyone what you made with boxes.

Little Box Safari

Set off to explore the wilderness . . . and keep your eyes open for tigers, hippos, and elephants!

You Will Need:

- various small boxes
- construction paper
- paints
- foam paper
- markers
- felt

More Ideas

Make an entire jungle scene with foam-paper rivers and waterfalls, papier-mâché hills, and box lions and turtles.

Or, select a different climate and create the animals that live there. Try making a desert scene, an Arctic scene, or an ocean scene.

To Invent an Animal

1 Paint a box or cover it with paper.

2 Cut out arms, legs, a tail, and other details from paper. Glue them on.

To Make the Lion

Paint a rectangular box. Cut out legs, a tail, and a head from foam paper. Glue them on. Add details with markers and cut foam paper.

To Make the Hippo

Paint a square box. Glue on foam-paper legs, a back, a tail, and a head. Add features with markers and cut paper.

Be on the lookout for all kinds of boxes, too. That's what you'll need to make these animals.

To Make the Tiger

Paint a box. Glue on legs, a tail, and a head cut from paper and felt. Add details with markers. Glue on felt stripes.

To Make the Monkey

Paint a box. Glue on cut-paper arms, legs, a tail, and a head. Add details with markers.

To Make the Elephant

Paint a flat rectangular box. Cut a body with legs on it from foam paper. Wrap it around the box and glue the sides to the box. Add a foam-paper trunk, ears, eyes, and toes. Add details with markers and cut paper.

To Make the Trees

Glue paper onto a rectangular box. Cut palm branches and coconuts from paper and glue them to the top.

Camera

Snap away the hours with a handmade toy camera.

1 To make the lens, cut the bottom inch from the paper cup. Glue it to the box.

2 To make the shutter button, glue on the plastic cap. Paint the camera. Add cut-paper details.

3 Braid yarn to make a neck strap. Glue the ends to the sides of the camera.

More Ideas

Draw and color your own snapshots, and put them in an album.

Use a larger box to make a toy video camera.

You Will Need:
- paper cup
- box (pudding)
- plastic cap
- paints
- construction paper
- yarn

Vacation Box

Keep games, postcards, and mementos in this box, and follow your travel route on the map.

You Will Need:
- extra map of your travel route
- box and lid (shoes)
- buttons
- hole punch
- yarn

1 Glue the map onto the box and lid. Put the part with your travel route on the lid, if it fits. Cut slits in two corners of the lid to make a long tab. Glue the tab to the box.

2 Glue a large button on a small button. Glue the small button to the front of the box. Punch a hole in the lid. Tie yarn through the hole. To close the box, wrap the yarn behind the button.

More Ideas

With a marker, trace your travel route on the map. See how many nearby towns, lakes, and rivers you can identify as you travel.

Keep a journal of things you do and sights you see on your trip.

Boxy Backpack

Take this backpack anywhere—it can hold toys, treats, books, and anything else you can't leave home without.

You Will Need:

- large box (cereal)
- paints
- felt
- button
- small boxes
- construction paper
- thick ribbon

More Ideas

Pack a lunch, throw it in your backpack, and get permission to go on a hike and a picnic.

Cover your backpack with aluminum foil and use it as part of an astronaut costume.

1 Cut the top from the box. Cut a V-shape in the front, and four horizontal slits in the back—two at the top, two at the bottom. Tape the bottom of the box closed. Paint the box.

2 Cut out a piece of felt with a V-shape on one edge to match the opening in the box. Glue the back and sides of the felt to the box. Cut a buttonhole in the bottom of the V. Glue a button on the box.

3 Cover small boxes with paper and glue them onto the sides and front of your backpack. Leave the tops off the boxes so that you can carry items in them. To make straps, weave two long pieces of ribbon through the slits in the back. Glue or tie the ends together inside the box.

Super Shadow Boxes

Try your hand at creating a three-dimensional scene, then decorate a wall, shelf, or windowsill.

You Will Need:

- small boxes (greeting cards; gifts) or box lids (gifts; oatmeal)
- paints
- construction paper
- fabric
- string
- foam paper
- other items

1 Decorate a box or box lid with paints, cut paper, or fabric.

2 Follow the instructions for a particular shadow box, or create your own.

3 Glue string on the back as a hanger, or set it on a shelf.

To Make the Apple Tree Scene

Use paints and foam paper to create the sky, grass, and clouds in the box. Add a toothpick fence. Cut out the top and the trunk of a tree three times from paper. Glue them in the box, one on top of the other, with tiny pieces of foam paper in between to add depth.

To Make the Butterfly Box

Glue lace around an oatmeal-box lid. Paint uncooked bow-tie pasta pieces, and glue them in the box. Glue a piece of chenille stick onto each bow tie.

More Ideas

If you use a greeting-card box, glue on the clear cover after you've finished.

Make a series of shadow boxes to show the same scene during the four seasons. Or, make a shadow box for each month of the year.

Use a large shadow box as the background for a finger-puppet play.

Place objects or figures in different locations within the box—see how much depth you can add.

To Make the Pinecone Girl

Decorate a wooden ball to make the girl's head. Use rickrack as hair and a button as a hat. Add plastic wiggle eyes and colored-pencil features. Glue the ball on top of an upside-down pinecone. Add winged maple seeds as arms. Glue the girl in the box.

To Make the Diamond-Shaped Box

Glue silk or dried flowers into a thimble or a cap. Glue the arrangement into the box at an angle. Decorate the box with ribbon.

To Make the Winter Scene

Decorate the inside of the box with twigs and feathers. Add rickrack as the snow on the ground. Glue small toys or wooden cutouts onto buttons or plastic lids. Glue them into the box.

To Make the Flower Box

Cut a flower, a butterfly, and grass from foam paper. Glue them into the box.

Berry Hot!

These fruity trivets will protect your table from hot dishes—and add some zip at the same time.

You Will Need:

- corrugated cardboard box
- pencil
- rubber bands
- paints
- felt

1 Cut one side from the box. To make a base, draw the outline of a fruit shape on the cardboard and cut it out.

2 Cut 1-inch-wide strips of cardboard from the box. Put glue on each strip and wind it into a coil. Keep winding strips around the coil until the trivet is as large as you'd like. Use rubber bands to hold the strips in place until the glue dries. To make grapes, wind individual strips into coils and glue them next to each other on the cardboard base.

3 Paint the trivet. Cut details from felt. Glue them on.

More Ideas

Make a trivet to look like your favorite food. Basic shapes, such as a tomato, an ice-cream cone, or an eggplant, are easiest.

Dancing Butterflies

This is the simplest craft in the book to make, but one of the most fun to play with.

You Will Need:

- box with a clear plastic cover (greeting cards)
- paints
- tissue paper

1 Remove the cover from the box. Paint the inside of the box. Cut small figure-8-shaped pieces of tissue paper. Twist the centers of two together to make a butterfly. Make a few.

2 Place the butterflies in the box and put the cover on. Rub your finger quickly back and forth over the cover. Watch the butterflies dance!

More Ideas

Paint a background inside your box. Cut various flying creatures from tissue paper.

Frog Box

No matter what you keep in this box, it's sure to catch everybody's attention.

You Will Need:

- foam paper
- plastic box with an attached lid (baby wipes)
- plastic-foam ball
- paints
- plastic wiggle eyes

1 Cut arms and legs from foam paper. Glue them to the box. Cut the plastic-foam ball in half. Paint each half, and add a wiggle eye. Glue them to the box lid.

2 Paint on a mouth, and glue on a foam-paper tongue.

More Ideas

Use the frog box as a tackle box. Keep your fishing lures and flies in it.

11

Fun on the Farm

Build a barnyard, and have a hoedown with the horses, roosters, and other box creatures.

You Will Need:

- boxes of various sizes
- paints
- cardboard or foam board
- markers
- construction paper
- foam paper
- ruler

To Make the House

Turn a box sideways. Cut the corner from a larger box so that the triangular shape fits on top of the first box. Glue it in place. Glue a small box to the front of the house. Paint the house. Cut a roof from cardboard. Paint it, and glue it on. Add details with markers, cut paper, and foam paper.

To Make the Tractor

Paint a small box or glue paper on it. Cut four wheels from cardboard and four from foam paper. Glue the foam paper to the cardboard. Glue on the wheels. Add details with cut paper and foam paper.

To Make the Fence

Cut two long, half-inch-wide strips of cardboard, and many shorter strips of the same width. Lay the long strips parallel to each other. Connect them by gluing the shorter strips onto them.

Making each piece is fun, but the best part starts after you've finished the whole farm. Hee-haw!

To Make the Barn

Lay a big box on its side. Cut the corner from another box so that the triangular shape fits on top of the first box. If the bottom box is too wide for only one triangular shape, cut another. Glue on the triangular shapes. Paint the barn. Cut a roof from cardboard. Paint it, and glue it on. Add details with cut paper and markers.

To Make the Chicken

Cut out the head and neck from cardboard. Glue them onto a tiny box. Paint the chicken. Cut wings and a tail from foam paper. Glue them on. To make legs, cut a small strip of cardboard, bend it in half, then bend the ends as feet. Glue the legs to the bottom of the box.

To Make the Silo

Paint a cylindrical box or glue paper to it. To make the roof, cut a circle from foam paper. Cut a slit from the edge to the middle and overlap the edges of the slit. Glue the slit closed, then glue the roof on the silo. Add foam-paper details.

More Ideas

Make people for your farm, along with cows, horses, and pigs. Add a farm pond with ducks and swans.

To make a working farmhouse or barn, get some ideas from the dollhouses on pages 24 and 25.

Piggy Bank

This little piggy will watch your coins.

You Will Need:

- construction paper
- square box (tissues)
- paper cup
- small box (pudding)
- wooden balls
- paints
- chenille stick
- markers

1 Glue paper over the hole in the tissue box. To make a nose, cut the bottom from the cup. Glue it to the pudding box. Glue the pudding box to the tissue box.

2 Glue on wooden balls as legs. Paint the pig. Cut a coin slot in the top.

3 Curl a chenille stick. Glue it in place as a tail. Add features with markers and cut paper.

More Ideas

Make an owl bank to remind you to save wisely.

Bookends

These clever bookends will blend right in with your book collection.

You Will Need:

- small stones or sand
- plastic bags
- boxes of various sizes
- paints
- construction paper
- markers

1 Put stones or sand in plastic bags. Close them with tape or twist ties. Put the bags in the boxes. Tape the boxes shut.

2 Paint the boxes, or glue paper to them. Add details with cut paper and markers.

3 Use them to hold books upright on a shelf.

More Ideas

Give these bookends as a gift to someone who loves to read.

Flying Butterfly Boxes

Let your imagination fly when creating this box mobile, then give it as a springtime gift.

You Will Need:

- large corrugated cardboard box
- small boxes
- paints
- construction paper
- markers
- hole punch
- yarn

More Ideas

Make a mobile to hang near a window. Use pictures of birds and flowers on the boxes.

Hang a bell from the bottom of each small box.

1 Cut a frame from the large box to hang the small boxes from. Paint the frame and the small boxes, or cover them with paper.

2 Cut butterflies from paper and glue them on the small boxes. Add details with markers.

3 Poke a hole in the top of each small box. Push a piece of yarn through it and glue it in place. Punch holes in the frame. Tie the yarn through the holes. Hang the mobile with yarn.

Big Box Band

Get some friends together and make your own musical box band. Instruments can be made from nearly any kind of box.

You Will Need:

- corrugated cardboard box
- paints
- hole punch
- jingle bells
- yarn
- boxes of various sizes
- chenille sticks
- rubber bands
- craft sticks
- pencil
- small plastic-foam ball
- fabric
- felt

To Invent an Instrument

1 Paint and decorate a box or a panel cut from a box.

2 Add a noisemaking feature, such as a rubber band to pluck, dried beans to shake, or a block of wood to strike.

To Make the Tambourine

Cut a strip of corrugated cardboard, bend it in a circle shape, and staple the ends together. Paint it. For each jingle bell that you want to attach, punch two holes in the cardboard. Tie on each jingle bell with yarn.

More Ideas

Make a maraca by putting dried beans in a small gift box and gluing it closed. Tape a craft stick to it as a handle.

Look around your house and see what other objects might work well as instruments. To make a gong, hit a baking pan with the striker. Turn a big can upside down, and use it as a drum.

Percussion instruments are sounded by striking, scraping, or shaking—here's how to make one of each kind, plus a stringed instrument.

To Make the Washboard

Peel off the top layer from cardboard, exposing the corrugated part. Cut this part into a square, and paint it. Cut a larger piece of cardboard in the shape of a washboard, and paint it. Glue the corrugated square onto the washboard.

To Make the Banjo

Cut a large hole in a box, and punch three holes below it. Tape the top closed, and glue a long, rectangular box on it. Punch three sets of two holes in a small box. Thread a short chenille stick through each set of holes and twist the ends together inside the box. Glue the small box onto the rectangular box. Paint the banjo. Tie yarn or rubber bands from the chenille sticks to the holes in the large box.

To Make the Xylophone

Cut a corner of a shoe box and one of the long sides along the bottom, forming a long tab. Push the tab toward the middle of the box. Cut off the excess on the bottom. Glue the edges closed. Glue three craft sticks together, ends overlapping, so that they are slightly longer than the box. Repeat with three more sticks. Glue both long sticks to the box, then glue five craft sticks across them.

To Make the Striker

Glue the pointy end of a pencil into a small plastic-foam ball. Cut out a square piece of fabric. Wrap it around the ball, and hold it in place with a rubber band. Cut a square piece of felt. Wrap it around the ball, and hold it in place with another rubber band.

Cuckoo Boxes

Make a whole family of colorful cuckoos from boxes, feathers, and straws.

You Will Need:

- boxes of various sizes
- paints
- construction paper
- feathers
- markers
- plastic-foam balls
- plastic drinking straws

1 To make the body, paint a small box or glue paper on it. Glue on a tail and wing feathers.

2 To make the head, paint another box, or cut a head from paper. Decorate it with paints or markers. Glue it to the bird's body.

3 To make the base, cut a plastic-foam ball in half, and paint one half. Poke two holes in the bottom of the body. Paint two straws, and glue them in the holes as legs. Glue the legs into the base.

More Ideas

Decorate your box bird to look like a pink flamingo, an ostrich, or an emu. Or, make a turkey and use it as a Thanksgiving centerpiece.

Recipe Box

Keep all of your favorite recipes together in a custom-made box.

You Will Need:

- box large enough to hold 4-by-6-inch cards
- paints
- pictures from old magazines

1 Paint the box.

2 Cut food pictures from magazines and glue them on the box.

More Ideas

Make section dividers with tabs to separate recipes for different types of foods.

Have a recipe-trading party with friends. Have everyone bring his or her favorite food, then eat, make recipe boxes, and trade recipes.

Fish Tank

Create an underwater world filled with plants and creatures.

You Will Need:

- box with a clear plastic cover
- paints
- construction paper
- markers
- clear plastic drinking straws

1 Set the cover aside, and paint the inside of the box. Cut fish, seaweed, and other things from paper. Add tabs to the seaweed and other objects that will be connected to the bottom. Add details with markers.

2 Fold the tabs back and glue the objects to the bottom. Cut straw pieces. Glue one end of each piece to the back of a fish. Glue the other end to the back of the box.

More Ideas

If you want to make a large fish tank, use a large box, then use plastic wrap to cover the front when you've finished.

Wacky Feet

These zany feet are funny to look at, but tricky to walk in. Be extra careful when trying them out!

You Will Need:

- corrugated cardboard boxes
- paints
- small boxes
- construction paper
- chenille sticks
- beads

More Ideas

Hold a wacky-feet party for your friends, and use the feet as part of a costume.

1 Cut the basic foot shape from corrugated cardboard. Paint it.

2 Cut a section from a small box (large enough for your foot). Paint it or glue paper on it. Staple or glue it to the large foot.

3 Make another wacky foot. Put your feet in them. Carefully try to walk.

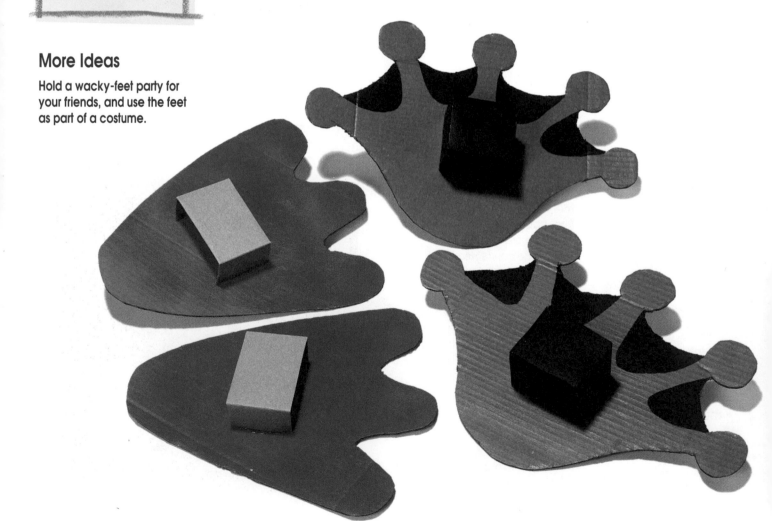

The trick to walking is to lift your knees high and keep your feet at a good distance from each other.

To Make the Duck Feet

Cut each foot in a triangle shape. Round off one point and cut three rounded toes in the opposite end.

To Make the Frog Feet

Cut each foot in a wide triangle shape. Round off one point and cut five webbed toes in the opposite end.

To Make the Pig Feet

Cut each foot in a teardrop shape, then cut a notch out of the point.

To Make the Clown Feet

Cut each foot in a pear shape. Glue on chenille-stick shoelaces and beads.

Scrapbook

Fill a scrapbook with your favorite photos and mementos.

You Will Need:

- thin cardboard box (cereal)
- paints
- pictures from old magazines
- hole punch
- paper
- yarn

1 Cut the front and back panels from the box, leaving part of the top flap attached to each panel. To create the cover, glue the flaps together.

2 Paint the cover and glue on pictures and letters or words cut from magazines. Punch matching holes in a stack of paper and in the cover. Tie the pages into the book with yarn.

More Ideas

Make a scrapbook for someone as a birthday gift. Include photos of the two of you, ticket stubs from events you attended together, and other keepsakes.

Funny Finned Friend

Hang up this creature and watch him flap in the breeze.

You Will Need:

- box (cereal)
- paints
- sponge
- construction paper
- plastic wiggle eyes
- yarn

1 Cut a long and a short corner from the box. Cut cardboard to fit over the open edges. Glue it in place. Glue the box corners together. Paint the box a light color. Let it dry. Dab on a darker color with a sponge.

2 Cut fins from paper and paint them. Glue them on. Add wiggle eyes. Tape yarn to the top of the creature so that it will hang straight. Once you find the right spot, poke a hole and glue the yarn in it.

More Ideas

Tie streamers onto your finned friend's tail, and use it as a windsock.

Campsite Diorama

Create a tiny world for your action figures or dolls. Play with it or use it as a decoration.

You Will Need:

- box (clothes)
- paints
- sand and stones
- plastic wrap
- construction paper
- twigs
- modeling clay

1 Cut the sides of the bottom of the box at an angle. The low part will be the front. Paint the box. Create a scene with sand, stones, and a stream made from painted plastic wrap.

2 Make trees and a campfire from cut paper and twigs. Stand the trees in lumps of clay. Make a tent from cardboard cut from the top of the box. Paint it and set it up in the scene.

More Ideas

Make a bead person by folding a piece of chenille stick in half, putting yarn in the fold, then pushing the ends of the stick through a bead. Add features with markers. Wrap another chenille stick around the body as arms.

Adorable Dollhouses

Playing with a dollhouse is fun, but it's even more fun when you've crafted it yourself.

You Will Need:

- large corrugated cardboard boxes
- ruler
- pencil
- paints
- craft glue
- wallpaper scraps
- construction paper
- cardboard or foam board
- markers
- small boxes (jewelry; gifts; toothpaste)
- foam paper

1 The back of the house will be the bottom of a large box. Cut off all but three or four inches from the sides of the box. With a pencil, draw lines inside the box where the floors and room dividers will be.

2 Decorate the walls in each room by painting them or by gluing on wallpaper scraps or construction paper. Add cut-paper windows, curtains, and other wall decorations.

3 Use cardboard or foam board as floors and room dividers. Make each floor an inch longer than the width of the house. At each end, bend the floor down a half inch to form a tab. Put glue on the tabs, and glue the floor in place. Cut room dividers long enough to fit snugly between the floors. Glue them in place.

Decorating the rooms and making the furniture will really let you show your style.

4 Design a roof from cardboard or foam board. Glue or tape it in place. Decorate the roof and outside of the house with paint, markers, and construction paper. Create furniture from small boxes or sections from a longer box. Paint them, then decorate them with foam-paper details.

More Ideas

Make a list of what you like best about the place where you live, then create these features for your dollhouse. Chimneys and fireplaces, staircases and bookcases, bathtubs, or even hot tubs can help to personalize your doll's home.

Go beyond the house and make a garage, a swimming pool, a doghouse, or a mini-playground. Create an entire neighborhood!

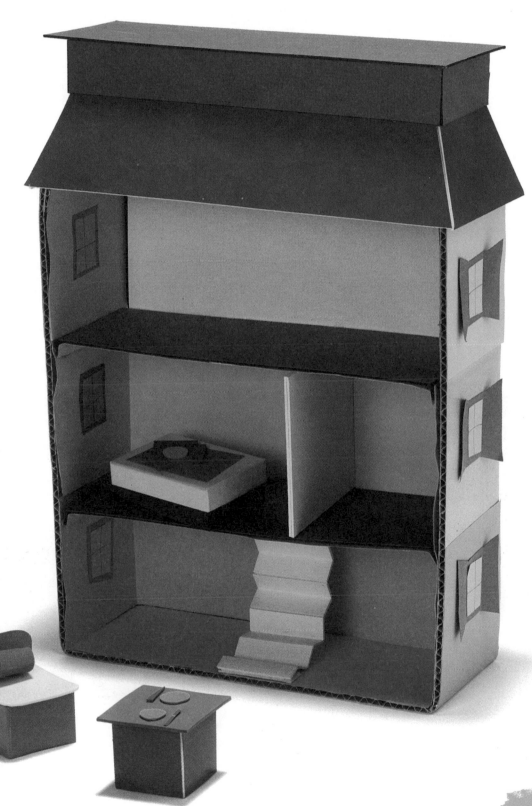

Boxes in the Kitchen

A kitchen is home to many boxy appliances. Here's how to make a sink, an oven, and a refrigerator.

You Will Need:

- boxes
- paints; markers
- construction paper
- cardboard or foam board
- craft glue
- foam paper
- other items

To Make the Fridge

Paint a box and lid. Cut shelves from cardboard or foam board. Make each shelf an inch longer than the width of the fridge. At each end, bend in the shelf a half inch to form a tab. Cover the shelves with paper. Put glue on the tabs, and glue the shelves in place. Cut the end off another box to make the snack drawer. Decorate it, and slide it into the fridge. Tape the side of the lid onto the box as the door. Glue on a foam-paper handle.

To Make the Sink

Cut a rectangular hole in the bottom of a box. Turn the box over. Glue cardboard or foam board on the back so that it stands up higher than the box. Cut two doors in the front panel. Paint the sink and decorate it with beads and foam-paper details. To make faucets, glue craft-stick pieces onto plastic caps. Paint them and glue them on the sink.

To Make the Stove

Turn a box upside down. Glue cardboard or foam board on the back so that it stands up higher than the box. Cut a door in the front panel. Paint the stove and decorate it with foam-paper details, beads, and markers.

More Ideas

Make a microwave, a toaster oven, a washer and dryer, a desk, or a stereo system.

Make mini-appliances to fit in a dollhouse. Use smaller boxes, and adapt the directions and supplies where necessary.

Marble Maze

Grab a stopwatch and challenge your friends to a marble-maze race.

You Will Need:

- large box
- construction paper
- markers
- marble

1 Decorate the box with construction paper and markers.

2 Cut a hole in one side to pop the marble through when starting the game. Cut a hole in the bottom at the opposite end for the finish.

3 Spread glue on paper. Roll it into a tube. Cut this into shorter tubes. Glue them in the box to form a maze.

More Ideas

Make dead ends by placing tubes against the sides of the box. Add other obstacles, such as trapdoor holes.

Picture Frame

This attractive, easy-to-make frame is a great place to display your favorite photos.

You Will Need:

- small box and lid (jewelry; gifts)
- wallpaper scraps
- craft glue
- ribbon
- photographs

1 Glue wallpaper scraps on the outside of the box and lid, and ribbon on the inside.

2 Join the edges of the box and lid together by gluing on two pieces of ribbon as hinges. Glue a photograph in each side of the frame.

More Ideas

Add a message and use it as a photo greeting card. Or, place a small gift inside and make it an all-in-one card and gift.

27

Boxcar Train Set

Get on board and create an entire railroad scene—trains, tunnels, buildings, and bridges.

1 Tape each box closed. Paint the boxes, or glue construction paper over them.

2 Follow the instructions for the craft you're making.

To Make the Tunnel

If using a tissue box, glue cardboard over the hole in the top before you paint it. Cut two arch-shaped holes on opposite sides of the box. Cut trees from paper. Glue them to the sides of the tunnel.

More Ideas

Make a floor scene for your train set. On poster board or an old sheet, draw train tracks, fields, and roads. Use aluminum foil to make a reflecting pond or river. Create pine trees by bending and stapling paper-plate halves into cones.

Experiment with different types of train cars. Make open-topped coal cars or birthday-express cars filled with presents.

Almost any box will do. We used boxes from toothpaste, tissues, soup, cereal, oatmeal, and raisins.

To Make the Buildings

Paint windows, doors, and other details on the boxes. Design a roof, cut it from cardboard, and glue it on. A corner cut from a larger box can be used as a roof.

To Make the Bridge

Cut the top three inches from a cereal box. Cut two strips of cardboard as wide as the top of the box. Tape them at each end of the top of the box. Cut an arch in the front and back of the bridge. Paint on details.

To Make the Water Tower

Remove the lid from an oatmeal container, and turn it upside down. To make the support poles, cut four rectangles from the open end of the container, leaving about an inch between them. To make the roof, cut a half-circle from paper, bend it into a cone shape, and glue it to the top. Glue on a drainage pipe cut from a straw.

To Make the Train

Add windows with passengers by cutting out faces from magazines or drawing your own. Glue them on. Cut wheels from cardboard and paint them. Glue two straw pieces to the bottom of each car, then glue the wheels onto the straw ends. Add details, such as a paper-cup smokestack and a cardboard-and-pompon headlight on the locomotive. Connect the cars with chenille sticks taped or glued in place.

Jewelry Box

Bangles, beads, and baubles—where to keep them all? Here's the answer.

You Will Need:
- large, flat box (candy)
- small boxes (jewelry; gifts)
- paints
- foam paper
- construction paper
- small mirror

1 Paint all the boxes and their lids, inside and out. Arrange the small boxes and lids inside the large box. Glue them in place.

2 Add details inside the boxes with paper. Glue the mirror inside the lid.

More Ideas

Replace the mirror with a small calendar, and use the box as a desk organizer.

Keep track of tiny craft supplies, such as beads, pompons, and sequins. Or, use it as a sewing box.

Happy House Doorstop

Open your door and welcome friends with a house doorstop.

You Will Need:
- large box (cereal)
- paints
- construction paper
- stones
- cardboard or foam paper

1 Cut the top two corners from the box, so that it's shaped like a house. Paint the box, and glue on cut-paper windows and a door.

2 Place stones inside the box, then glue a cardboard or foam-paper roof over the hole in the top of the box.

More Ideas

Decorate your doorstop to look like a small-scale version of the building where you live. Or, use a tiny box and make a house paperweight.

30

Fire Truck and Station

Here's a fire truck that's ready for rescue. You can also make a station to park it in.

You Will Need:

- five boxes (crackers; four smaller ones)
- paints
- construction paper
- foam paper
- twine

To Make the Fire Station

Cut the flaps from one end of a cracker box. Glue a smaller box to the side as the hose tower. Paint the fire station. Cut windows and other details from construction paper and foam paper. Glue them on.

To Make the Fire Truck

Glue two small boxes to the end of a long rectangular box. Paint the truck shape. Cut wheels, ladders, and other details from foam paper. Glue them on. Roll up some twine, and glue it on the truck.

More Ideas

Make a car that fits in a garage, a plane that fits in a hangar, or a train that fits in a roundhouse. Or, try making a stacking box puzzle with several boxes that fit inside one another.

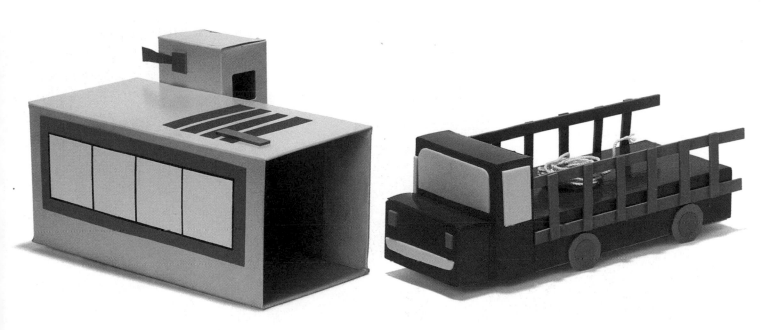

A Bunch of Box Games

Whether you like shooting hoops, tossing coins, or going fishing, you can find a way to make your favorite game with boxes.

You Will Need:

- boxes of all sizes
- paints
- construction paper
- chenille sticks
- hole punch
- foam board
- markers
- stickers; beads
- foam paper
- poster board
- yarn
- paper clip
- stick or dowel
- coins
- plastic cup
- coins
- table-tennis ball

1 Paint each box, or glue construction paper onto it.

2 Follow the instructions for the game you're making.

To Make the Coin Toss

Decorate boxes of various sizes with stickers. Paint a point value on each box: give boxes with large openings a low point value, and boxes with small openings a high point value. To play, arrange them on the floor. Each player tries to toss three coins into the boxes. The player with the highest score wins.

To Make the Basketball Hoop

Cut a backboard from foam paper or construction paper. Decorate it with markers, and glue it onto a box. Cut the bottom from a plastic cup. Glue or tape the cup to the bottom of the backboard. Use a table-tennis ball as a basketball.

When the competition begins, you can even keep score on a boxy scoreboard.

To Make the Fishing Game

Cut several slits in a box. From poster board, cut out a fish with a tab on the bottom, and punch a hole in the top. Decorate it with paints, markers, and beads. Make several. Stick them in the slits. To make a fishing pole, tie yarn and a bent paper clip to a stick or dowel.

To Make the Scoreboard

To make team-name hooks, poke two holes about 6 inches apart on the front of a box, toward the top. From inside the box, thread a chenille stick through the holes so that each end sticks out. Curl the ends into hooks. To make score hooks, poke two holes about 2 inches apart below each team-name hook. Thread a chenille stick through each set of holes, as before. From construction paper, make team-name cards and four sets of number cards from 0 to 9. Punch a hole in each. Make a "scoreboard" sign from foam board. Decorate it with markers, stickers, and foam paper. Glue it to the top of the scoreboard.

More Ideas

Create a bowling game with pins made from quart-sized milk cartons. Make a soccer game by cutting a plastic berry basket in half, and attaching the halves, or goals, to opposite ends of a large gift-box lid. Use crumpled foil as a ball.

Puppet Theater

Design your own puppet theater, and have a blast putting on puppet shows for your friends.

You Will Need:

- large corrugated cardboard box
- ruler
- paints
- construction paper
- markers
- foam paper

More Ideas

Make your own puppets (see pages 36 and 37), and write your own scripts.

Play television by decorating the box to look like a TV and putting your head behind it.

1 Cut off the back of the box, leaving a 1-inch border. Cut a square section from the front of the box, leaving a larger border.

2 Paint the theater. Make curtains and a sign from paper. Decorate them with markers.

3 From foam paper, cut a ruffle and tiebacks. Glue the curtains, ruffle, tiebacks, and sign onto the theater.

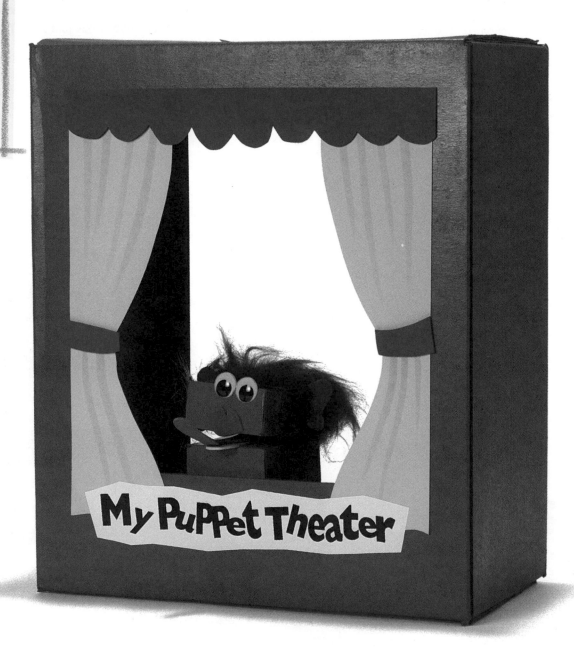

My Puppet Theater

Mailbox

Here's a place for your messages when you're not in your room.

You Will Need:

- box (shoes)
- foam paper
- cardboard
- craft stick
- metal paper fastener

More Ideas

Make a play tent for toys or dolls using the same shape, but replace the front with tent flaps.

1 Cut the box, as shown, with a door in one end.

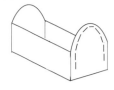

Cut on dotted line

2 Glue foam paper over it so that it forms a round top. Cover the front and back of the mailbox, too. Glue a foam-paper handle and a sign on the door.

3 Make a flag and a holder from cardboard and a craft stick. Put a paper fastener through the holder, the bottom of the flag, and the mailbox. Put the flag up when you have mail.

Box Baskets

Keep anything from food to flowers in these decorative baskets.

You Will Need:

- corrugated cardboard boxes
- paints
- fabric
- toothpicks or craft sticks
- cardboard
- metal paper fasteners

1 Cut off the top flaps, then paint the boxes or cover them with fabric. Add details, such as a fence made from toothpicks or craft sticks.

2 Make a handle from cardboard. Glue it on, or attach it with paper fasteners.

More Ideas

Leave two flaps on top, if you wish to cover whatever's inside. Fill a basket with gift items, and use it as a present.

Playful Puppets

These goofy puppets will liven up any puppet show—grab some boxes and make a whole cast.

You Will Need:

- boxes of various sizes
- paints
- construction paper
- foam paper
- plastic wiggle eyes
- fake fur
- plastic-foam balls

1 Make the basic puppet. Paint it or glue on construction paper or foam paper.

2 Follow the instructions for the puppet you're making.

3 Put your hand in the puppet to make it talk or fly.

To Make the Basic Puppet

If you're using a long, narrow box, glue on the lid if it has one. Find the center and cut one long side and both short sides (almost cutting the box in half). Fold the box on the uncut side.

If you're using two boxes, tape them shut at one end. Cut off the flaps at the open ends, then make a hinge to connect the boxes by taping them or by gluing on paper.

Stretch your imagination. Try making these, or invent some silly creatures of your own.

To Make the Monster

Glue on wiggle eyes and fake fur. Cut out and glue on ears, a mouth, and a tongue from foam paper.

To Make the Crocodile

Glue wiggle eyes onto plastic-foam-ball halves. Make paper eyelashes and a tongue, and foam-paper teeth and nostrils. Glue them on.

To Make the Butterfly

Decorate the wings with cut-paper shapes. To make the body, roll foam paper or construction paper into a tube. Glue it on. Add a plastic-foam-ball head decorated with foam-paper features.

More Ideas

Birds, bears, lions, or lizards can all be made by following the basic instructions then adding different details. Make the puppet theater on page 34 and entertain your family and friends.

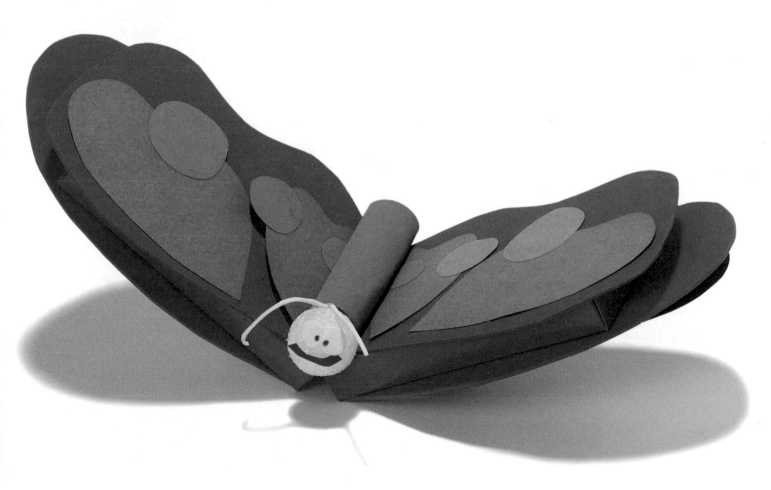

Elephants Never Forget

... to write back!
Here's a great way to keep your paper and envelopes handy to write to your pen pal.

You Will Need:
- three cardboard boxes (cereal; cake mix)
- paints
- construction paper
- small paper cups

1 Cut the tops from the boxes. Paint the bottom parts, then glue them together.

2 Cut an elephant's head, ears, eyes, nose, and tail from paper. Glue the head on the front of the holder and the tail on the back.

3 To make legs, paint four paper cups and glue them on.

More Ideas

Use it to hold anything from new craft supplies to old greeting cards. Or, give it to an adult to use as a file box.

Keepsake Box

Favorite jewelry, tiny toys, or dried flowers are just a few of the treasures you can keep in this box.

You Will Need:
- box and lid
- paints
- foam paper
- beads

1 Paint the box and lid. Cut shapes from foam paper.

2 Arrange the shapes and beads in a design on the lid. Glue them in place.

More Ideas

Decorate the box with natural materials, such as shells, dried beans, and seeds.

Put a small present inside and use it as a gift box that you don't have to wrap.

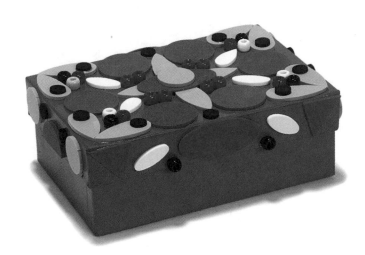

Terrific Tiles

These tiles are fun to make, long lasting, and will look great anywhere in your house.

You Will Need:

- box lid
- modeling clay
- ruler
- objects to press into the clay
- plaster of paris
- paints

1 Cover the inside bottom of the lid with a half-inch layer of clay. Press objects into the clay to make a design, then remove the objects.

2 Following the directions on the plaster of paris container, mix up a batch and pour it into the lid so that it's about a quarter-inch deep.

3 When the plaster dries, take it out of the lid, remove the clay, and paint the tile.

More Ideas

Before the plaster dries, press objects such as dried beans and walnut shells into it and leave them there. You'll have designs on both sides of the tile.

Make a welcome plaque for your house. If you want to make letters, write them in mirror image. Place a hanging hook into the edge of the plaster before it dries.

Instead of using clay as your base, press objects into wet sand, then remove them and add the plaster of paris. It'll look like a sand sculpture.

Boxes on the Go!

By boat, by truck, by racecar, by bus—make all of your traveling toys from boxes.

You Will Need:

- boxes of all sizes
- paints
- construction paper
- foam paper
- cardboard
- plastic drinking straw
- ruler
- plastic lids
- markers
- milk carton
- small cardboard tubes
- cotton

1 Tape the boxes closed. Paint them or glue on construction paper or foam paper.

2 Follow the instructions for the craft you're making.

To Make the Truck

Glue together a rectangular box and a smaller box. Cut wheels from cardboard. Paint them, and glue them on the truck. Paint a straw, and glue it between the boxes. Cut details from foam paper and construction paper, and glue them on.

To Make the Car

Lay a box on its side, and cut a U-shaped hole in the top. To make the windshield, fold and glue the flap that you cut. To make the seat, cut a U-shape from foam paper. Glue it in the hole. To make the spoiler, cut a cardboard rectangle about 2 inches longer than the width of the car. Fold each end in one inch, and glue the ends to the sides of car, toward the back. Use painted plastic lids as wheels. Add details with markers and foam paper.

The more you make, the more fun it becomes. Soon you'll be making fleets of vehicles.

To Make the Bus

Cut wheels from cardboard. Paint them, and glue them on the bus. Add windows and other details with markers and cut paper.

To Make the Bulldozer

Cut a section from a cardboard tube, paint it, and glue it to the front of a box. Cut windows in a smaller box. Glue the smaller box onto the larger box. Add foam-paper details.

To Make the Boat

Cut and tape one end of a large rectangular box so that it forms a point, or use a milk carton. Cut a smaller box at a slant. Cut a window in each side, and glue it onto the larger box. Cut a cardboard tube at a slant, paint it, and glue it to the top of the boat. Add painted cotton as steam and other details cut from foam paper and construction paper.

More Ideas

To float the boat, glue it on a plastic-foam tray.

To make wheels that turn, poke a hole in the center of each wheel and in the places on the vehicle where each wheel will go. Attach the wheels with metal paper fasteners.

Make a racetrack and several cars. Or, create a larger town scene with a river, roads, and a construction site—places to put all of your vehicles.

Big Box Car

Drive this car anywhere—through the living room, across the backyard, or down the sidewalk. It doesn't need gas and it won't get a flat.

You Will Need:

- large corrugated cardboard box
- cardboard
- paints
- construction paper

1 Cut the bottom from the box. On the top, glue the two long flaps inside the box. To make the spoiler, fold back one of the short flaps and glue it in place.

2 To make the hood, tape or glue the other short flap to the sides of the car. Cut wheels and other details from cardboard, and glue them on. Paint the car, then add cut-paper details.

More Ideas

Make a horse, an airplane, a dinosaur, or anything you'd like to ride or drive.

Tie two strings onto the car and hang them over your shoulders.

Have a friend make one, and drive around together.

Kangaroo Keeper

This handy kangaroo's pouch can hold a lot more than her joey. There's plenty of room for books and some magazines, too.

You Will Need:

- large box (cereal)
- pencil
- paints
- construction paper
- fabric
- markers

1 Cut the top from the box. With a pencil, draw the basic outline of a kangaroo's head and pouch on both sides. Cut along the line.

2 Paint the box. Cut details from paper and fabric, and glue them on. Add features with markers.

More Ideas

Instead of a kangaroo, make a koala or an opossum. Or, design the sides to look like your favorite book or magazine.

Message Board

This happy character will pass along important messages.

You Will Need:

- corrugated cardboard box
- craft glue
- fabric
- poster board
- markers
- construction paper

1 Cut two rectangles the same size from the box. Glue one on top of the other. Glue fabric over one side, and poster board on the other.

2 From poster board, cut a head, hands, and feet with a tab on each. Glue them to the message board, along the edges. Add details with markers and cut paper.

More Ideas

Design it to look like a mail carrier or a pony-express horse.

Rolling Box Buddies

Once you start making these, you'll really get rolling. Make a bunch, and give them as gifts.

You Will Need:

- boxes (shoes; cake mix)
- paints
- twine
- corrugated cardboard
- fabric
- construction paper
- metal paper fasteners
- felt
- cotton balls
- plastic wiggle eyes
- foam paper
- glitter
- markers

1 To make the body, turn a shoe box upside down, and paint it. To make the head, paint a smaller box and glue it on. Poke a hole in the front of the body. Thread twine through it, then tie a knot at both ends.

2 Cut wheels from cardboard, and glue fabric or construction paper on them. Poke a hole in each wheel, and holes in the body where the wheels will go. Attach the wheels with paper fasteners.

3 Follow the directions for the craft you're making.

These cooperative pets will follow you anywhere. Plus, they don't cost a penny to care for.

To Make the Lamb

Cut legs and ears from felt and glue them on. Then, glue painted cotton balls all over the head and body. Add wiggle eyes, a foam-paper nose, and a glittery mouth.

To Make the Duck

Cut wings and a tail from construction paper. Decorate them with markers, and glue them on. Add a foam-paper beak, wiggle eyes, and cut-paper eyelashes.

To Make the Dog

Cut spots from fabric, and other features from paper. Glue them on. To make the tail, cut fringe in a wide strip of paper, curl it up, then glue it on.

More Ideas

Leave the shoe box right side up to make an all-in-one wagon-pet. You can cut a notch in the bottom of the head to attach it to the body. Make a wagon-pet from a large box, and use it as a portable toy box.

Lion and Cage

Let this likable lion hang around in his cage or wander out for a stroll.

You Will Need:

- boxes (clothing; cake mix)
- paints
- plastic drinking straws
- construction paper
- foam paper
- markers
- plastic wiggle eyes

1 Cut a side panel from a large box. Glue the lid on. Cut a square in the front panel. Paint the cage. Glue on painted straws as bars.

2 Cut a smaller box in half lengthwise. Glue construction paper on it. Glue it inside the cage as a stand for the lion.

3 Fold paper in half and cut out the shape of a lion's body. Use paper, foam paper, and markers to make a tail, a mane, and a head. Add wiggle eyes.

More Ideas

Make an entire zoo, or a circus train, where each train car holds an animal.

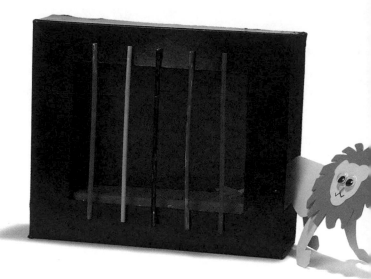

Secret Treasure Chest

We're not going to tell you what to keep in this chest. (Then it wouldn't be a secret!)

You Will Need:

- shoe box and lid
- poster board
- yarn
- construction paper

1 Cut the top from poster board. Glue it to the front and back of the lid. On poster board, trace around the half-circle shapes at each end of the lid. Cut them out, and glue them on.

2 To attach the lid to the box, cut a slit at each back corner of the lid to make a long hinge. Put glue on the inside of the hinge, and glue it to the box. Decorate the chest with cut-paper details.

More Ideas

Make a large chest for blanket or sweaters.

Make a secret panel underneath the lid.

Building Box Cards

You're the architect here—build countless creations with these easy-to-make cards.

You Will Need:

- corrugated cardboard boxes
- paints

More Ideas

Experiment with building cards of different shapes—triangles, circles, and hearts can work.

1 Cut as many cardboard rectangles as you like. Make them all the same size.

2 Cut six slits in each card— two on each long side, one on each short side. Make them in the same places on each card.

3 Paint the cards, and build away!

Title Index

Subject Index

Look What You Can Make With
PAPER BAGS

Over 90 Pictured Crafts and Dozens of Other Ideas

Edited by Judy Burke

Look What You Can Make With

Paper Bags

Edited by Judy Burke
Photographs by Hank Schneider

Boyds Mills Press

Craft Coordinator:

Carrie Abel

Contributors:

Sharon Addy
Caroline Arnold
Jenny Bak
Laura G. Beer
Anne Bell
Doris Boutin
Marie E. Cecchini
Diane Cherkerzian
Nancy Dunlea
Gladys Emerson
Julie Fultz
Mavis Grant

Edna Harrington
Carmen Horn
Ellen Javernick
Janet Kent
Garnett Kooker
Kathleen Peelen Krebs
Karen Kremsreiter
Twilla Lamm
Ruth Everding Libbey
Lee Lindeman
Doreen Macklen
Clare Mishica

June Rose Mobly
James W. Perrin, Jr.
Luella Pierce
Simone Quick
Necia Sneed Ramsey
Kathy Ross
Mary Jo Rulnick
Beth Stevens
Sharon Dunn Umnik
Lynn Wasnak
Linda Weissinger
Doris Woodliff

Copyright © 1999 by Boyds Mills Press
All rights reserved

Published by Bell Books
Boyds Mills Press, Inc.
A Highlights Company
815 Church Street
Honesdale, Pennsylvania 18431
Printed in China

Publisher Cataloging-in-Publication Data
Burke, Judy, editor.
  Look what you can make with paper bags : over ninety pictured crafts and dozens of other ideas /
edited by Judy Burke ; photographs by Hank Schneider.—1st edition
[48]p. : col. ill. ; cm.
Summary: Toys, games, and other ideas all from paper bags.
ISBN 1-56397-717-6
1. Handicraft—Juvenile literature. 2. Paper bags—Juvenile literature.
[1. Handicraft. 2. Paper bags.] I. Schneider, Hank, ill. II. Title.
745.54—dc21   1999   CIP
Library of Congress Catalog Card Number 97-77904

First edition, 1999
Books in this series originally designed by Lorianne Siomades
The text of this book is set in 10pt Avant Garde Demi, titles 43pt Gill Sans Extra Bold

10 9 8 7 6 5 4

Getting Started

This book is filled with fun, easy-to-make crafts, and each one begins with a paper bag. You'll find a wide variety of things to make, including toys, games, and gifts.

Directions

Before you start each craft, read the directions and look closely at the photograph, but remember—it's up to you to make the craft your own. If we decorate a craft with markers, but you want to use glitter paint and stickers, go for it. Feel free to stray from our directions and invent new crafts.

Work Area

It's a good idea to keep your work area covered. Old newspapers, brown paper (yet another use for grocery bags!), or old sheets work well. Also, protect your clothes by wearing a smock. A big, old shirt does the job and gives you room to move. Finally, remember to clean up when you've finished.

Materials

You'll need a lot of paper bags, so start saving now. Ask friends and relatives to help. Keep your craft-making supplies together, and before making each craft, check the "You Will Need" list to make sure you have everything. In this list, we'll often specify which type of paper bag we used. For most crafts, however, any type of paper bag will work. When selecting a bag, think about what size you want your finished craft to be.

Other Stuff

When we show several similar crafts, we'll often list numbered directions that apply to all of the crafts, then specific directions for each craft.

Here's a painting tip: Sometimes department-store bags have a shiny coating, and poster paint won't stick to them. Try mixing liquid soap with the paint. It takes longer to dry, but it works. Acrylic paints also work.

That's about all. So, find a bunch of paper bags, select a craft that you like, and have some fun. Before you know it, you'll be showing everyone what you made with paper bags.

Bag Animal Bonanza

Gather bags of all sizes, and use your creativity to turn them into friendly beasts.

To Make the Animals on This Page

1 Turn the bag upside down. Use a pencil to draw the animal shape, using the corner folds as legs. Draw a head on one side and a tail on the other side of the bag. Cut out the animal.

2 Cut a piece of cardboard to fit inside each leg, and fold it lengthwise so it matches the fold in the leg. Glue each piece of cardboard in place to strengthen the legs.

To Make the Giraffe

Fold the neck up and glue it in place. Draw spots and other details on the body with markers. Glue on a mane cut from construction paper.

To Make the Skunk

Paint the skunk. Let it dry. Using a pencil, poke a few holes in a line along the center of the tail, and weave a chenille stick through them. Shape the tail as you wish. Glue on a pompon as a nose.

To Make the Turtle

For the turtle's shell, cut out a piece of construction paper and decorate it with markers. Glue it on. Draw a face with markers.

Start with the creatures shown here, then see what others you can make.

To Make the Animals on This Page

1 For the head, stuff a bag half full with newspaper.

2 For the body, glue paper over a box.

3 Cut out legs, wings, or ears from cardboard.

To Make the Tiger

Glue the bag closed. Glue it on the end of the body, with the bottom of the bag as the face. Glue on cardboard ears and legs. Paint the tiger. Use markers to add stripes. Glue on a chenille-stick tail and whiskers, a pompon nose, and eyes cut from paper.

To Make the Bird

Fold the end of the bag to form a beak. Glue it to secure it. Glue the head on top of the body. Glue on cardboard wings and legs. Paint the bird. Add a feathery tail and wiggle eyes.

To Make the Elephant

Twist the end of the bag into a trunk. Wrap it with masking tape. Glue the head on the end of the body. Glue on cardboard ears and legs. Paint the elephant. Add a braided yarn tail and a yarn mouth. Draw eyes and other details with markers.

More Ideas

Try to think of other ways a bag can be used to make an animal. You might stuff a bag with newspaper to create a body, and glue on paper features.

Make a habitat for your animals. Create trees, ponds, flowers, and other features from paper bags.

Broom Friend

Dance together, or just keep each other company.

You Will Need:

- grocery bag
- paints
- broom
- newspaper
- string
- scissors
- construction paper
- glue
- pencil
- accessories

1 For the head, turn the bag upside down and paint a face on one side.

2 Wrap the broom with newspaper. Place it in the bag. Add more newspaper to fill out the head. Tie the bag closed.

3 For hair, glue on strips cut from construction paper. Curl the ends around a pencil. Add an old hat and a scarf for decoration.

More Ideas

Create several broom characters and put on a play.

Make a hobbyhorse by creating a horse's head from a bag and attaching it to a broom.

Body Drawing

Personalize a wall hanging with pictures of your favorite things.

You Will Need:

- grocery bags
- scissors
- tape
- pencil
- old magazines
- glue

1 Cut open the bags. Tape the ends together to make a piece of paper that is a little longer and wider than yourself. Lie down on the paper, and ask a friend to trace around you with a pencil. Cut out the shape.

2 Cut out pictures of things you like from magazines. Glue them to the shape. Hang up your body drawing.

More Ideas

Create a jumbo paper doll and clothes. Attach the clothes to the doll with self-adhesive Velcro pieces.

Magnificent Mobiles

Decorate for a party or spice up your room with these colorful mobiles.

You Will Need:

- grocery bags
- paints
- glue
- scissors
- construction paper
- newspaper
- stapler
- crepe paper
- reinforcement rings
- yarn and thread
- tape
- pinecones

1 Turn a bag upside down. On one side, paint a face or glue on cut-paper features. Stuff the bag with newspaper. Staple the bag closed. Glue the end down.

2 Poke two holes an inch apart on top of the head. Add reinforcement rings to the holes so the paper doesn't rip. Tie a long piece of yarn through the holes for a hanger.

To Make the Witch

For hair, glue on crepe paper. Tie a knot about two inches above the head. Cut a circle from construction paper for the brim of the hat. Make a hole in the center, and pull the yarn through, letting the brim rest on the knot. To make the top of the hat, roll a piece of paper into a cone shape. Thread the yarn through the hat and tape the top of the hat to the brim. Glue on yarn as a hatband.

To Make the Owl

Poke two holes on each side of the bottom of the bag. Tie a long piece of thread through each set of holes. A few inches from the owl's body, wrap each piece of thread around an upside-down pinecone. Wrap another pinecone below. Glue cut-paper features on the pinecones so they look like little owls. Glue cut-paper wings on the sides of the large owl.

More Ideas

Design a mobile to match a party theme. If it's a Fourth of July party, paint the American flag on a bag, and hang mini stars and streamers from it. If it's a birthday party, paint a cake on a bag, and hang tiny wrapped boxes from it as presents.

Make a wind-chime mobile by decorating the main bag festively and hanging jingle bells, cans, or other noisy objects from it. Hang it where there's a breeze.

Rustic Log Cabin

You're the architect! Design a house, roll up some paper logs, and create a log cabin.

You Will Need:

- grocery bags
- corrugated cardboard
- scissors
- bakery box with a plastic window
- markers
- tape and glue
- pencil
- plastic drinking straws
- paints
- sand

1 From cardboard, draw and cut out four walls with tabs. Each wall should have two tabs, one at the top of the left side and one at the bottom of the left side. Cut holes in the walls for windows and doors.

2 To make windows, cut squares from the window of a bakery box. Use a marker to draw panes. Tape the windows behind the cut-out window holes on the walls.

3 Put glue on the front of the tabs, and assemble the walls, with the tabs inside the cabin. To make each "log," cut a strip from a paper bag, roll it around a pencil, and glue the edges. Glue the logs on the walls. Let the end of every second log stick out to interlock with the logs from the other walls, as shown in the photo.

Then make a woodland setting, complete with a lake and trees.

4

From cardboard, cut out a roof to fit the cabin. Glue it on. Make a chimney from cardboard. Cut the bottom to fit the angle of the roof. Glue it on. Glue the cabin on a piece of cardboard. Add details with a marker. Add a porch roof and other details with cardboard and paper rolls.

To Make the Trees

Cut a long, 3-inch-wide strip from a bag. Draw a line diagonally across it. Cut fringe on one side of the line. Starting with the end with the short fringe, wrap the strip around a plastic straw, gluing it and bending out the fringe as you go. Tape down the end. Cut a square from cardboard and cut a slit in the middle. Insert the straw end through the slit, cut the end in half vertically, and tape the two straw parts to the cardboard.

To Make the Lake

Cut out a lake shape from a paper bag. Paint it, leaving the beach section unpainted. Spread glue on the beach section and sprinkle sand on it. Let it dry. Create a dock by gluing paper logs onto a piece of cardboard.

More Ideas

Adapt the rolled-paper technique to add a 3-D effect to other crafts. Decorate a photo frame or a pencil can to look wooden by gluing on rolled paper-bag strips.

Breeze Catchers

With the help of some string and a little creativity, send those bags soaring into the blue.

You Will Need:

- long bags
- grocery bags
- markers
- scissors
- construction paper
- foil
- stapler
- fabric
- hole punch
- reinforcement rings
- string
- glue
- crepe paper
- paints

To Make the Streamer Kite

Fold over the top edge of a grocery bag to form a cuff. Glue crepe paper under the cuff and near the bottom of the bag.

To Make the Fish Kite

Use markers and cut paper to create a face at the open end of a long bag. Glue on scales cut from construction paper and foil. Staple on a knotted fabric tail.

To Make the Nautical Wind Sock

Paint nautical flag symbols on a long bag. Punch two holes at the closed end, glue on reinforcement rings, and tie a long string through each hole. Cut out paper rectangles and paint them. Fold them in half around the strings, and glue them in place.

1 Follow the directions for the kite you want to make.

2 Punch two holes near the open end of the bag. Add reinforcement rings to the holes so the paper doesn't rip. Tie a long piece of string through the holes and knot it.

3 To fly your kite, hold it by the string and run in the wind.

More Ideas

Create your own kite designs. Try an airplane, a hot-air balloon, or an eagle.

10

Winter Warm-Up Bag

This is the perfect gift on a wintry day: a decorative bag filled with delicious hot-cocoa mix.

You Will Need:

- lunch bag
- white paper
- scissors
- glue
- glitter
- 2 cups instant dry milk
- 1 cup sugar
- 1/2 cup unsweetened cocoa
- plastic sandwich bag that zips
- ink pen
- ribbon

1 To decorate the bag, fold a square piece of paper several times. Cut out triangles and other shapes from the edges. Open the paper, and glue it on the bag. Add glue-and-glitter decorations.

2 Mix together the dry milk, sugar, and cocoa. Put the mixture in the sandwich bag. Write the following directions on a piece of paper:

Place three heaping teaspoons in a cup,
Add boiling water, stir, and drink it up!

3 Put the sealed sandwich bag and the directions in the decorated bag. Tie it closed with ribbon, and give it as a gift.

More Ideas

Decorate the bag for any occasion. In the summer, use iced-tea or lemonade mix instead of hot cocoa.

Basket of Flowers

Ring in spring with this bright bouquet.

You Will Need:

- grocery bags
- compass
- pencil
- scissors
- glue
- markers
- construction paper
- yarn

1 Cut open the bags. Use a compass to draw two large circles of equal size. Cut them out. Cut one circle in half. Glue the curved edge of one half onto the other circle, forming a pocket. Use markers to decorate it.

2 Cut flowers from construction paper. Place them in the basket. Make a hole in the top of the basket. Tie yarn through the hole as a hanger.

More Ideas

On the back of each flower, write a chore that you're willing to do, and give the bouquet as a gift.

Make an autumn decoration by cutting out paper vegetables instead of flowers.

Wear It on Your Head!

Throw on one of these wacky hats, and see how many smiles you get. You can also use these hats as starting points for some unique costumes.

You Will Need:

- grocery bags
- white bags
- ruler
- scissors
- stapler
- construction paper
- chenille stick
- pencil
- glue
- markers
- hole punch
- yarn
- cotton balls
- ribbon
- paints
- plastic wrap
- cardboard tubes

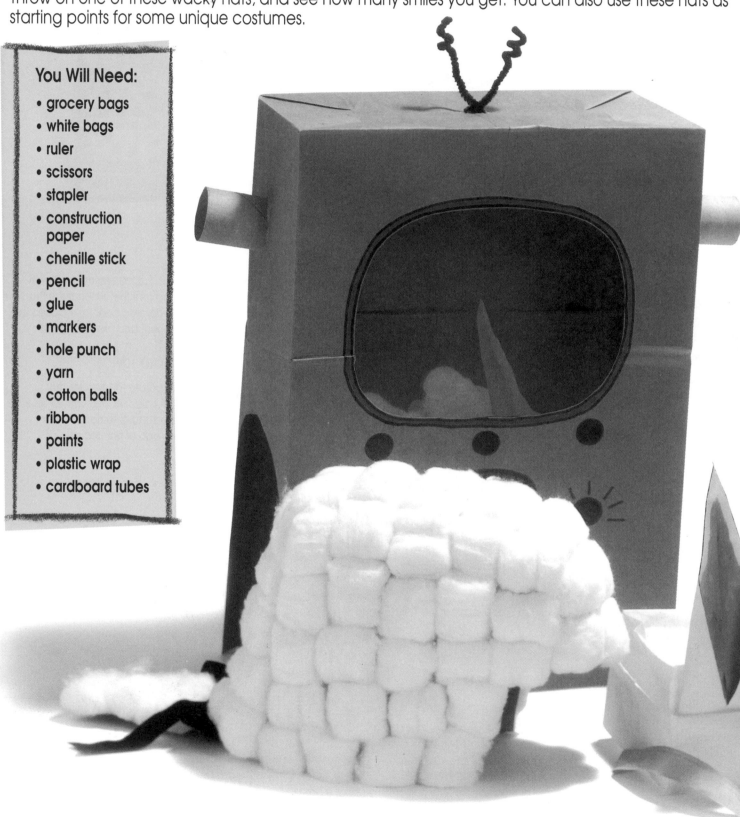

To Make the Spaceman Mask

Put a grocery bag over your head. Place your hand on the bag where it covers your face. Remove the bag, leaving your hand on that spot. Draw an oval-shaped window where your hand was, then cut out the window. Glue a piece of plastic wrap over the window. Cut a hole in the bag below the window. Decorate the mask with markers.

For antennae, curl the ends of a chenille stick around a pencil. Fold it in half and staple it to the top of the mask. For each "ear," snip slits around one end of a short cardboard tube. Cut a matching hole in each side of the mask. Insert the tubes, slit end first, then flatten the slits against the inside of the mask and glue them in place. On each side of the mask, cut out a U-shaped piece at the bottom so the mask can fit comfortably on your shoulders.

To Make the Colonial Wig

Cut a grocery bag in the shape of a wig with a ponytail in the back. Spread glue over a section of the wig, and press cotton balls onto it. Continue until the entire wig is covered. Let it dry. Tie a ribbon in a bow around the ponytail.

To Make the Rabbit or Donkey Ears

Use a paper bag that will fit on your head. Cut the bag so it's about 6 inches long. Fold the open end up 2 inches all around, then fold it once again. For the ears, cut two triangular pieces from a bag. Fold the bottom corners inward, and glue them in place. Glue the ears into the fold of the hat. Decorate the ears with paints or markers. Add ribbon ties.

To Make the Eagle Hat

Find a white bag that will fit on your head. Cut one of the narrow sides down the middle to the bottom of the bag, then cut straight across the bottom. Fold in the resulting flaps and glue them down. Fold the opposite corner inside. Glue this down.

From construction paper, cut out two sides of a beak. Glue them together along the top end. Glue the beak to the hat, and glue the top of the hat closed. Let it dry. Use a marker to draw eyes. Fold up the bottom of the bag for strength, then punch holes along this border. Lace yarn ties through the holes.

To Make the Mouse Hat

Cut out a 9-inch square from a grocery bag. Fold it into a triangle. For the band, cut an 11 1/2-inch-by-1 1/2-inch strip from the bag. Staple the band to the corners opposite the fold. Glue on cut-paper ears, eyes, and a nose. For the tail, staple on a chenille stick and curl it around a pencil.

More Ideas

To make a bonnet, make a larger version of the doll's hat on page 33. To make a long-hair wig, find a brown bag that fits on your head, then cut long fringe in the sides and back of it. Try these: cowboy hats, berets, sailor caps, or sun hats.

Gift Stocking

Make a personalized stocking to hang by the chimney with care.

1 Cut two stocking shapes of equal size from a bag. Hold them together and punch holes around the edges, about an inch apart. Lace them together with yarn, and make a loop at the end.

2 From construction paper, cut out a cuff and snowman. Decorate them with markers and glue them on.

More Ideas

Make a stocking card. Cut out two stocking shapes and lace them together on the long straight side. Decorate the front of the card, and write a message inside.

Make a stocking for your pet, and fill it with treats and toys.

You Will Need:

- grocery bag
- scissors
- hole punch
- yarn
- construction paper
- markers
- glue

Hanukkah Banner

Use this banner as a decoration or as a fire-safe menorah. The "flames" are removable.

1 Cut open a bag, and cut out a large rectangle for the banner. Lay a long piece of yarn along the top. Fold the paper over it, then glue it in place. Tie the yarn ends together to form a hanger. Use a pencil to draw a menorah on the banner. Go over these lines with glue, then add glitter. Let it dry.

2 For each candle, roll a square piece of paper bag into a tube. Add glue, then place them on the banner. Make "flames" by inserting tissue-paper pieces into the candles. Use markers to write "Happy Hanukkah" on the banner.

More Ideas

Make a birthday banner with a paper cake and candles (as in step 2). Add things that are special to the person whose birthday it is.

You Will Need:

- grocery bag
- scissors
- yarn
- glue
- pencil
- glitter
- tissue paper
- markers

14

Wreaths for All Seasons

Twist, curl, or mold a bag into a festive wreath for any occasion.

You Will Need:

- grocery bags
- scissors
- tape
- yarn or twine
- pinecones, dried flowers, and sticks
- ruler
- gift wrap
- glue
- ribbon
- paper plate
- pencil
- construction paper

To Make the Curly Wreath

Cut out the center of a paper plate. Use the donut shape as the base for your wreath. Cut 7-inch-by-3-inch pieces from a paper bag. At both short ends of each piece, cut fringe 3 inches deep. Curl the fringe around a pencil, then glue the uncut parts onto the base. When the base is covered, crush small pieces of construction paper into balls and glue them on. Add a paper bow. Tie on a twine hanger.

To Make the Pinecone Wreath

Cut a paper bag down one side, and cut off the bottom section. Roll the paper into a tube, crumpling it as you go. Shape the rolled paper into a circle. Tape the ends together. Decorate the wreath with yarn, and tie on pinecones, dried flowers, and sticks. Add a yarn loop as a hanger.

To Make the Tiny Wreath

Cut a 3-inch-by-36-inch strip of paper from a grocery bag. Crush and twist the strip tightly together so it looks like a rope. Shape it into a circle. Tape the ends together. Cut out hearts from gift wrap, and glue them on. Tie on a ribbon bow.

More Ideas

Make a wreath for any season. Tie on flowers, toy birds, and ribbons for spring. Add seashells, sandpaper castles, and paper suns for summer. Glue on nuts, leaves, and pinecones for autumn. Add cotton-ball snowmen, foil ice-skates, and ice-cream-stick skis for winter.

Paper-Bag Party!

It doesn't take much to throw together a party that's fun and inexpensive. Just grab some bags and make your own games, toys, and decorations.

You Will Need:

- paper bags
- markers
- stickers
- streamers
- glue
- scissors
- construction paper
- string
- treats and small toys
- newspaper
- stapler
- plastic film canisters
- dried beans
- pencils
- tape

To Make the Lantern Decorations

For each decoration, cut down the back seam of a lunch bag and cut off the bottom to get a large rectangle. Decorate it with markers, then fold it lengthwise. Cut slits on the fold about an inch apart. Open it up, and glue the short ends together. Cut a strip from another bag as a handle and glue it on. Set it on the table or hang it up.

To Make the Place Mats

For each place mat, cut off one large side from a grocery bag. Cut the edges in a wavy pattern. Decorate it with markers.

To Make the Piñata

The bottom of a bag will be the top of the piñata. Use markers, stickers, streamers, and cut paper to decorate it. Leave 3 inches by the open end blank. At the top of the piñata, poke two holes on opposite sides. Thread a 3-foot-long string through one hole and out the other. Knot the ends together. Fill the piñata with treats and small toys. Use old newspaper as filler. Close the open end of the piñata, fold it down, and staple it closed.

How to Play

With an adult's permission, hang your piñata, have someone blindfold you, and swing at the piñata with a plastic bat. Take turns with others until the piñata breaks. Share the treats and toys.

To Make the Maracas

For each maraca, decorate a lunch bag with markers. Fill a film canister halfway with dried beans, and put on the lid. Wrap it in a piece of newspaper and put it in the bag. Stuff the bag halfway with newspaper. To make a handle, stick a pencil in the middle of the newspaper, and gather the bag opening around it. Wrap the handle with tape to secure it.

More Ideas

Make a gift bag for each guest as a party favor. See pages 20 and 21 for ideas.

Play a mystery-bag game. Place different objects in lunch bags. Have the guests feel the objects and try to guess what they are.

17

Autumn Scarecrow

This fellow is too friendly to scare away crows, but he'll look great as an indoor autumn decoration.

You Will Need:

- paper bags
- scissors
- newspaper
- stapler
- tape
- twine
- construction paper
- straw hat
- bandanna

1 For the body, turn a bag upside down. Poke a hole in each side near the top for arm holes. For arms, roll newspaper into a tube, and push it through the holes. Stuff the body with crumpled newspaper, then fold and staple the open end shut.

2 For the head, stuff a smaller bag with newspaper. Twist and tape the bag closed to form a neck. Make a hole in the top of the body, and insert the neck. Tape it in place.

3 Roll newspaper for legs. Staple brown paper around them, leaving some newspaper sticking out at the bottom. Staple the legs to the body.

4 Tie twine near the ends of the arms and legs, then cut fringe in the newspaper. Glue cut-paper patches and facial features on the scarecrow. Add a straw hat and a bandanna.

More Ideas

To turn your scarecrow into a backpack, don't stuff the body with newspaper. Cut around the top part of the body to form an opening, and add two ribbon straps to the back.

Make a floppy shelf doll with fabric legs. When you set it on a shelf, the legs will hang loosely over the edge.

Souvenir Trunk

This is the perfect container for treasures—letters, movie stubs, invitations, and other keepsakes.

You Will Need:

- grocery bag
- scissors
- glue
- shoe box and lid
- tissue paper
- ribbon
- gold gift wrap

1 Cut open the bag, and glue the paper on the outside of the shoe box and lid. Glue tissue paper inside them.

2 Put the lid on the box. To make straps, glue two pieces of ribbon around the box. Start at the front of the lid, and end at the front of the box.

3 Cut out a latch and other details from gold gift wrap. Glue them on.

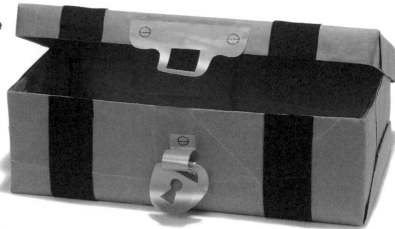

More Ideas

Decorate a clothes storage box to match the season when the stored clothes are worn.

Decorate the outside of a stationery box with used stamps, maps, and postcards. Create stationery and envelopes to put inside.

A Journal Just for You

Create poems and stories, write about your adventures, or jot down the day's events in this leather-like journal.

You Will Need:

- paper bag
- glue
- blank notebook
- soft cloth
- brown cream shoe polish
- markers

1 Rip a bag into pieces, and glue them over the entire cover of the notebook.

2 Using the cloth, rub a little shoe polish smoothly over the cover. Let it dry.

3 Cut out a rectangle from another bag. Fold in the sides to form a frame. Glue it on the cover, and add polish. Write "Journal" with markers.

More Ideas

Make a travel journal. On the cover, glue pictures of wherever you're going. Inside, write about what you see on your trip.

Decorative Gift Bags

Spice up a plain old brown bag and transform it into a handsome gift holder.

You Will Need:

- paper bags
- construction paper
- glue
- pencil
- scissors
- ribbon
- markers
- tissue paper
- old greeting card
- paper doily
- glitter
- hole punch
- string
- blunt table knife
- potato
- paints
- pompon

To Make the Reindeer Bag

Fold down the top 4 inches of a bag to form a flap. From construction paper, cut out antlers, a bow tie, a tongue, eyes, and eyelashes. Curl the eyelashes around a pencil. Glue the antlers near the fold of the flap, glue the eyes, eyelashes, and tongue on the flap, and glue the bow tie below the flap. Add a pompon as a nose.

To Make the Lion Bag

From construction paper, draw and cut out the front view and the back view of a lion. Glue them onto the front and back of a shopping bag with handles. Add details with markers.

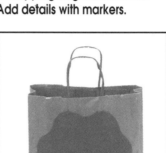

To Make the Happy-Lady Bag

Fold down the top 3 inches of a bag to form a flap. On one piece of paper, draw and color a person's head with a hat and collar, then cut it out. On another piece of paper, draw and color a person's body, then cut it out. Glue the head part on the flap. On the bag under the flap, glue the body. Under the neck, poke two holes through the flap and the bag. Thread ribbon through the holes and tie a bow. This will hold the bag closed.

Use your creativity, and people will admire the bag as much as the gift inside!

To Make the Bag for Mom or Dad

Cut out a picture from an old greeting card. Glue it onto a paper doily, then glue both of them onto a paper bag. Use markers, glue, and glitter to decorate and write a message on the bag. Place a gift inside. Fold in the bag's opening about 1 inch. Close the bag and punch holes across the top. Lace string through the holes and tie the bag closed.

To Make the Birthday Bag

Glue construction paper onto the wide sides of a grocery bag, from the bottom to as high as you want the handles. With a pencil, draw a line around the bag a few inches below the top of the construction paper. Draw a handle on each wide side. Cut off the top of the bag, cutting around the handles. Then cut out the insides of the handles. Decorate the bag with ribbon and markers. Place some tissue paper in the bag.

To Make the Star-Print Bag

Cut a potato in half. With an adult's help, use a table knife to carve an upraised moon shape on one half and an upraised star shape on the other half. Press the potato halves into poster paint, then press them onto a bag to make star prints and moon prints. Let the paint dry. Put a gift in the bag. Fold over the top of the bag, and punch holes through the flap. Lace yarn through the holes, and tie it.

More Ideas

Weave your own gift bag by cutting wide strips in a bag from the opening to the bottom, then weaving strips cut from another colored bag horizontally through the bag strips. Glue or tape the ends in place, and glue on paper handles.

Cover a paper shopping bag with scrap-fabric patches, or glue brightly colored yarn around it.

Autograph Hound

This pooch is perfect for displaying all of your friends' signatures.

1 Cut out a large rectangle from the grocery bag. Fold it accordion-style.

2 Open the paper. Use markers to draw a dog across the whole piece of paper.

3 Have your friends sign the card at the end of the school year. Keep it as a memento.

You Will Need:
- grocery bag
- scissors
- markers

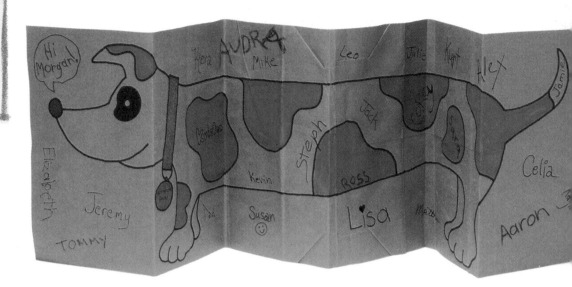

More Ideas

Use the autograph hound as a get-well card from a group of people.

Make a similar card using another long animal, such as a giraffe, lizard, otter, or snake.

Toadstool Pencil Holder

Is there mush-room for pencils in this holder? There certainly is!

You Will Need:
- lunch bag
- rubber band
- paints

1 To form the cap of the toadstool, carefully turn the open end of the bag so that a few inches of it hang over the sides.

2 Put a rubber band around the section beneath the cap.

3 Paint the toadstool, and let it dry. Put your pencils, pens, and markers in it.

More Ideas

For a puppet-show set, make palm trees by cutting palm fronds from the folded part of the bag.

Invent your own funny creature by cutting hair from the folded part and painting on a face.

Strings of Bag Beads

Roll them, twist them, or bend them. Then string them up and wear them!

You Will Need:

- grocery bags
- scissors
- markers, glitter, or paints
- glue
- toothpick
- hole punch
- yarn or string

To Make a Tube Bead

Cut a long strip from a grocery bag. Make it as wide as you'd like your bead. Use markers, glitter, or paints to decorate a few inches at one end of it. Then, starting at the plain end, roll the strip around a toothpick. Glue down the end.

To Make the Accordion-Style Bead

Cut a strip from a bag. Decorate it on both sides with markers or paints, then fold it accordion-style. Punch a hole in each section between the folds.

To Make a Necklace, Bracelet, or Anklet

Create as many beads as you like, then arrange them on your work space. Wrap tape around the end of a length of string or yarn, then thread it through the beads. Trim the string, leaving enough room at both ends to tie them together.

More Ideas

For a twisted bracelet, cut a 2-inch-by-1-foot piece from a paper bag. Decorate both sides of it. Crumple it until it's soft and wrinkled, then hold each end and twist it. When it's twisted as much as you like, tape the ends together. Slide it onto your wrist.

23

Barnyard Bag Games

Whether you're a city kid or a country child, you're sure to think these games are a hoot.

You Will Need:

- paper bags
- boxes
- gift-wrap tube
- scissors
- tape
- paints
- glue
- small rocks
- construction paper
- newspaper
- cylindrical container
- markers
- fabric
- dried beans
- rubber bands
- stapler
- plastic berry baskets
- cotton balls
- thin cardboard
- other accessories

To Make "Feed the Pig"

For the snout, cut off a short, tube-shaped section from a large cylindrical container. Trace around it onto a large box, and cut out the circle. Cut open a bag and use the paper to cover the box and the snout. Glue the snout into the hole in the box. Paint the pig. Glue on cut-paper ears and use markers to add eyes and feet. Curl a chenille stick, and glue it on the back as a tail.

For the feed, cut out three circles from fabric. Place dried beans in the center of each circle, then gather the edges and hold them with a rubber band. Try to toss the feed into the pig's mouth.

To Make "Bell the Cow"

On the top of a box, trace around the end of a gift-wrap tube. Cut out the hole. Wrap the box with paper. Cut a hole in the paper to match the hole in the box. Tape the paper in place, but leave one narrow side open. Paint the tube, and let it dry. Cut tabs in the bottom of the tube. Insert the tabbed end of the tube into the hole in the box, and glue the tabs against the opposite side. Let it dry. Fill the box with small rocks through the open side. Seal that side, then paint the box and let it dry.

Turn a white bag upside down, and paint it to look like a cow's head. Glue on cut-paper ears. Stuff some newspaper into the head, and tape it around the end of the tube.

To make each belled collar, cut down the seam of three lunch bags and cut off the bottom sections. Twist each long rectangular strip, then tape them together into a circle. (It should fit over the cow's head.) Paint the ring and let it dry. Tie on a large jingle bell. Try to toss the belled collar onto the cow.

To Make "Cornfield Bowling"

Use a pencil to draw an ear of corn on six lunch bags. Leave a few inches of blank space at the top of each bag. Paint the corn and let it dry. Outline the corn with a black marker. Stuff the bags with newspaper. Fold down the tops of the bags, and staple them closed.

To play, arrange the corn in a triangle, then use a rubber ball to bowl over as many as you can.

To Make "Hens and Chicks"

Game Board

Create a large triangular board out of bag paper. Paint the board, and let it dry. Use markers to draw spaces at least 2 inches long. Make the same number of spaces on each side of the triangle. From paper, create a short path with 3 spaces leading out from each side of the triangle. Leave space to glue the nests on the ends.

Spinner

Cut out a circle from cardboard and paint it, as shown. Add numbers from 1 to 4. Glue it in the middle of the game board, and let it dry. Cut an arrow out of cardboard and paint it. Poke a hole in the arrow, the spinner, and the game board. Fasten the arrow loosely to the board with a metal fastener.

Nests

Cut a few inches from the top of a lunch bag, then fringe the sides and curl the ends around a pencil. Glue the nests onto the ends of the paths leading out from the board.

Chicks

Dip cotton balls in paint and let them dry. Make four red chicks, four brown chicks, and four yellow chicks. Glue on paper beaks and feet, and use a marker to add eyes. Place the matching chicks in the nests.

Hen Baskets

Cut a hen shape from the side of a paper bag and paint it. Paint one red hen, one brown hen, and one yellow hen. Glue each hen in a plastic berry basket. Poke a hole in each corner of the board, and tie on the hen baskets. Tie the red hen directly across from the nest with the red chicks, and the other hens across from the matching chicks.

How to Play

Three players are needed. The point of the game is to move your chicks from the nest to the matching hen. Each player takes a turn with the spinner. You are allowed to move one chick per spin, and you can move to the left or the right around the board. You can have all of your chicks on the board at once, if you wish. If you land on a space with a chick already on it, send the chick that was there back to the nest to start over. Whoever is the first player to move all of his or her chicks safely to the hen basket wins.

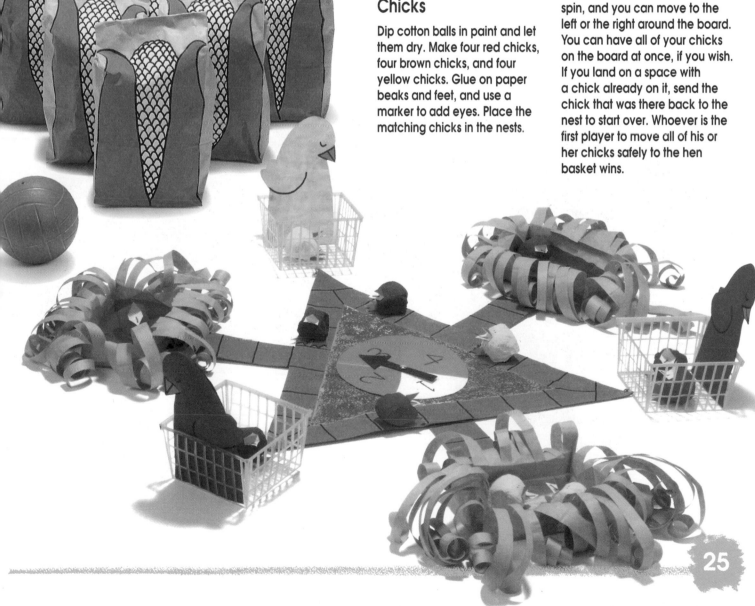

Coiled Baskets

With only a few materials and some patience, you can create a sturdy, attractive coiled basket.

You Will Need:

- grocery bags
- scissors
- ruler
- large-eye needle
- strong thread, string, or twine

1 Cut down one seam of a bag and cut off the bottom section. Cut the rectangular piece into long 3-inch-wide strips. Twist each strip into a tight rope.

2 Thread the needle. Form a small loop at the end of one twisted-paper rope. Wind the thread end (opposite the needle) six or seven times around the rope to hold the loop in place. Coil the rope once around the loop.

3 Pass the needle through the center of the loop, from top to bottom, to hold the coil. Make another stitch through the loop about a half-inch from the first. Make more stitches all the way around until you have a complete coil.

4 When you begin the next coil (and all the others), pierce the needle through the preceding coil every half-inch or inch to make a stitch. Add twisted-paper ropes when you need them by inserting them under the end of the coiled rope. Make the basket as large as you wish.

5 To finish the basket, knot the thread, then trim the rope end.

More Ideas

Decorate your basket with paints or markers, if you wish.

Use it as a fruit basket or a candy dish.

Gingerbread Men

These friendly fellows make any scene festive. String them over doorways or around a tree.

You Will Need:

- grocery bag
- scissors
- pencil
- paints

1 Cut a long strip from the bag. Fold it accordion-style. On the top section, draw a gingerbread man with the hands and feet touching the folds.

2 With the paper folded, cut out the man, but do not cut through the folded paper at the hands and feet.

3 Unfold the paper. The gingerbread men should be in a row, with hands and feet touching. Paint them.

More Ideas

Create other strings of things, such as kissing fish, leaping dolphins, a fleet of jets, or a line of ducklings.

Paper-Bag Snowman

This smiling snowman can sit inside all winter without melting.

You Will Need:

- paper bags
- newspaper
- rubber band
- pencil
- tape
- scissors
- construction paper
- glue
- cylindrical snack container
- twigs
- felt

1 For the body, stuff a large bag with newspaper. Gather the bag at the opening and secure it with a rubber band.

2 For the head, stuff a small bag with newspaper. Stick one end of a pencil in the opening. Gather the bag around the pencil and secure it with tape to form a neck. The other end of the pencil should be sticking out. Stretch open the rubber band on the body, and insert the neck in the opening.

3 For a hat brim, cut out a paper circle, and glue it on the head. Cut off one end of the snack container, glue paper onto it, and glue it on the brim. For arms, stick a twig into each side of the body. Add a felt scarf, a hatband, and paper details.

More Ideas

Make other characters, such as Uncle Sam or a favorite story character.

Mask Mania!

Invent all kinds of masks—funny ones, scary ones, animals, or other creatures.

You Will Need:

- grocery bags
- scissors
- ribbon
- pencil
- markers
- paints
- construction paper
- glue

To Make the Ponytailed Lady

Cut out the bottom of a bag. Cut fringe around the top, gather it, and tie it with ribbon. Ask an adult to curl the ribbon with scissors. Use this bag and follow step 1 under "To Make the Square Masks." Add details with markers.

To Make the Square Masks

1 Put a bag over your head. Place your fingers where your mouth and eyes are. Remove the bag from your head, leaving your fingers there. Draw eyes and a mouth. Cut them out.

2 Trim a few inches from the opening of the bag, or cut curved slots in the sides so the mask can rest on your shoulders.

3 Follow the instructions for the mask you want to make.

To Make the Clown

Paint eyes, eyebrows, a nose, and a mouth on the front of the bag. Make a bow tie and a hat from construction paper, and glue them on. For hair, cut wide fringe in construction paper, and glue it on. Curl the ends around a pencil.

28

It's fun and easy to do, using large paper bags and a few other supplies.

To Make the Frog

Glue blue construction paper on the front of the bag. Cut out the paper eyeholes where they're already cut out of the bag. Cut out a frog, fly, and lily pad from paper and glue them on. Position the frog so that its eyes are above the top of the bag, and so that your eyeholes are the frog's nostrils.

To Make the Chick

Cut out eyes and a beak from construction paper. Add details with markers. Glue them on the front of the mask. For the feathers, cut out strips of paper. Glue them on the mask, and curl the ends around a pencil.

To Make the Bearded Man

Draw facial features and glasses with a marker. Cut out ears from a paper bag, and glue them on. For the beard, cut wide fringe in paper, and glue it on. Curl the ends around a pencil.

More Ideas

Before Halloween, have a mask-making party where all of the guests invent their own paper-bag masks.

For variety in your masks, use different materials, such as fake fur, feathers, chenille sticks, and scrap fabric. Some different masks to try making are elves, bears, cats, goblins, dogs, ghosts, and lions.

Fish Out of Water

These adorable fish are fun to make—and quick! Make a whole school of them.

You Will Need:
- paper bags
- glue
- newspaper
- rubber bands
- paints
- markers
- scissors
- construction paper

1 To form the nose, fold back and glue the two corners at the bottom of a closed bag. Stuff the bag with newspaper. A few inches from the open end, gather and hold it closed with a rubber band. For the tail, fan out the ends.

2 Paint the fish and decorate it with markers. Cut out fins from construction paper, and glue them on. Set your fish on a shelf as a decoration or attach a string and hang it up.

More Ideas

Make fish and other creatures, and have a party with an underwater theme.

Create a mobile by hanging small fish from a dowel.

Bright Yellow Duck

This duck doesn't swim, but it's still lots of fun.

You Will Need:
- white bag
- yellow paint
- newspaper
- string
- masking tape
- scissors
- construction paper
- glue
- markers

1 Paint the bag and let it dry. Fill it halfway with newspaper. Gather and tie it with a string above the filled part. Fill the rest of the bag with newspaper. Tape it closed.

2 Cut out wings, feet, eyes, feathers, and a beak from paper. Glue them on. Add details with markers.

More Ideas

Use the duck as a favor and place card for a party. Write the guest's name on the front. Fill it with peanuts (with the shells on), other treats, and small toys.

Spooky Halloween Crafts

Ghosts suspended in midair, pumpkins grinning without care, a house with ghouls in every nook—you've found the scariest crafts in the book!

You Will Need:

- grocery bags
- foil
- scissors
- yarn
- stapler
- white bags
- glue
- markers
- clear fishing line
- flashlight

To Make the Trick-or-Treat Bag

Fold over the top of a bag several times to make a cuff. Cut a jack-o'-lantern from foil and glue it on the bag. For the handle, braid three bunches of yarn strands and knot each end. Tie the handle ends to the sides of the bag.

To Make the Floating Ghost

Cut out two arms from white paper. Glue them to the sides of a white bag. Use markers to draw a face on the front of the bag. Stuff the bag with newspaper, and staple it closed. Tie on clear fishing line as an "invisible" hanger.

To Make the Haunted House

On the front of a bag, use markers to draw and color a house. Cut out windows and doors. Place a flashlight inside the bag to create an eerie glow.

More Ideas

For a jack-o'-lantern centerpiece, stuff a paper bag with newspaper, tie the top with yarn, and decorate it.

31

Design a Doll

"Paper doll" takes on a whole new meaning with this classy trio.

You Will Need:

- grocery bags
- scissors
- ruler
- cotton balls
- string and yarn
- markers
- chenille sticks
- cardboard tubes
- glue
- rubber band
- needle and thread
- paints
- pompon
- plastic cap

To Make the Basic Doll

1 Crumple up a paper bag until it is a small ball. Uncrumple the bag and smooth it out. Do this again and again until the bag is very soft. For the head, cut a 5-inch square from the soft paper bag. Wrap cotton balls in the center of the square. Tie it with string to form a neck. Use markers to add facial features.

2 Roll a 6-inch-by-3-inch piece of the soft paper around a chenille stick to form the arms. Tie the ends with string. Place the neck over the center of the arms and tuck the neck into a tube. Cut two notches out of the tube to set the arms in.

3 At the bottom end of the tube, cut a slit in the front and the back to form two legs. Use markers to add shoes.

More Ideas

Make a whole family. When making children, use shorter tubes and make the heads and arms smaller.

They may look complex, but they're surprisingly simple to make.

To Make the Red-Haired Doll

For the pleated skirt, cut a strip from the soft paper, and use a marker to add a stripe along one side. Make a fold every half-inch or so. Glue the skirt around the waist. For the blouse, cut out a rectangular piece from the soft paper. Cut a slit in the center for the neck. Decorate it with markers. Place it over the head, with one end in front and the other in back. Make a sash from the soft paper, add a stripe along the middle, and tie it around the doll's waist. For hair, tie yarn strands together and glue them on the head.

To Make the Sailor Doll

Paint the body and the arms. For a neckerchief, cut out a triangle from the soft paper and paint it. Glue it around the sailor's shoulders. For the hat, glue a pompon on a plastic cap and glue it on the head.

To Make the Black-Haired Doll

For the skirt, cut out a large circle from the soft paper. Decorate around the edge with a marker. Cut a hole in the middle and slide it onto the waist. Use a rubber band to hold it in place on the underside. Cut out a vest from the soft paper. Decorate around the edges with a marker and poke two holes in the sides for the arms. Put it on the doll. Punch a hole on each side in the front and tie string through them. For the shawl, cut a long strip from the soft paper and fold it over once. Cut fringe in the ends and drape it around the arms. For hair, tie yarn strands together and glue them on the head. For the hat, cut out a large circle from the soft paper. Ask an adult to help you sew a running stitch around the edge of the circle. Pull the thread ends to gather the hat, then tie them in a bow. Place the hat on the doll's head.

Costumes for Kids

Big, boxy paper bags are great for quick and clever costumes. Try making the ones below, or come up with your own costume ideas.

You Will Need:

- grocery bags
- scissors
- paints
- construction paper
- glue

1 Turn a bag upside down. Cut out a hole in the bottom section for your head. Or, to make a hole for your face, put a bag over your head. Place your hand on the bag where it covers your face. Remove the bag, leaving your hand there. Draw an oval shape at that spot. Cut out the oval.

2 Cut arm holes in the front of the bag or the sides. Or, cut off the sides of the bag completely. Paint the costume or cut out paper or fabric decorations and glue them on. Add other details, such as a paper lion's tail or paper-doily apron.

3 Create any props that you'll need, such as a shield.

More Ideas

Try these other costumes: a robot, a star, a box of your favorite cereal, or a bookworm (decorate the bag as the book, and yourself as the worm).

Brown-Bag Scrapbook

The heavyweight paper from a grocery bag is the perfect material to use for a lasting scrapbook.

You Will Need:

- grocery bags
- scissors
- yarn
- old magazines
- glue
- markers

1 Cut the large sides off of several grocery bags. Place the sheets on top of one another and fold the stack in half to make a book.

2 Open the book to the middle and poke two holes in the fold. String yarn through the holes and tie the ends together.

3 Cut letters from a magazine to spell the words "My Scrapbook." Glue them on the cover. Decorate with markers.

More Ideas

Create a calendar using seven large sheets. Turn the book sideways so the yarn is at the top. Create a drawing and a calendar grid on each spread.

Easy Book Covers

Give your books a personalized look while protecting them from wear and tear.

You Will Need:

- grocery bags
- scissors
- hardback book
- pencil
- markers

1 Cut down the seam of a bag, then cut off the bottom to form one long rectangle of paper. Position it horizontally in front of you.

2 Place a book in the center of the paper. Trace along the top and bottom of it onto the paper. Remove the book. Fold along each line.

3 Place the book in the center of the paper again. Fold over each side of the paper to form flaps. If you wish, insert the book cover into the flaps. Decorate with markers.

More Ideas

Decorate your book covers with school symbols or colors, cut-paper decorations, ribbon, or fancy writing.

Village Scene

Create this colorful town using paper bags, paints, and cutouts from magazines.

You Will Need:

- paper bags
- pencil
- paints
- glue
- stapler
- old magazines
- scissors
- thin cardboard
- tape

To Make the Buildings

1 Lay a bag flat on your work surface. Leaving the top few inches blank, use a pencil to draw a building. Add details, such as a roof, shrubs, steps, windows, curtains, and a door.

2 Paint the design and let it dry. Open the bag, then close the top and fold it back three times. Staple or glue it closed. Position the building so it stands upright.

3 Make various kinds of buildings for your village, such as houses, apartment buildings, a grocery store, a barbershop, and a variety store.

Invent a town of your own, or model your scene on a place you've visited.

To Make the Cutouts

1 From old magazines, cut out pictures of people, cars, trees, and other objects for your paper-bag village.

2 Glue the cutout pictures onto thin cardboard, then cut around them.

3 To make a stand for each figure, cut out a triangular piece of cardboard that is slightly smaller than the figure, and tape it on the back.

More Ideas

Make a model of the area where you live. Draw the buildings near you, and add streets, bridges, and other landmarks. For people cutouts, use a mix of photos cut from old magazines and photos of your family and friends.

Look at postcards for ideas of other cities and towns that you can make.

Wise Old Owl

Whooo can make this owl in no time flat? Youuu can!

You Will Need:

- paper bags
- newspaper
- stapler
- glue
- scissors
- markers

1 Fill a bag halfway with newspaper. Close the bag, fold the top down twice, and staple it. Glue the stapled part down so it is as flat as the bottom of the bag. This will be the bottom of the owl.

2 From another bag, cut out feet, a face, wings, and feathers. Glue them on the owl. Add details with markers.

More Ideas

Use smaller paper bags to make baby owls.

Make other birds, such as a penguin, a puffin, a toucan, or a parrot.

Big Pink Bunny

This cheerful rabbit will brighten up any room.

You Will Need:

- paper bags
- pink paint
- newspaper
- ribbon
- scissors
- construction paper
- markers
- glue
- ice-cream sticks
- pompon
- cotton ball

1 Paint two bags and let them dry. Fill one bag with newspaper. Carefully pull the other bag over the top of the filled bag. Tie a ribbon around the bags for the rabbit's neck.

2 Cut out feet, eyes, and ears from construction paper. Add details with markers, and glue them on. Glue an ice-cream stick behind each ear for support. Draw whiskers and a mouth with markers, then glue on a pompon as a nose and a cotton ball as a tail.

More Ideas

Instead of stuffing the bunny with newspaper, fill him with a mixture of tissue paper and treats, such as wrapped candies or sandwich bags filled with cookies. Give the bunny as an Easter gift, along with a note with instructions to remove the top bag and look inside.

King-Size Octopus

It's hard to resist smiling back at these big friendly creatures.

You Will Need:
- grocery bags
- paints
- newspaper
- stapler
- glue
- ruler
- chenille sticks
- construction paper
- scissors

1 For the body, paint a grocery bag and let it dry. Stuff it with newspaper. Fold and staple the opening closed. Glue it in place so it is as flat as the bottom of the bag. Add cut-paper features for the face and glue them on.

2 For the legs or tentacles, cut down one side of a grocery bag and cut off the bottom section. Cut the large rectangle into long 5-inch-wide strips. Twist chenille sticks together, end to end, as long as each strip. Glue each paper strip around connected chenille sticks. Make eight legs. Paint them. Staple them onto the octopus's body and bend them to shape.

More Ideas

Make a jellyfish by gluing on wavy strips of tissue paper instead of legs.

Make a paper-bag caterpillar by stuffing a long bread bag with newspaper and gluing on short paper legs with chenille sticks in them.

Wrap It Up!

Why buy gift wrap when you can create your own? There are countless ways to decorate it.

You Will Need:

- grocery bags
- scissors
- newspaper
- sponge
- paints
- paintbrush
- large-eye needle
- ribbon
- glue
- paper plates
- tape

1 Cut down the seam of a bag, and cut off the bottom section. Use the large rectangle that's left. If you want a larger piece of gift wrap, tape together the paper from several bags.

2 Cover your work space with newspaper. Follow the instructions to decorate the gift wrap of your choice.

3 Wrap a gift with the paper, and add a bow or other trim on top of it.

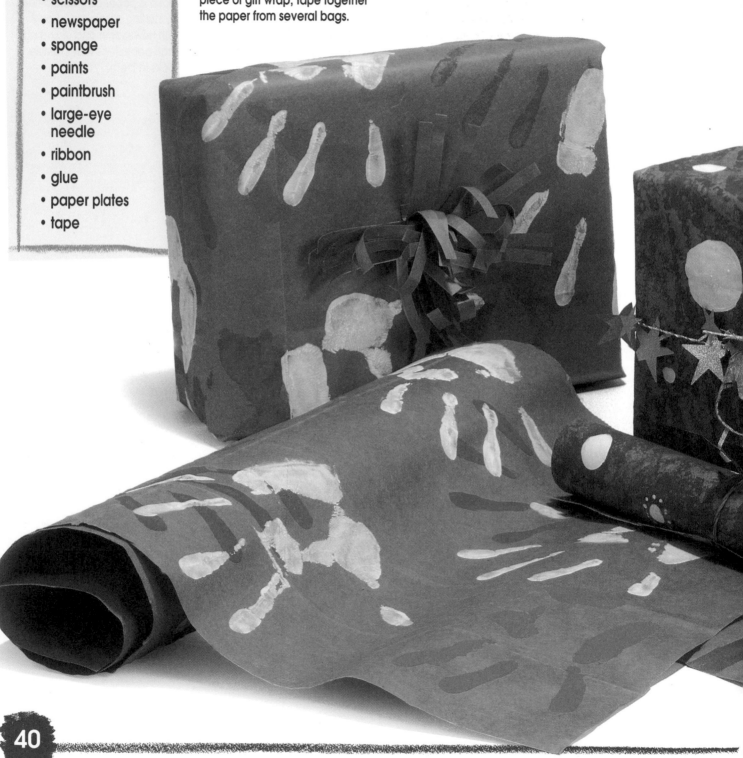

Use handprinting, sponge-painting, or ribbon-weaving, then make bows for on top.

To Make the Sponge-Print Paper

Dip a small section of sponge in some paint, and dab it over the entire surface of the paper. Let it dry. Use a paintbrush to add white dots.

To Make the Woven-Ribbon Paper

Thread a large-eye needle with ribbon. Weave it through the paper and glue down the ends. Glue wider ribbon between some of the woven ribbons.

To Make the Handprint Paper

Spread some paint on a paper plate. Press your hand in it, then press your hand all over the paper. Use several colors if you wish, but use a different paper plate for each color, and wash your hands in between colors. Let the paint dry before overlapping handprints.

To Make the Fringed Paper Bow

Cut fringe along one side of several rectangular strips of paper. Fold the strips into squares (with the fringe all facing the same way), and glue them in place. Put glue around the squares near the bottom, and glue them together in a cluster. To glue them on a package, cut tabs from the bottoms of the outside squares, and glue the tabs to the package. Curl the fringe around a pencil.

More Ideas

Decorate gift wrap by finger-painting it, tracing around cookie cutters, or painting animals or balloons on it.

To make a greeting card or a gift tag for on top, see "Cards from Bags" on page 47.

Fruit-Filled Cornucopia

This horn of plenty makes a great autumn centerpiece. For other seasons, arrange the fruits in a basket or bowl.

You Will Need:

- paper bags
- pencil
- paints
- scissors
- markers
- masking tape
- plaster of paris
- chenille sticks
- glue
- acrylic paints

1 Roll down the top few inches of a paper bag. Twist the bag tightly from bottom to top. At the top edge, gently open out the bag to form a cone shape.

2 On the sides of a grocery bag, draw and paint leaf shapes. When the paint dries, cut them out and add details with markers. Place them in the cornucopia.

3 To make the fruit, crumple bag paper into a fruit shape. Wrap masking tape around the shape.

4 Tear paper into tiny pieces. With an adult's help, mix plaster of paris according to the directions on the package. Add the tiny pieces of paper. Apply this mixture around the fruit shape, and let it dry.

5 To add a stem, poke a hole in the dried fruit, insert a chenille stick, and add glue. Paint the fruit with acrylic paints. Let it dry.

More Ideas

Make other kitchen decorations, such as artificial rolls, pretzels, and muffins.

Don't Litter! Bag

Help keep your family's car clean by making a litter bag for it.

You Will Need:

- paper bag
- scissors
- construction paper
- glue
- hole punch
- yarn

1 To form a cuff, fold down the top of the bag twice.

2 Draw and cut out pictures from construction paper. Glue them on the bag.

3 On one side of the bag, fold a small piece of paper over the cuff. Punch two holes through the cuff and the paper. For a hanger, thread a loop of yarn through the holes.

More Ideas

Notice if any rooms in your house, such as a basement or a workshop, could use a litter bag. Create a few and decorate them to match those rooms.

Paper-Bag Pilgrims

This jolly couple would look terrific as a centerpiece on your Thanksgiving table.

You Will Need:

- lunch bags
- paints
- newspaper
- stapler
- construction paper
- scissors
- glue

1 For the bodies, paint two lunch bags and let them dry. Stuff them with newspaper, then staple the tops closed.

2 Create heads from construction paper and glue them on the bodies. Add cut-paper collars, arms, hands, feet, and other details.

More Ideas

Make decorations for other holidays, such as cupids, leprechauns, bunnies, or groundhogs.

Puppets Take the Stage

Throw together an entire puppet show with a few bags, some supplies, and your imagination.

You Will Need:

- lunch bags
- grocery bags
- paints
- markers
- felt
- scissors
- glue
- construction paper
- buttons
- yarn and string
- chenille sticks
- ribbon
- pompons
- other decorations

To Make the Rabbit Puppet

Lay a bag smooth side up. Use markers to draw a rabbit face and paws. Glue on a pompon nose. Cut out ears from another bag, and glue them on the back of the head. Cut a short, vertical slit in the bag behind each ear and glue a small paper loop on the back of each ear for your fingers. Glue on a cotton ball as a tail.

To Make the Bear Puppet

Draw and paint a bear on the large side of a grocery bag. The lower section of the bear should be wide enough to put your hand through. Let it dry, then cut it out. Add details with markers. Trace around the bear onto another bag section. Cut it out. Glue the two shapes together at the edges only. Leave the lower section open. When it's dry, stuff the bear's head with paper.

To Make the Woodland Creature Puppet

On the bottom section of a lunch bag, paint a face and let it dry. Add details with markers and glue on a pompon nose. Paint an oval on the bag below the head. Cut out ears, legs, and a tail from another bag. Paint details on them. Cut fringe in the tail and weave a chenille stick through it. Glue the ears, legs, and tail onto the bag. Glue an acorn between its paws.

To Make the King Puppet

Lay a bag smooth side up. Cut out a crown from gift wrap, and decorate it with ribbon and sequins. Glue it at the top of the bag. Below the crown, glue on wiggle eyes and a mustache cut from felt. Below the mustache, cut two holes in the front of the bag. (For arms, stick your fingers through the holes.) Cut out a cape from felt and decorate it with rickrack. Glue it to the bag in the back. Punch two holes in the front of the cape and use string to tie the front corners together.

To Make the Lady Puppet

Use markers to draw a face on the bottom section of a lunch bag. Draw her top lip on the bottom section and her lower lip on the bag beneath it, so you can move her mouth. Use markers to draw her blouse. Cut a paper doily to make a lace collar. Glue it on. For a bow, poke two holes near the collar and tie a ribbon through them. Glue on a few buttons. For hair, poke holes along the top of her head and tie pieces of yarn through them.

To Make the Elf Puppet

Glue cut-paper eyes on the bottom section of a lunch bag. Cut out a hat from construction paper, and glue it above the eyes. Tie a jingle bell on the end of the hat. Glue a cut-paper shirt on the bag below the head. Add details with glitter and markers. Blow up a balloon partway and knot it. Poke a hole below the eyes, and insert the balloon knot through it.

More Ideas

For any puppet where you're using your fingers as arms, you might wish to make its clothes to match gloves that you have, so that the arms will match the body. You can also do this for rabbit or donkey ears—poke two holes in the top of the puppet and stick your gloved fingers through them as ears.

Here are some more ideas for puppets: a frog that opens its mouth to catch flies, a singer who carries a microphone, and a snake with a forked tongue (that's really your finger with a paper V taped on it).

Spirit Pennant

Make a pennant to show your support for a team, a club, or even your favorite person.

1 Cut out a triangular shape from the large side of a paper grocery bag.

2 Paint it and let it dry. Use markers to add sayings and decorations.

3 Glue folded paper strips on the ends.

More Ideas

To decorate for a holiday or a party, string together a row of colorful pennants that spell out a saying. Put one letter on each pennant.

You Will Need:

- grocery bags
- scissors
- paints
- markers
- glue
- construction paper

Handy Backpack

This whimsical backpack can hold a light lunch, some toy animal friends, or an extra sweater.

1 Fold the top of the bag down twice. On one large side, cut four 2-inch-wide slits: two near the top and two near the bottom. Paint the bag. Let it dry.

2 Pull a long strip of fabric through each set of slits. Staple the strips in place near the top of the backpack. Tie the strips to fit you.

More Ideas

Make a gift backpack by placing some tissue paper and a gift inside. Add a bow and a card. It's two gifts in one!

You Will Need:

- grocery bag
- scissors
- ruler
- paints
- fabric
- stapler

Cards from Bags

Turn those paper bags into thoughtful, handmade greeting cards or festive, colorful gift tags. Mail them to friends and relatives, or tie them onto gifts for a personal touch.

You Will Need:

- paper bags
- scissors
- large-eye needle
- yarn and string
- paper
- glue and tape
- hole punch
- photo
- paints
- colored pencils
- markers

1 Fold a section cut from a paper bag into the size you want your greeting card or gift tag to be.

2 Follow the instructions for the card you want to make.

3 For cards, write a greeting on the inside. For tags, punch a hole in the corner and tie it to a package with a string.

To Make the Duck Card

With a pencil, draw a duck on the card. Thread a needle with yarn, and sew a running stitch around the duck. Tape down the yarn ends. Add details with markers or colored pencils.

To Make the Photo Card

On the front of the card, cut out a shape that is slightly smaller than the photo. Tape the photo behind the shape. Paint hearts around the photo. Add details with colored pencils.

To Make the Tree Card

Cut out two trees from different colored paper. Glue one on top of the other so they don't line up exactly. Punch holes in the tree. Cut out a pot from paper. Glue the tree, pot, and punched circles on the card.

To Make the Gift Tags

Press your thumb in some paint, then press it on the tag to make a print. Let it dry. Decorate it with markers.

More Ideas

Create invitations and announcements from paper bags.

Try making a pop-up card by gluing a folded section inside.

Title Index

Subject Index

Look What You Can Make With
TUBES

Over 80 Pictured Crafts and Dozens of *More Ideas*

Edited by Margie Hayes Richmond

Look What You Can Make With

Tubes

Edited by Margie Hayes Richmond
Photographs by Hank Schneider

Boyds Mills Press

Craftmaker:

Lorianne Siomades

Contributors:

Maureen Murray Casazza   Edna Harrington

Kathy Murray Pietraszewski   Olive Howie

Margie Hayes Richmond   Matthew Stockton

Lorianne Siomades

Copyright © 1997 by Boyds Mills Press
All rights reserved

Published by Bell Books
Boyds Mills Press, Inc.
A Highlights Company
815 Church Street
Honesdale, Pennsylvania 18431
Printed in China

Publisher Cataloging-in-Publication Data
Look what you can make with tubes / edited by Margie Hayes Richmond ; photographs by Hank Schneider.—1st ed.
[48]p. : col.ill. ; cm.
Summary : Toys, trinkets and other terrific craft ideas all from cardboard tubes.
ISBN 1-56397-677-3
1. Paper sculpture—Children's literature. 2. Handicraft—Children's literature.
[1. Paper sculpture. 2. Handicraft.] I. Richmond, Margie Hayes. II. Schneider, Hank, ill. III. Title.
745.54—dc20   1997   AC   CIP
Library of Congress Catalog Card Number 96-80396

First edition, 1997
Book designed by Lorianne Siomades
The text of this book is set in 10pt Avante Garde Demi, titles 43pt Gill Sans Extra Bold

10 9 8

Getting Started

This book is crammed full of fun, easy-to-make crafts that each begin with a cardboard tube. You'll find a wide variety of things to make, including holiday decorations, gifts, toys, and games.

Directions

Read all the directions for each craft before you start. Big, beautiful photographs make following the step-by-step directions a snap. This really is a time when "a picture is worth a thousand words." The picture will help you better understand how to make the craft and will inspire you to make yours beautiful and unique. When we tell you to "decorate," that means use paint, crayons, markers, or whatever you like to make your craft colorful and personal. Let your imagination soar, but always remember that paint and glue need time to dry!

Work Area

It's always best to protect your clothing and work surface. So you may want to wear a smock or apron. A parent's or older sibling's old shirt works nicely, too. Simply trim off or roll up the sleeves. Next, cover the floor, table, or counter top where you will work with paper. Old newspapers are great. Or you can cut up large brown-paper grocery bags and tape a few together. Some craft-makers use old worn-out sheets. Remember to clean up when you're done!

Materials

Start now to save and store cardboard tubes. Enlist the help of your friends and relatives, especially around the December holidays. Gather supplies and put them into a box or basket. The picture below shows most of the basic supplies you will need. Add others as you think of them. There is a list of materials for each craft. Get those things before you start. If you intend to make only one of the crafts, compare the directions and the materials list. You may not need all the items that are listed.

Very Important

You'll find that many crafts have ideas for three or four different crafts based on one basic idea and set of directions. Plus every craft is presented with a *More Ideas* section. You'll also think of new ideas of your own once you get rolling. So browse through these pages, choose a craft, and have some creative fun. Before you know it, you'll be exclaiming, "Look what I *made* with cardboard tubes!"

Clowns, Cadets, and Cowboys

You can make a whole cast of cardboard characters. And they don't all have to begin with "C." The characters you can make are limited only by your imagination.

You Will Need:

- cardboard tubes
- cardboard or foam board
- glue
- scissors
- paint or markers
- construction paper
- various items for decoration: pompons, yarn, plastic eyes, rickrack, twine, chenille sticks

More Ideas

How about making a cowgirl, cook, or captain (for more "C" words). Or try a butler, a police officer, a nutcracker, an astronaut, or a self-portrait.

If you celebrate Christmas, make an entire nativity scene. Follow the basic directions to make Mary, Joseph, shepherds, and Wise Men. Can you figure out how to make a baby from a small tube held horizontally? For a real challenge, make a crib. Glue two small tubes together in an X shape. Then use two more to make another X. These will be the crib's legs. Make the bed part from cardboard. Look at the raft on page 14 for general ideas of how you might make a stable.

To Make the Basic Character

1 Choose "who" you want to make and select a tube for the body. We used parts of wrapping paper tubes for our characters. Any size tube will work. Maybe you'll want to make characters of several different sizes.

2 Plan how you want to dress your character. Sketching it out first might be helpful. Gather all your costume needs and get to work. Try pretending you are a toy designer.

3 Think of the tube in three parts—head, body, and legs. All you have to do to form the legs is draw a line from the bottom of the tube. Stop the line at a point less than halfway, but more than one-third of the length of the tube—unless you want a character with extra-long legs. Of course, you won't draw in the legs until you've painted the tube or covered it with paper.

So stock up on cardboard tubes of all sizes. Your friends are going to want to make a crowd of their very own creations.

To Make the Clown

We covered our clown's body and legs with yellow construction paper and then drew in the line to form the legs. Decorate two small tubes for arms. Look at our picture to judge where to glue them on to the "body" tube. Attach big feet made from foam board or cardboard. Decorate your clown. We used construction-paper hands, ears, mouth, and hat; plastic eyes; a pompon nose; and yarn hair. Isn't he funny looking!

To Make the Cadet

His uniform is gray construction paper wrapped around the tube. The jacket features strips of white paper highlighted with gold foil. The buttons are metal fasteners. Ask an adult to help you make the holes. Put a dab of glue by each hole to help secure the metal fastener once it is inserted. Gold garland epaulets and cord trim finish off the jacket. We used foam-paper shoes and made a hat from construction paper and foam paper. Add some gold cord, an aluminum-foil shield, and a chenille-stick plume to the hat. Draw on facial features, and you're ready to march.

To Make the Cowboy

His face and hair are done with black pen and colored pencil. His shirt is red construction paper and the pants are denim, of course. Belt, boots, and hat are made from foam paper, but lightweight cardboard will work just as well. Don't forget to decorate the boots before you put them on. A twine lasso and a gingham kerchief are the finishing touches. Howdy, "pardner."

Shaggy Dog

Make a "pet-able" toy for yourself or to give to a friend.

You Will Need:

- cardboard tube
- cardboard egg carton
- paint
- yarn
- glue
- various items for facial features: plastic eyes, buttons, felt, construction or foam paper

1 Cut two sets of two connecting cups from a cardboard egg carton for the dog's front and back feet. Cut two individual cups for the head and tail. Paint them.

2 Use a cardboard tube for the body. Glue it to the sets of feet. Glue on the head and tail cups. Cut pieces of yarn for hair and glue in place. Then decorate the head. We used plastic eyes, a button nose, and foam-paper ears.

More Ideas

Make a purring kitty or a poodle using ribbon curls instead of yarn.

Wind Chime

Delight in the sounds of a gentle breeze.

You Will Need:

- cardboard tube
- paint or paper
- string, yarn, or ribbon
- seashells

1 Choose a tube for your chime and decorate it. We painted ours, giving it a "marbled" look. Wouldn't gluing on sand and other natural seashore materials be nice?

2 Punch holes near the bottom of the tube. Thread lengths of string through the holes and the shells. (You'll be surprised at how many shells have natural holes.)

More Ideas

Instead of shells, tie on pretty, shiny metal buttons.

Turn the chime into a room freshener. Instead of shells, tie on cinnamon sticks and tiny net bags filled with spices.

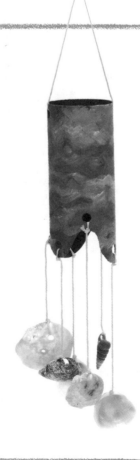

Tubie the Robot

Aren't there times when we all wish we had a robot of our own to help out with chores or just to keep us company? You can make your own robot—figuring out those magic powers might be tougher!

You Will Need:

- cardboard tubes
- box, such as a small cereal or cake-mix box
- paint or construction paper
- scissors
- glue
- various items for decoration: felt, glitter, beads, chenille sticks

More Ideas

Hide a small portable radio on or near your robot. When someone approaches, turn on the music to surprise them. Or better yet, use a tape recorder and make a tape using your "robot voice" to greet visitors.

Dress yourself as a robot for a costume party or Halloween and take your "robot" along in the parade. You might want to attach a curved strip of cardboard to the head for a handle.

1 Decide how big you want your robot to be and choose cardboard tubes. A section of a sturdy wrapping paper tube works best for the body. Decorate the tube. We made our robot look like silver metal and decorated his control panel with assorted buttons, beads, glitter, pieces of felt, and strips of masking tape that were painted red.

2 Choose and decorate tubes for the robot's legs and arms. Cut two 1" slits across from each other at the top of each leg. Looking at our picture will help you determine where to put these slits.

3 You can make hands and feet from cardboard tubes, too. We cut a 4" section from the sturdy tube and then cut it in half to make our feet. For hands, we cut two 1" rings from a tube and then cut out a ½"-1" piece. Decorate and attach the hands and feet.

4 Attach the legs by slipping the body into the slits. For extra security, apply glue or tape. We attached the arms with metal fasteners so they can move. (You'll need to punch holes in the body and in the arms first.)

5 Decorate the box for the head. We used beads, felt, and glitter. Our eyes are an old contact-lens case with black circles and "glass" buttons attached. Then we added some chenille-stick antennae.

Tag-Along Tubes

Decorating tubes and then stringing them together makes a great toy or room decoration to hang on the wall or across a window or top of a doorway. Be sure you have lots of tubes for this one.

You Will Need:

- cardboard tubes
- paint, crayons, markers
- yarn, ribbon, or thread
- paper punch
- construction paper
- plastic straws
- various items for decoration

1 Decide what kind of tag-along you want to make and how long you want it to be. Obviously, the longer you make it, the more tubes you will need. Gather your tubes and be sure you have plenty of thread, yarn, or ribbon. Fishing line is another good choice because it's so strong.

2 Cover your tubes with paint or paper. Punch a hole at each end of each tube. The holes should be about ½" in from each end of the tube, and they should be directly across from each other. It might help to make one hole and then draw a straight line from it to the other end on the outside of the tube. That will show you exactly where to make the second hole. Naturally, the tube for the front (or head) and the end (or tail) of your tag-along will need only one hole.

3 Cut lengths of yarn to be used to tie your tag-along pieces together. (The number of lengths of yarn you need will be one less than the number of tag-along pieces you have.) Make sure to cut the yarn at least an inch longer than you want the distance between your tag-along pieces to be. For example, if you're making the train and you want 2" between the cars, cut your yarn into lengths of at least 3". You'll see why in Step 4.

More Ideas

Decorate your tubes, tie them together, and hang them vertically. Make lots of them and hang like streamers to decorate for a party. Or make curtains like the bead curtains that were popular in the 1970s. A grown-up can show you what we mean.

Decorate a sturdy paper plate, punch holes around the edge, and tie on four or five tag-alongs. You've got a great moveable mobile.

Instead of train cars, decorate each tube with a letter of your name. Hang this nameplate on your door. Make one for a friend.

If you're really ambitious, make a number line of 1 to 10 or an alphabet row for a preschooler.

Read the directions before you begin. There are some slight variations that you need to be aware of early in the creative process.

4 Use the yarn to tie your tag-along pieces together. Thread the yarn into each hole and tie carefully, making secure knots. It's these knots that require the extra yarn. If the lengths of yarn are too short, you'll find it's almost impossible to tie them. In fact, it might be smart to make lengths of really long yarn and then cut off the extra once you've tied the knots. Another helpful hint is to dip the ends of the yarn in glue to make the threading process easier.

5 Cut a length of a plastic-drinking straw for each piece of your tag-along. The straw should be about an inch shorter than the tag-along piece. Affix this straw to the top of the tag-along tube. (The top is the opposite of where you punched the holes.) Use strong glue and/or tape. Thread a long length of yarn or fishing line through the straws. It should be at least 18″ longer than your tag-along when it is all stretched out.

To Make the Train

Add details to your decorated tubes. We used construction paper for our sets of wheels. Cardboard, foam board, buttons, or milk lids will make great wheels, too. The cab of our engine is made from cardboard with a foam-board top. And the grill is a section of a tube. The smokestack is the top of an old marker. When your train is done, have someone help you tie each end to something sturdy— a chair, a doorknob, or even bedposts. Make sure the yarn or fishing line is taut. Now "guide" your train on a journey.

To Make the Snake

When you decorated your tubes in Step 2, did you make a colorful, silly snake like ours? Or did you choose a specific kind of real snake to make? Nature's colors and patterns are really cool, too. Don't forget to add eyes and a tongue. We just wanted our snake to lie on the "ground," so we didn't do Step 5. You can decide which way you want to do yours. Either way, your snake can slither along.

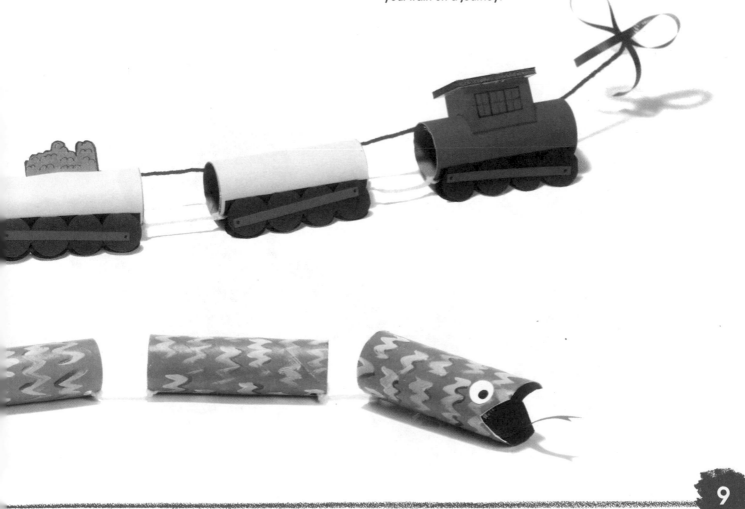

Finger Puppets

Get ready to wave your magic wand, play ball, or clown around. With finger puppets like these, you can "be" whatever you choose.

You Will Need:

- bathroom tissue tube
- colored paper
- paint, crayons, markers
- scissors
- glue
- various items for decoration: yarn, rickrack, fabric, chenille sticks, felt, netting, sequins

1 Decide which puppet you want to make. Cover the tube with paper or fabric. The number of pieces you need will depend on your design. We used three different pieces (head, shirt, pants) for the baseball player and two pieces (head and body) for both the fairy and circus clown.

2 Decorate. Remember to make all designs from the center so the face, shirt buttons, and pants line up properly. We created facial features with colored pencils and black pen. For the baseball player, we made clothes and a baseball glove from colored paper. Our clown is dressed in plaid wrapping paper, rickrack, and yarn. He has yarn hair and paper hands and feet. Our fairy also has yarn hair. She is wearing a felt and netting dress, and has wings and a magic wand made from chenille sticks. Don't forget a star for the wand.

3 Carefully glue the pieces made in Step 2 in place on the tube. We made hats from construction paper. Cut a half-circle of paper—a small one for the baseball cap and a bigger one for the clown. Curve into a cone shape and glue. Don't forget to add a bill to the baseball cap.

More Ideas

Make and give the puppets as party favors, or your guests can make their own. Make several puppets and group them together as a centerpiece.

Tube Tower Puzzle

Three-dimensional puzzles are quite popular. Make one like ours or create some of your own.

You Will Need:

- cardboard tube of any size
- paint, crayons, markers
- scissors

1 Think about a design for your puzzle. We did an easy one, using an abstract design of bright colors. How about making a building, a rocket, or a penguin?

2 Carefully cut your "tower" into three or four pieces. Lightly squeeze the tube to get your cuts started. Jagged or slanted cuts are the easiest. Your cuts need to be exact so the pieces will fit together. If you want to make curvy cuts, ask an adult to help you.

More Ideas

Make puzzles that have interchangeable parts. Making heads, bodies, and legs of people or animals that you could mix and match would be lots of fun.

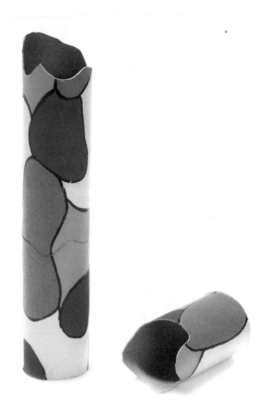

Hanger Wreath

For a holiday or any day, a wreath is a wonderful decoration.

You Will Need:

- cardboard tubes
- wire hanger
- paint
- ribbon
- colored paper
- tissue paper
- scissors
- glue

1 Ask an adult to help you bend the wire hanger into a circle shape.

2 You'll need 10-15 tubes. Make horizontal cuts in the middle of each tube; stop when you are halfway through. Decorate the tubes and then push the slit of each tube onto the hanger.

3 Cut out leaves and glue them between the tubes. Look at our picture for help. Crumple tissue papers and attach. Add a colorful bow at the top.

More Ideas

Change the colors and make a wreath for each season.

Soaring Tubes

Let your imagination soar as you create these "high-flying" crafts. Aren't tubes perfect bodies for planes, rockets, and helicopters?

You Will Need:

- cardboard tubes
- lightweight cardboard or foam paper
- paint, crayons, markers
- construction paper
- scissors
- glue or tape
- chenille sticks
- metal fasteners
- decorative items

1 Choose the aircraft you want to make. Then decide how big you want the body to be and get the right-sized tube. We used bathroom tissue and paper towel tubes, but wouldn't a rocket made from a big, sturdy wrapping paper tube be fun?

2 Decorate your tube. If you use paint, use a thick one that covers well. The cardboard that most tubes are made from is hard to cover with paint—the glued sections show through. We used lots of acrylic paint on our helicopter. Choosing a dark color works best. Sometimes it's better to glue white paper to the tube as described in Step 3 and then paint the paper the color you want.

3 You can skip Step 2 and just cover your tube with colorful construction paper. Measure the length or height of your tube and trim your paper to fit. Then lightly wrap the paper around the tube to see about how much paper you need. Cut the paper to the correct size, apply glue, and attach the paper to the tube. Smooth the paper carefully as you wrap it around the tube.

Soar even more as you pretend to pilot these aircraft on wondrous adventures to exciting places. Today you can be giving city traffic reports from a helicopter. Tomorrow, be an astronaut.

To Make the Helicopter

Make the body. Punch four holes in the tube and insert landing gear made from chenille sticks. Next cut a 1" section from another tube and trim away two small arcs from its bottom so it will fit neatly on the tube body. Decorate. Cover the open top with a paper circle and set aside. For the tail section make a long, thin cone. Next make propellers of two different sizes from lightweight cardboard or foam paper and attach with the metal fasteners. Attach the top section to the tube, slide the cone onto the back, and secure with glue or tape. You're ready to whirl away.

To Make the Rocket

Decorate the tube as described in Step 2 on page 12. One way to make the cone is to cut a half-circle out of construction paper, roll one side in, and tape or glue. We made ours about 3" tall. Attach the cone to the top of the tube. Cut out two or four tail fins from lightweight cardboard or foam paper. Use lots of glue to attach the fins to the rocket body securely. Add details with paper cutouts, markers, or other materials. We even used some sequins. It's blast-off time!

To Make the Airplane

Make the basic body. We covered ours with colored construction paper. We made windows with paper cutouts and markers. Make a short cone for the nose of the plane and decorate before attaching. We added a foil point to ours. Cut wings and triangular tail sections from cardboard or foam paper. Attach with lots of glue. Now fly, fly away.

More Ideas

Make several different soaring tubes, attach fishing line, and hang them from the ceiling of your room.

Instead of a passenger jet, make a military plane. Or try your hand at making an old-fashioned prop plane, a modern glider, or an ultralight plane.

Use several tubes and design your own space shuttle or orbiting space station.

Raft of Tubes

Get away from it all as you pretend to float away downriver.

You Will Need:

- cardboard tubes
- ice-cream sticks
- paint or colored paper
- yarn
- scissors
- glue

1 Decorate your tubes for the raft's bottom. We used six paper towel tubes. Glue on an ice-cream stick floor. We made a railing from pieces of tiny tubes (from fabric softener) and yarn.

2 Attach two tubes to the floor for the roof-support poles. Decorate the roof tubes and begin to cut them in half, stopping before going all the way through. Bend and glue them to each other and then to an ice-cream stick. Glue the stick to the support poles and attach another tube in the bend.

More Ideas

Glue a plastic-foam tray to the bottom and your raft will float.

Make-It Monster

A monster isn't quite so scary when you create it yourself.

You Will Need:

- cardboard tubes
- paint
- scissors
- glue
- various items for decoration

1 Design and sketch your monster. Then cut out pieces of tubes. We used a variety of sizes. Paint the tubes inside and out. We used the naturally curved parts of the tubes to make wings, feet, and a tail. If you want the jagged look, ask an adult to help you cut the tubes.

2 Glue the tubes together, allowing time for the glue to set. Then add facial features. We used chenille sticks, paper circles, and pompons.

More Ideas

Instead of a monster, make a modern art sculpture like you might see at playgrounds.

Roaring Tubes

Make your own trucks, buses, cars, and construction equipment. Don't forget to make the *roaring* sound as you play.

You Will Need:

- cardboard tubes
- lightweight cardboard or foam board
- construction paper or foam paper
- chenille sticks
- plastic-drinking straws
- paint, markers, or colored pencils

1 Choose a vehicle to make. Look at our pictures for help in deciding on the shape. Notice the sleek windshield of the race car. Making the rounded cab of the truck and the bulldozer's curved blade is easy because of the tubes' rounded shape.

2 Cut your tubes and decorate them. We drew windows on our bus and used construction paper and foam paper to cover some of the vehicles' cabs and windshields.

3 Make holes where the wheels will go on your vehicle. Use a hole punch if it will reach. Otherwise, ask an adult to help you. Also make holes so the van and trailer can be attached. We used a chenille stick, but yarn will work, too.

4 Put a plastic-drinking straw through the holes you made in the body of your vehicle so that the straw is inside, like an axle. Or, simply glue the straw to the bottom of the vehicle where you want the wheels to go. If you do this, you can skip Step 3.

5 Cut out wheels and punch a hole in the center of each one. Cut pieces of chenille stick that are at least ½" longer than the straw pieces. Push a chenille stick through the straw, and thread the wheels on its ends. Twist and you're ready to roll.

More Ideas

Make an engine and train cars. String them together with yarn. Or make and give these vehicles as stocking stuffers.

Have a transportation-themed birthday party. Surround the cake with a variety of these vehicles. Give a roaring tube to each guest as a party favor. Or even better, let guests make their own.

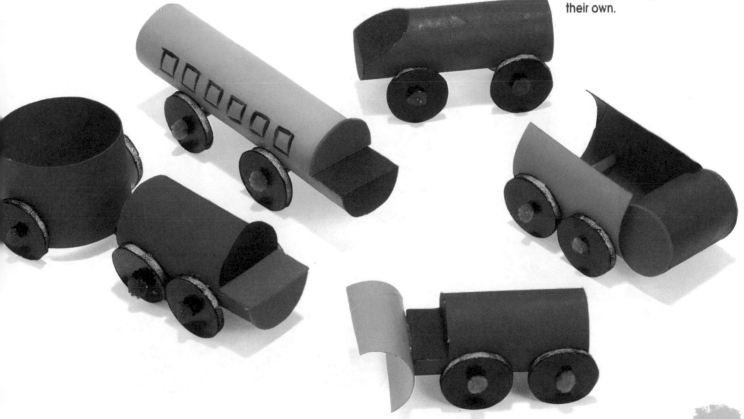

Musical Tubes

Sing a song, dance a jig, play a tune, keep the beat—all fun ways to enjoy these musical crafts. Isn't it amazing how many instruments are shaped like cardboard tubes?

You Will Need:

- cardboard tubes
- paint or colored paper
- scissors
- glue
- waxed paper
- rubber bands
- paper cup
- aluminum foil
- metal fasteners
- dried beans or popcorn kernels
- various items for decoration: yarn, foam paper, rickrack, ribbon

To Make the Basic Instrument

Choose the instrument you want to make and read the directions. Each one calls for some different materials, so you won't need all the items included in the list. Decorate your tube with paint or cover it with some colorful paper of any type—wrapping, construction, even tissue paper.

To Make the Bass Bog

We used a 7˝ section of tube. (That is a good size for an average rubber band to stretch around.) Then we covered the tube with paper that we had already painted with watercolors. Make two small cuts on opposite sides of one end of the tube. Do the same on the other end, keeping those cuts in line with the first cuts. Stretch a large rubber band and place it in the cuts. Pluck the rubber band at one of the open ends. Does it sound like a frog?

To Make the Rhythm Tube

Decorate your tube. Put a little glue around one of its ends and cover that end with layers of aluminum foil, carefully placing the edges of the foil on top of the glue. Let it dry. Pour beans or popcorn kernels into the open end of the tube. Then glue a piece of foil to that end. Add yarn circles, tassels, or other decorations, and you're ready to keep the beat for the neighborhood band.

Invite some friends, have an instrument-making party, and then strike up the band. Perform for your families—just pick some favorite songs that you all know.

To Make the Clarinet

Choose a tube and decorate it. Maybe you'll want to make yours look more like a real clarinet than we did. Ours is short and colorful. Ask an adult to help you use a large nail or pointed scissors to make four or five holes that are about ¼" across. Put them about 1" apart. Cut off the bottom of a small paper cup and discard it. The rest of the cup will be the "bell" of the clarinet. First decorate the cup and then glue or tape it to one end of the tube. Cover the opening of the bell with waxed paper. We used a rubber band to hold it in place. Move your fingers over the holes while you hum a tune into the open end.

To Make the Rain Stick

Decorate your tube. We put patches of brightly colored paint directly on a paper towel tube. Ask an adult to help you use a very small nail to poke holes in the tube. Put a tiny drop of glue around each hole and insert a metal paper fastener in each one. Cover one end of the tube with aluminum foil and glue it in place. Pour in large dried beans and cover the other end with foil and decorate. Gently turn the tube on end and listen to the sound of rain as the beans fall against the metal fasteners. Instruments like these were used by native peoples of Central and South America to invoke rain.

To Make the Kazoo

Nothing could be easier than making a kazoo, so why not make lots of them—they're great party favors! Decorate your tube. A bathroom tissue tube is just the right size, or cut the length you want from a longer tube. We covered our tube with colorful plaid wrapping paper. Attach a piece of waxed paper to one end of the tube. Use glue or hold it in place with a rubber band. We put a decorative piece of foam paper around each end of ours. Hum a tune into the open end of the tube.

More Ideas

Use the basic clarinet directions and make a recorder. Make a "mouthpiece" by squeezing the tube at the open end. Make holes of different sizes in this order from the mouthpiece: one medium, two large, one medium, one large, and two sets of two small ones side-by-side. Remember that the bell of a recorder is smaller than a clarinet's. Can you figure out how to make a flute?

Menorah

Candles are an important part of celebrations. You see them for all seasons and special occasions. Using a cardboard tube is an easy way for you to begin your own candle making.

You Will Need:

- cardboard tubes
- cardboard
- red, orange, and yellow tissue paper
- paint or colored paper
- scissors
- glue
- ribbon

1 Cut two rectangular pieces of cardboard. (We cut up a gift box.) Our base is 11" long and 5" wide. The upper candle-holder part is 15" long and 3" wide. Paint both and let dry.

2 Paint your cardboard tubes or cover them with colored paper. We used a total of seven bathroom tissue tubes. We cut four of the tubes in half to make eight shorter tubes.

3 Decorate the "posts" by wrapping ribbon around two of the tubes. Attach the candle-holder part and base cardboard to these tubes. The tubes go between the two pieces of cardboard as shown. Use lots of glue around the rims of the tubes and position them carefully. Hold in place until the glue is set.

4 Cut out nine sets of 5" squares of red, orange, and yellow tissue paper. Overlap and twist each set to form a flame shape. Glue to the inside of the nine candle tubes.

5 Glue the one remaining tall tube, called the Shamos, in the exact middle of the candle-holder cardboard. Glue it securely and then glue the short candles in place as shown.

More Ideas

Celebrate Christmas with an Advent candle ring. Use a sturdy paper plate as a base. Make one pink and three purple candles, gluing them in a circle shape. Depending on your faith, you may want to make a red or white center candle.

Celebrate Kwanzaa with a kinara. Make cardboard base and candle-holder parts like the menorah's. There are seven kinara candles. To depict the order of lighting and the relative amount of time the candles have "burned," you can make them differ in length. For example, if the longest is 4 ½" tall, the next one will be 4", the next 3 ½", and so on, with the shortest being 1 ½". Glue them on the cardboard in order from longest to shortest, left to right. The three tallest candles should be red, the middle one black, and the others green.

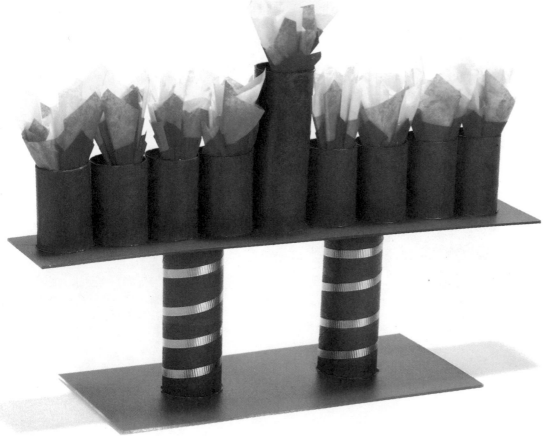

Talking Tubes

Communicate like the children of long ago.

You Will Need:

- cardboard tubes
- waxed paper
- rubber bands
- 10´-20´ of heavy thread or dental floss
- paper clips
- paint or construction paper
- scissors
- glue or tape

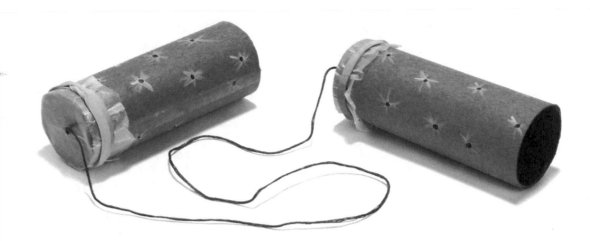

1 Decorate two tubes. Cut two circles of waxed paper and poke a tiny hole in the center of each. Insert one end of the thread through each hole. Tie a paper clip to the end of the thread.

2 Put the paper clip inside the tube and secure the waxed paper to the tube with a rubber band. Give a friend one tube and you keep the other. Go far enough apart so that the string is tight and start talking!

More Ideas

Create a mystery play where you'll need to use your talking tubes. For even more fun, make up a secret code.

Napkin Rings

Brighten your table with these easy-to-make crafts.

You Will Need:

- cardboard tubes
- scissors
- glue
- tape
- various items for decoration

1 Cut 1˝ to 2˝ sections from tubes. Paper towel or bathroom tissue tubes are just the right size.

2 Decorate your sections. We wound yarn around one, ribbon around another, and covered one with paper with ribbon borders. Choosing holiday colors or colors that match your dishes would be nice.

More Ideas

Attach paper cutouts to the top of your napkin rings. Try flowers, bunnies, autumn leaves, or circles with each guest's name.

Games Galore

We all know that playing games can be a lot of fun. Now you'll see that making the games can be great fun, too. We'll give you directions for making a few games. You'll probably think of others to make.

You Will Need:

- cardboard tubes
- plastic-foam trays
- cardboard or foam board
- colored paper
- scissors
- glue
- paint, crayons, markers
- plastic rings
- clothespins
- uncooked macaroni
- foam ball
- die

1 Choose the game or games you want to make. Think about the materials you will need. You will probably need lots of tubes, so your first step may be to start saving tubes several weeks ahead of time. Or contact your neighbors and friends and ask them to start saving tubes. It's amazing how fast tubes will accumulate when lots of folks are saving them.

2 Look at the pictures of the game or games you want to make so you can get the correct number and size of tubes. Asking an adult to help will make the cutting easier and safer. Paint or cover the tubes with construction paper. Letting your imagination run wild as you decorate can be fun, too. Our tubes are plain but colorful.

To Make the Ring Toss

Decorate a large plastic-foam tray. Ours is 9" x 12". Be sure to have at least two different colored sections. Ours are white and deep pink. Put a number, such as 10, on your decorated tube and glue the tube to the tray. Put numbers in the other sections. Looking at our picture will help. Get two rings that are 2"-3" across. We made ours by cutting out the insides of plastic lids. Ask an adult to help you or use an old bangle bracelet. Or make cardboard rings from large wrapping paper tubes. You're ready to toss the rings and keep score. With our board, we give 10 points for ringers, 5 points if the ring is mostly in the white area, and 2 points for the dark pink. Rings that fall totally on the floor don't get any points.

Why not have an Olympics party? Set up lots of different games like these for your friends to try—remember to reward effort and improvement, too.

To Make the Clothespin Game

Paint a plastic-foam tray, a piece of cardboard, or a piece of foam board. We used a 5" x 9" piece of foam board. Glue your decorated tube to the center of the board. Don't you like our polka-dotted, ribbon-based one? Grab a friend and some clothespins—it's game time. See how many times each of you can get a clothespin into the tube out of ten tries. To make the game more challenging, try dropping the clothespins faster and faster and/or by raising your arm higher and higher.

To Make the Macaroni Marathon

Decorate a piece of cardboard or foam board. We painted a 7" x 20" piece of foam board, but the bottom of a large cardboard box will work just as well. Cut out sixteen pieces of tube that are each about 1 ½" high. Decorate them as two different sets. Cut out four pieces of tube about 3" high. Decorate two to match each set of your short tubes. Put START and FINISH on each pair. Attach the tubes to your board as shown in the picture. Play as a toss game for two players, seeing how many tosses it takes to get from START to FINISH or see *More Ideas* for directions on how to play it as a relay game.

To Make the Bowling Pins

Choose at least three different sizes of tubes. We made six pins, but you could make ten, like in a bowling alley. Decorate your pins. Make them colorful like ours that are covered with construction paper. Or paint them to look more "real." Set the pins up and try to knock them down with a foam or yarn ball. Keep score as though you were really bowling.

More Ideas

To play Macaroni Marathon as a relay, each player puts ten pieces of macaroni in the START cups. Take turns rolling a die and moving your pieces up your side. The first player to reach the FINISH cup with all pieces wins. Hint: You can break up a roll—for example, if you roll a six, you can move one piece up by four cups and a different piece up by two.

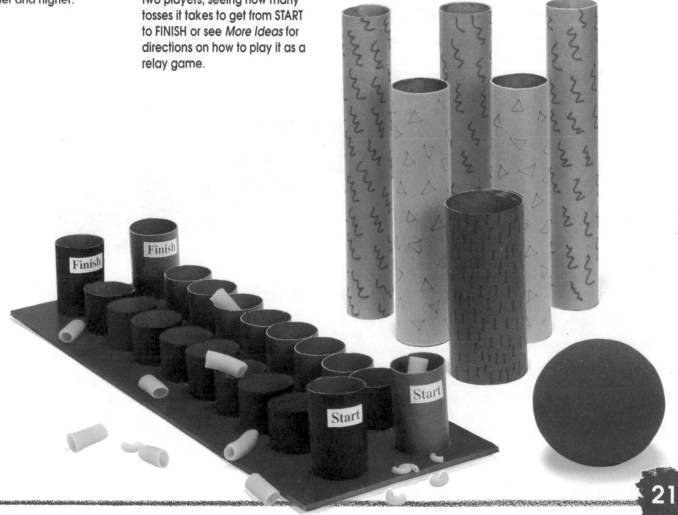

Desk Organizer

Make your own holder to keep supplies handy and neat.

You Will Need:

- cardboard tubes
- colored paper
- paint
- plastic-foam tray
- scissors
- glue
- various items for decoration

1 Design your organizer. Choose a variety of tubes and cut sections of differing heights. Decorate with paint and/or colored paper. We painted our tubes and trimmed them with wavy strips of painted paper.

2 Paint the tray and let dry. Then decorate the tray. Finally, glue the tubes to the tray. Hold them in place until the glue sets.

More Ideas

Instead of a plastic-foam tray, use a shoe box lid or trim the bottom 2" from a tissue box. Add MOM or DAD letters for a "special day" gift.

"Write" Props

Decorate or play with these oversized and kooky crafts.

You Will Need:

- cardboard tubes
- construction paper
- colored pencils, paint, or markers
- scissors
- glue or tape

To Make the Pencil

Make and decorate a cone for the pencil's point. Ours is about 3" long and made from paper that we decorated with marker and colored pencils. Paint or cover a large tube to look like a pencil. Don't forget the eraser. Insert the wide part of the cone into the other end of the tube and glue or tape.

To Make the Crayon

Choose a color for your crayon. Form a cone for the point from a 2" x 5" rectangle of decorated paper. Cover the opening with a small circle of paper. Decorate the tube. Looking at a real crayon will help with the details. Insert the cone into the tube and secure it with glue or tape. Glue a paper circle over the open end.

More Ideas

To help a preschooler learn colors, make a set of crayons in basic colors.

Make the eraser part of the pencil from a paper cup or piece of tube that is slightly larger than the pencil. Slide the eraser off and store pencils or other surprises inside the tube.

Tube Tea Set

It's fun to dress up and pretend to serve tea to your friends. And it's just as much fun to make a tea set of your own design.

You Will Need:

- cardboard tubes
- paint
- colored paper
- plastic-foam tray
- scissors
- glue
- various items for decoration: buttons, beads, rickrack, stickers, glitter, chenille sticks

1 Cut a section from a large wrapping paper tube for the teapot. Ours is 4" tall. Cut sections from a medium-sized tube for your cups. We used smaller tubes for our cream and sugar containers, but you can use whatever size you choose.

2 Decorate your tubes. We sponge painted ours, but covering them with wrapping paper or fabric would look terrific. How about an old-fashioned flowered design? (Don't forget to paint the insides of the tubes, too.)

3 To make the spouts, first cut triangular shapes from the tubes. It's easiest to start at the edge, like our creamer. Ask an adult to help if you start below the edge, like our teapot. The spouts are made from pieces of colored paper folded and glued inside the tubes.

4 Make handles from strips of colored paper or lightweight cardboard. Chenille sticks would work well, too. Just form a curve and glue the two ends to the container.

5 Make cone-shaped lids from sheets of half-circle paper. Glue on a button or bead knob. Put the set on a decorated plastic-foam tray, and you're ready to say, "Tea is served."

More Ideas

Make a complete set of pretend dinnerware. Decorate large and small paper plates and soup bowls to match your tea set.

More Games Galore

You probably never realized how many games involve tube-shaped elements. Here are a few more that are easy to make. Collecting the tubes could be the hardest part.

You Will Need:

- cardboard tubes
- cardboard or foam board
- construction paper
- small paper cup
- paint, crayons, markers
- scissors
- glue
- yarn
- large button
- small buttons or coins
- marbles

1 Look at the games pictured here. Decide which one you want to make. Maybe you'll decide to make them all. Just be sure you have enough tubes—plan ahead and start saving early.

2 Decorate your tubes with paint or cover them with construction paper. If you use paint, remember that some cardboard tubes really soak up paint, so you have to use a lot and give it time to dry. That's true for all the crafts in this book. If you cover them with paper, you'll find that it's smart to measure and trim your paper before you start to glue or tape it to the tube.

To Make the Tunnel Game

Decorate five or more tubes. Cut out a ½"-¾" strip from the length of the tube. Looking at our picture will help. Paint the insides of the tubes and then glue them together with the open side down. That's all you really have to do for this game except assign a point value to each tunnel. We made ours fancier by painting and then attaching a foam-board top. Then we used more foam board to make a wavy backdrop to display the point values. Cardboard will work, too. Get your marbles, and try to roll them into the tunnels. How high can you score with ten tries?

Not only are games fun to play and to make, they are great gifts. Everyone really likes to get something that you've made yourself.

To Make the Coin Game

Cut and decorate a large piece of cardboard or foam board. Ours is 8" x 14" and painted bright gold. Decorate ten bathroom tissue tubes. We covered ours with construction paper, and used sticker-type numbers to show the point value of each tube. Writing numbers on with a marker or crayon will work just as well. Glue the tubes to the base. Be sure all your numbers face the same way. We placed our tubes with the high point values in the middle and the lower ones near the edges of the board. You're ready to get a friend and take turns trying to toss a coin into one of the tubes—the higher its point value, the better. Don't stand directly over the board. As you become good at the game, stand farther and farther away.

To Make the Thread-the-Tube Game

Decorate a bathroom tissue tube anyway you like. We painted ours green and then glued on stripes of yellow construction paper. Punch a hole near one end of the tube. Get a piece of yarn or ribbon that is 12"-18" long. Tie one end through the hole in the tube and the other to a large button. To play, hold the tube in an upright position as shown in the picture. Swing the button in an upward motion, trying to get it to go into the tube. We think making the game is much easier than playing it!

To Make the Button-Toss Game

Decorate a bathroom tissue tube and attach a small paper cup to one end. We painted both pieces red. Decorate a piece of cardboard, foam board, or a plastic-foam tray. Create sections like those in our picture. We drew two ovals about 2" apart. That left four corner areas. Then we assigned a point value to each area. Glue the tube in the center of the base and assign it a point value. Step back and try to toss your buttons into the cup. Play by yourself or with a friend. How many points can you get with five buttons?

More Ideas

Instead of tossing buttons in the Button Toss Game, put the game board on a table and try to flip or flick the buttons up and into the cup.

Can you figure out how to use four tubes and a cardboard base to make a football goalpost? Use a button or small ball as your football and try to "kick it" through the goalpost with your thumb and index fingers. To make the game even more challenging, keep moving your "football" farther away.

Story-Time Mobiles

All mobiles are fascinating to watch. And they can be just as fascinating and fun to make. These are really special—you can use them as puppets, too. Preschoolers will really like watching them.

You Will Need:

- cardboard tubes
- ice-cream sticks
- yarn or ribbon
- paint, crayons, markers
- construction paper
- lightweight cardboard or foam paper
- scissors
- glue
- various items for decoration: plastic-foam ball, plastic eyes, tissue paper, chenille sticks

1 Choose a tube that is no smaller than a paper towel tube. We used 24" wrapping paper tubes. Choose a theme and decorate your tube with paint or construction paper. We painted our tube first and then added other decorations.

2 Ask an adult to help you make holes in the tube. The first one should be about 3" from the end. Make another hole directly beneath it. Make two more pairs of holes—one set in the center and the other set 3" from the opposite end of the tube.

3 Make three 12"-15" pieces of yarn and tie each to the center of an ice-cream stick. Thread the other yarn end through a pair of the holes in the tube. Pull down until the stick rests on the top of the tube. Tie a hanging object to the end of each piece of yarn.

For the Ocean Theme

We made an octopus from a plastic-foam ball with foam-paper tentacles. Our crab is painted cardboard and chenille sticks. Our cute clam is a simple circle colored and folded in half with eyes peeking out.

For the Space Theme

We made a silver foam-board spaceship with tissue paper exhaust and used foam paper for our three-eyed friendly green alien and crescent-moon man.

More Ideas

Make up a story about your mobile. Then act it out. Of course, you know you can make a mobile with any theme you want!

Ribbon Holder

This "hound" will keep your ribbon where you need it.

1 Decorate a section of tube for the dog's body. Cut out the dog's front and back from cardboard or foam board, decorate, and attach to the tube with glue.

2 We made our tail section removable so ribbon holders can slide on. Just cut a 2" section of tube, cut out a tiny slice, and tape the edges of the cut back together. This makes it slightly smaller than the dog's body so it will slip inside it easily.

More Ideas
How about a holder that looks like a dinosaur or a centipede?

Sitting Scarecrow

Make a friend for your indoor garden, mantel, or table.

1 Choose a tube for the head and body. Ours is 7" long. Decorate and add facial features. We used a checked fabric for the shirt and brown paper for the head.

2 Create arms and legs from fabric or paper. Ribbon will work, too. We used burlap. We covered the lower part of the tube, too. Glue to the bottom and back of the tube.

3 Add hands, feet, and hair. We used yarn and added a burlap hat.

More Ideas
Use red felt and make a sitting Santa or green for St. Patrick's Day leprechauns.

A Crowd of Creatures

Creatures, creatures everywhere and all such fun to make! Make "real" ones or imaginary friend ones—just put on your creative thinking cap.

You Will Need:

- cardboard tubes
- cardboard or foam board
- paint, crayons, markers
- construction paper
- various items for decoration: moveable plastic eyes, chenille sticks
- stapler
- scissors
- glue

1 Choose a creature to make. Create one of these or imagine one of your own to test your crafting skills. Get a tube that suits the size you want your creature to be. How about working with a really large wrapping paper tube to create a giant creature for your room? Just don't get carried away and get your room too crowded.

2 You may want to trim the ends of your tube to give your creature a distinctive head and tail. You'll be surprised at how easy it is and what a difference it makes. See how the mouths of our lobster, fish, and dinosaur differ. Look at their tails, too. We'll tell you how we did it in the directions that follow.

To Make the Lobster

Cut a 1 ½" wedge from one end of a paper towel tube. Then make a place for the claws by cutting a 1" slit on each side. You can see in our picture exactly where to put the slits. You can also see how to cut the shape of the lobster's tail. Ask an adult to help you make three holes in each side of the tube and two more holes for its eyes. Paint or cover the tube with construction paper. Make a tail and claws from construction paper. Insert and glue the claws in the slits. Then insert the tail, squeeze the end of the tube, and staple. Insert chenille-stick legs and "eyes." Add beads and your lobster is ready for fun.

Isn't it great to give each creature an expression that reveals its personality? We think our fish is happy and our porcupine puzzled. Do you agree?

To Make the Fish

Choose a tube and decorate it. We painted a bathroom-tissue-sized one. A couple of simple cuts will create a mouth for your fish. Ask an adult to help you make a 2" slit in the fish's back. Create a tail and fins—ours were made with colored pencils on blue construction paper cut into wavy shapes. Glue on the side fins. Push the top fin into the fish's mouth and pull it up through the slit. Insert the tail fin, squeeze the back of the tube, and staple. Add moveable plastic eyes and display your fish.

To Make the Porcupine

Choose a tube and decorate it. We painted a bathroom tissue tube gray. To make the quills, we cut out six 4" x 5" rectangles. Then we cut out triangular sections about 3 ½" tall to make the spikes. This leaves a ½" tab at the bottom. Wrap each strip around the tube and glue it on. Fold up the spikes. Add cardboard or foam-board legs and a paper tail. Make a head of your own design or like ours, which is construction paper with moveable plastic eyes and marker-made ears, nose, and mouth. Your porcupine is ready to roam.

To Make the Dinosaur

Our dinosaur is made from a 10" section of a sturdy wrapping paper tube. We covered it in green speckle-painted paper. V-cuts were made for the mouth and a slant cut for the tail. Ask an adult to help you cut if your tube is real thick. Our foam-board legs are covered with the same paper as the body. Then we added back plates and a tongue made from construction paper. Marker-made eyes complete our creature.

More Ideas

Crocodiles, caterpillars, and centipedes would be natural additions to your crowd of creatures. Can you figure out how to make an octopus from a ball and eight tubes?

Write a story about your creature. If you make the whole crowd, try to write one story that involves them all.

Make a school of different kinds of fish. Find pictures of real fish and try to make lifelike models. Wouldn't that be a great science project?

29

Tube Turkey

Here's the perfect Thanksgiving table decoration.

You Will Need:

- cardboard tubes
- construction paper
- lightweight cardboard
- feathers
- markers or crayons
- scissors
- glue
- stapler

1 Our turkey's tail is seven brightly painted paper towel tubes. His body is a 6" section of a large wrapping paper tube. The head, chest, feet, wattle, and beak are construction-paper cutouts.

2 Mount the body on a piece of cardboard to keep it steady. Ask an adult to help you make a 1 ½" slit for the tail. Squeeze the bottoms of the long tubes, hold them together like a fan, and staple. Insert the "tail" in the slit you made and glue. The feathers are the finishing touch.

More Ideas

Make a bright peacock.

Flags for All Seasons

People love to decorate with flags.

You Will Need:

- cardboard tube
- paint or construction paper
- yarn or chenille sticks
- fabric or felt
- scissors
- glue

1 Paint or cover a long tube with paper.

2 Cut out a fabric or felt rectangle. Our spring flag is a 9" x 12" piece of felt. The flower is made from pieces of felt and pompons glued to the rectangle. Make three holes along one side and attach to the tube with yarn or chenille sticks.

More Ideas

Covering the pole with plastic or aluminum foil and making the flag from an old shower curtain will make it more waterproof so that you can hang it outdoors.

A Host of Handles

You can make lots of things with handles from cardboard tubes. *Lots of* handles—that's what we mean by a *host of* handles.

You Will Need:

- cardboard tubes
- construction paper
- lightweight cardboard
- paint, crayons, markers
- scissors
- glue or tape

More Ideas

Wouldn't these crafts make great props for a play? Or you could use them in an advertising display for a playground clean-up day.

Make pretend housecleaning tools. For a broom, you could insert a bundle of straw. A bundle of yarn would make a great head for a mop.

Make sports equipment. A golf club or hockey stick will be easy. Can you figure out how to create a lacrosse stick or rackets for tennis or badminton?

1 Get a long cardboard wrapping paper tube for each tube tool you want to make. Or, you can make a long tube from two or three paper towel tubes. Just tape or glue the tubes together. If you use glue, it will help to squeeze one tube as you insert it into the other.

To Make the Hoe

Use a tube with at least a 4" diameter. You can also use an oatmeal box to give you a curve like the hoe we made. Cut out a section shaped like the one in our picture. It is about 7" long with a 5" curve with a tab cut to fit up into the handle. Paint and attach to the inside of the handle with glue or tape.

To Make the Shovel

From lightweight cardboard, cut out a shovel-shape as shown. (Don't forget to include a long tab.) Paint it. Shading its center with pencil will make it look more realistic. Attach to inside of the handle.

2 You can leave the tube handles their natural brown color, paint them like we did, or cover them with colored paper.

To Make the Rake

Use a wrapping paper tube with about a 2" diameter. Cut out a section like ours, about 10" long with a tab at the top. Paint it. Ask an adult to help cut out the tines—the forklike sections of the rake. Insert the tab into the handle and attach it securely with tape or glue.

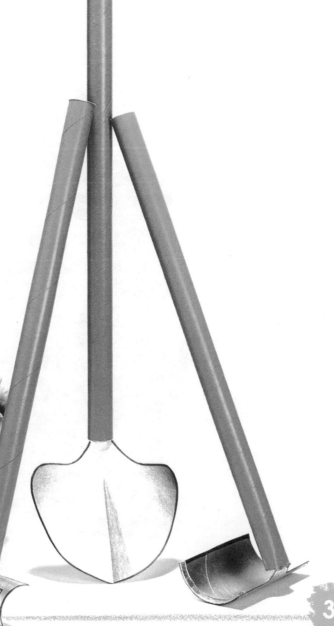

Ye Olde Tube Town

Hear ye, hear ye! This jolly play town is easy to make—and even more fun to play with. Fire up your imagination, get or make some medieval action figures, and begin a grand adventure.

You Will Need:

- cardboard tubes
- scissors
- construction paper
- glue
- tape
- paint, crayons, markers

1 Gather lots of cardboard tubes—short ones, tall ones, skinny ones, fat ones. Make a plan for the buildings you want to create for your town. Making a rough sketch will help. Ask an adult to help you cut the tubes to the various lengths needed for your plan.

2 Think about what you want your village to look like. Choose your colors and get a supply of paint, markers, crayons, and/or construction paper or paper that you can decorate yourself.

3 Decorate your tubes. We painted ours "building" colors: brown, rust, tan, and gray. (Remember paint needs time to dry.) Then we used markers and paint to create windows and doors. We even added some grass and shrubs around the bottom. It's easy to draw or paint stones, but for a more realistic look, glue on some small rocks and pebbles.

Wouldn't this be a great stage backdrop for a puppet play performed by you and your friends? Invite all your parents and serve old English tea and peasant black bread.

4 Create roofs for your buildings. We used cones made from construction paper. (One way to make a cone is to start with a paper or lightweight cardboard circle, cut out a wedge like a slice of pie, and then tape or glue the edges together.) We also made thatched roofs from construction paper decorated with markers and colored pencils. (You could also glue dried grass or hay to a piece of cardboard.) Start with a rectangle with wavy edges, fold it in half, and then fold one edge under to form a tab. Glue the tab to the top of the building.

5 Arrange the tubes to make the building you sketched in Step 1. Don't put the tubes in a straight row. Stagger them in and out, placing some behind others. You can vary the placement of the towers on your buildings as we did, too. Just make two cuts in the bottom of a short tube and slide it over the front side of another taller tube. Finally, glue the tubes together to form several different groups of buildings .

More Ideas

Create other parts for your town. Can you figure out how to make trees, bridges, and fences from cardboard tubes?

Use the ideas for finger puppets on page 10 to create some medieval characters for your town. Remember to "size" the puppets according to how big your buildings are.

Make a moat for one of your castles. Cut a paper towel tube in half lengthwise, place it so it looks like a ditch, and paint in "water." Make a drawbridge from lightweight cardboard and yarn or chenille sticks.

If modern cities are more to your liking, decorate the tubes to look like high-rise skyscrapers. For a futuristic look, wrap the tubes in foil or paint them with wild colors of metallic paints.

Lions, Tigers, and Bears

Oh my! These beasts are more friendly than fierce. Wouldn't they look great decorating a baby's or toddler's room? Just put them out of reach of little hands.

You Will Need:

- cardboard tubes
- cardboard
- scissors
- glue
- construction paper
- chenille sticks
- plastic lids
- paint, crayons, markers
- various items for decoration: plastic eyes, fuzzy pompons, felt, fabric, and fake fur scraps

1 For legs, cut four tubes of equal length. Ours are 3" to 4" long. Decorate the legs. Cover them with paper or fabric, or paint them and set aside to dry.

3 To make the head, use paper, cardboard, or plastic lids. Here's what we did: For the lion, we cut a construction-paper circle, fringed the edges, and drew in lines to make it look like a mane. For the tiger, we glued a construction-paper circle onto a plastic lid, and we covered a plastic lid with furlike fabric for the bear. Then we added facial features, using plastic eyes, pompons, construction paper, marker, and chenille sticks.

2 Cut a cardboard square for the body. We made ours about 4" x 4", but you can make one as large or small as you like. Decorate the body to match your animal's legs.

4 Assemble your animal. First glue the legs to the body, and let the glue set. All four of our legs touch. If you're making a bigger animal, attach the legs to the four corners of the body. Glue on the head.

5 Make tails and attach. We twisted chenille sticks together for the tiger, attached a small fur square to the bear, and partially covered chenille sticks with felt for the lion.

More Ideas

Make a whole zoo! Use the basic body instructions to make rhinos, zebras, and elephants. Longer legs and a paper-tube neck make a stately giraffe. Let your imagination run "wild!"

Find some tiny tubes like those from fabric softener rolls, make little animals, and turn the raft on page 14 into Noah's Ark.

Candle Canister

What a lovely way to present a gift of candles or to store your own!

You Will Need:

- cardboard tube
- paint or paper
- scissors
- glue
- ribbon or other decorative items
- 2 small paper cups

1 Choose a tube—a section of a wrapping paper one will work best. Cut three sections from the tube. Our bottom is 8" and the top is 4". The third section, about 1 ½", is needed to slide the top on, so cut a slit, squeeze slightly, insert it into the bottom section, and attach with glue.

2 Decorate your tube with paint or cover it with paper. We sponge-painted ours and added a ribbon bow. Cut the bottoms off two small paper cups. Then close off the open ends of the canister by inserting the cup bottoms and gluing them in place.

More Ideas

Use the canister to store fireplace matches or knitting needles.

Decorate a canister with your school colors and keep your pens and pencils handy and neat in your bookbag.

Give a painted canister to an artist friend to store brushes in.

Christmas Crackers

Guests twist and pull these traditional holiday favors and goodies pop out.

You Will Need:

- cardboard tube
- wrapping paper
- string, yarn, or ribbon
- various items for decoration

1 Cut the tube in half and place the two pieces back together. Use a tiny piece of tape to hold them in place while you wrap the tube with paper. Be sure your paper is at least 3"-4" longer than your tube.

2 Twist the paper at one end and tie. Pour in small candies and/or prizes through the open end of the tube. Twist the paper and tie. Decorate with ribbon, stickers, garland, or glitter.

More Ideas

In craft stores you'll find an insert that makes the crackers open with a "bang." Or, make a unique package for a present. Leave the tube whole and wrap it. Don't pull it apart; just unwrap!

Mighty Marionettes

Tubes seem to be perfect for making the moveable sections of marionettes. Aren't ours cute? Have a marrionette-making party. Your creations will be cute, too!

You Will Need:

- cardboard tubes
- paint, crayons, markers
- construction paper
- lightweight cardboard or foam paper
- ice-cream sticks
- yarn
- thread, twine, or ribbon
- scissors
- glue

1 Choose the marionette you want to make. If you don't do one of ours, sketch out your plan. It's almost impossible to figure out all the parts and pieces without something to look at as you go along. It's best to decide now how long your strings will need to be. Gather all your materials and get them organized before you begin.

2 For the marionette guide bar, cover a cardboard tube with paper or paint it. Attach two ice-cream sticks as shown in the picture. Use lots of glue. Tie lengths of thread to each end of the stick, wrapping the thread around the stick a few times. Adding a drop of glue will help. The length of the strings is critical to the success of your project, so measure and cut carefully. When you hold the guide bar, the leg strings need to fall straight. If you're new at this, shorter strings are a little easier to work with.

3 Cut sections of cardboard tubes to suit the size of your creature's body, head, tail, and feet. (We'll tell you more about our alligator and giraffe later.) Decorate your tubes. Make tiny holes in the tube where you want to attach the guide thread. Use larger holes for where you'll use yarn to connect the neck and legs to the body.

Creating a marionette is quite a fun-filled challenge, but making it perform can be the most fun of all. Can you "do" the alligator walk? How about making the giraffe nibble from a tree?

4 Insert the guide thread. Dipping the end of the thread (and yarn, too) in glue will make it stiff and easier to get through the holes. Make a big knot or tie a button on the end to hold the thread in place inside the tube. Next pull the yarn through the creature's parts and tie, but don't make it too tight. The head and body need to be able to bend.

To Make the Alligator

Use a 9" section of tube for the body, a 3" head with a mouth cut out, and a 4" squeezed-together tail section. Make feet from four 1" sections of tube. Insert your marionette strings as described above. We used foam-paper circles with holes in the middle to cover the "feet." Then we connected the head, body, tail, and feet with yarn. Don't forget eyes and teeth.

To Make the Giraffe

The body is a 5" section of a wrapping paper tube. The head is a smaller tube about 3 ½" long with a slanted section cut out in the nose area. The feet are 1" tube sections. Our giraffe has a black nose and sleepy eyes. Attach the marionette threads carefully and look at the picture to see how to connect the giraffe's parts with yarn. Don't forget the foam-paper circles, ears, or the yarn tail!

More Ideas

There is no limit to the creatures you can imagine and make.

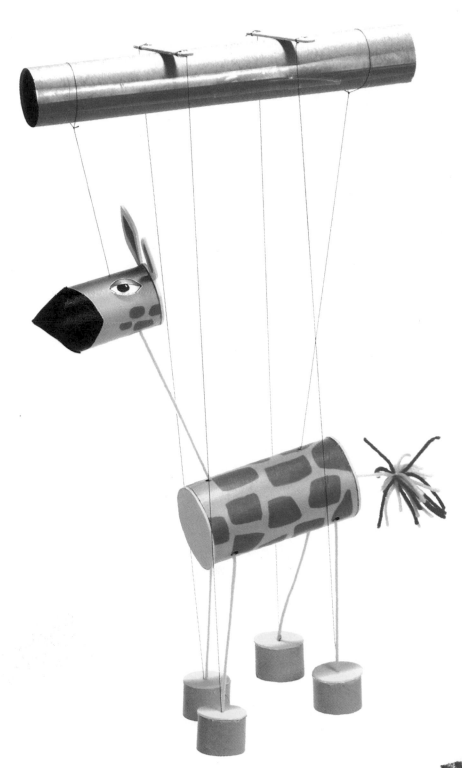

"Bird Feeder" Tube

Use this simple craft as a decoration or hang in a protected area of a porch.

You Will Need:

- cardboard tube
- paper or plastic cup
- plastic lid
- plastic-drinking straw or dowel
- yarn or chenille stick
- glue
- scissors

1 Decorate a bathroom tissue tube, or use a section from a wrapping paper tube. We covered ours with sponge-painted paper. Cut a door and punch holes near the tube's bottom. Insert a straw or dowel.

2 Glue a plastic lid to the bottom. Punch holes and insert a chenille stick hanger in the bottom section of a paper cup. Cover the top of the tube with the cup as shown.

More Ideas

To make the feeder more waterproof, cover the tube with plastic wrap or aluminum foil.

Put a fake bird on the straw for an even prettier decoration.

Tube Binoculars

Set out on a pretend safari or bird-watching expedition with your own "binoculars."

You Will Need:

- cardboard tubes
- paint or paper
- bottle cap
- yarn or ribbon
- construction paper or foam paper
- scissors
- glue

1 Paint two bathroom tissue tubes or cover them with colored paper. We used thick gray paint and then trimmed the tubes with black eye circles and yellow strips of paper.

2 Glue the tubes together. Use a paper clip to hold in place until the glue sets. Glue on the bottle cap as shown. Punch holes at the sides and add a yarn or ribbon strap.

More Ideas

Make your own pretend telescope from tubes of different sizes. Can you mount it on a wrapping-paper-tube tripod?

A Fantastic Fort

Build a big, full-sized fort for you and your friends. Or, build a smaller one for your action figures or dolls. Isn't it fun to pretend to be part of the Old West?

You Will Need:

- cardboard tubes
- heavy cardboard or foam board
- paint, crayons, markers
- large ice-cream stick
- chenille sticks
- scissors

1 Plan to make this craft after the holiday season because you will need as many wrapping paper tubes as you can find, especially if you plan to make a person-sized fort. Remember to ask others to save tubes for you. We used more than three dozen tubes. It's not necessary for all the tubes to be the same.

2 Think about how you want your fort to look. Having a plan will help as you start to glue the tubes together lengthwise. You'll notice we didn't decorate our tubes, but you can paint yours or cover them with paper.

3 Make one wall of your fort at a time. Punch holes in the end tube of each wall. Put them near the top and near the bottom so you can join the walls with twisted chenille sticks. This will allow you to take your fort apart for storage. If you are making a small fort, you can glue the walls together at the corners.

4 Make gates from two pieces of cardboard decorated with paint or markers. Make a latch with chenille sticks and a large ice-cream stick.

5 Make a play ladder from two cardboard tubes and ice-cream sticks. It's really easy. Use it inside or outside the fort.

More Ideas

Make forts for your toys. Just cut sections of tubes whatever size you want. Or how about using the small tubes from fabric softener rolls?

Build a house. Just make sure the tubes for the walls are all the same height. Follow the directions for the raft on page 14 to make a roof. Turning the tubes sideways instead of upright will make your house look like a log cabin.

A fence is another thing you can make using shorter tubes.

Great Growers

Cardboard tubes are the perfect shape for vases of all sizes and styles. But we bet you never thought of using tubes as flowerpots. We'll show you how.

You Will Need:

- cardboard tubes
- heavy plastic sandwich bags or other food-storage bags
- rubber bands
- plastic lids
- plastic-foam tray
- various items for decoration: colored paper, ribbon, yarn, buttons
- paint, crayons, markers
- scissors
- glue
- grass and herb seeds
- small plants
- potting soil

To Make the Basic Holder

1 Choose a cardboard tube sized to fit your plan. Decorate it with paint, crayons, or markers, or wrap it with colored paper. We explain exactly how we decorated ours in the steps on these pages.

2 Make a fringe at the bottom of the tube by making cuts in the tube about ½" long and spacing the cuts ¼" to ½" apart. Fan the pieces out. You might need to fold them out and up to form a crease. Glue the fanned-out sections to a plastic lid or plastic-foam tray. Looking at our pictures will help.

3 Open a plastic bag and push it down through the tube. The bag's bottom should rest on the tray or lid. Some of the plastic bag should be sticking out of the top of the tube. Fold that over, then wrap a rubber band around the top twice to hold the bag in place. Trim away any excess plastic.

4 Fill the bag with dampened potting soil. (Spreading it out on a paper plate and sprinkling it with water will probably work best.) After you plant your seeds or plants, water often and carefully. Make sure the soil isn't too wet—your seeds and plants will rot. Plants need sun, too, so find just the right spot—not too cold or too hot.

In addition to tubes, you'll need to gather some seeds and/or seedlings. And don't forget your "green thumb."

To Make the Herb Garden

We used tubes of three different sizes on a plastic-foam tray. You can use a larger tray and more tubes if you want to plant several kinds of herbs. We covered our tray with patches of cut tissue paper and then painted it with a clear varnish. Plant herbs such as mint, parsley, chives, basil, or thyme. You might even try growing a tomato plant. When your plants outgrow the pots, transfer them to a plot outdoors.

To Make the Flowerpot

We spatter painted our tube and used a plastic-lid base. Then we added some decorative ribbon. We put in some silk flowers just to show you how pretty the ones you plant will look. Plant a few wildflower seeds or dried beans. You might even try a tulip or daffodil bulb. Certainly you can plant a small petunia or marigold. Don't forget the sun and water.

To Make the Grass Head

We made ours look like a person. We painted the bottom part of the tube red, added buttons, and topped it with blue ribbon. We used a marker to make the nose and mouth and glued on plastic moveable eyes. We attached our guy to a plastic lid and then "fed" him some soil, grass seed, and water. Soon he had a head of tall, green, grassy hair.

More Ideas

There are dozens of ways to decorate your pots. Try to make them look like clay or decorate them with drawings or stickers. Or make one for a special person, featuring his or her name or initials. Covering the tube with a light coating of glue and wrapping it in yarn or ribbon will make a pretty pot.

Give your grassy-head guy some arms and legs.

Make a pretend fishbowl. Cut a section out of the side of the tube. Put in the plastic bag filled with water and a plastic floating fish. Or attach a tiny toy fish to fishing line and tape the line to the tube. Position the fish so it shows through the opening.

Tubeful Bouquets

The shape of a cardboard tube makes it a natural holder for flowers. Choose one of these and sit it on a table, hang it in a window, or display it on the wall.

You Will Need:

- cardboard tube
- cardboard or foam board
- yarn or ribbon
- dried or silk flowers
- paint or colored paper
- scissors
- glue or tape

To Make the Basic Vase

Choose the flowers you want to display and then pick your cardboard tube according to the size vase you want to make. Decorate it with paint or cover with paper.

To Make the Hanging Bouquet

Make the basic tube. We painted ours with metallic shades of paints. Cover the bottom of the tube with a paper circle or insert the bottom of a paper cup. Punch two holes near the top of the tube and tie on a piece of ribbon or yarn. Arrange flowers, hang, and enjoy.

To Make the Tabletop Bouquet

Make the basic vase. We sponge painted ours. Cut a base from thick cardboard or foam board and decorate it with paper or paint. We made a square, but you can design your own. How about a flower shape? Glue the tube to the base and let it dry. Remember lots of glue needs time to set. Arrange your flowers in the tube.

To Make the Wall Bouquet

Choose your tube and then decorate it. We painted ours with pretty swirls. Hold the tube horizontally, punch holes near its ends, and make a ribbon hanger. Glue or tape flowers in each end. Add a ribbon bow.

More Ideas

Make an apple tree. Decorate the vase like a tree trunk. Use chenille sticks for branches and paper or pompons for apples. In fact, you can make a fruit orchard—lemon, lime, orange, grapefuit, peach, pear, cherry.

Bangles and Bracelets

Plain or fancy—you can make them, wear them, or give them.

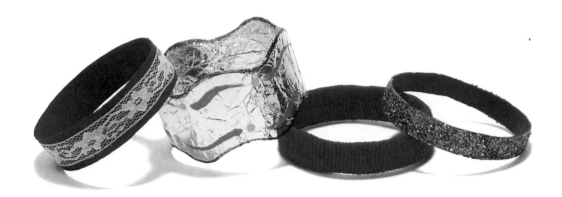

You Will Need:

- cardboard tubes
- wrapping paper
- scissors
- glue
- various items for decoration: yarn, lace, paint, glitter, aluminum foil, permanent markers

1 Find a tube large enough to fit over your hand. Decide how wide you want your bracelets to be, and ask an adult to help you cut. Slightly pinching the tube to get started will help.

2 Decorate. We made one curvy and covered it with foil and painted-on designs. We wrapped another in yarn. (Just secure the ends of the yarn with glue.) We painted two others, rolled one in glitter, and glued lace to another.

More Ideas

Have a bracelet-making party. Then give them to residents of an elder-care center. You'll brighten their day and yours.

Use smaller tubes to make bracelets for dolls. Have your friends bring their dolls over and have fun making and exchanging bracelets.

Tube Barrettes

More great crafts to make and wear. And they make gift-giving a snap.

You Will Need:

- cardboard tubes
- ice-cream stick
- various items for decoration, such as paint, fabric, paper, ribbon, rickrack

1 Cut sections from a tube. Tubes that are 2" or 3" in diameter work best. Cut each section in half to form two half circles. Decorate. We used printed fabric, felt, and paper.

2 Paint an ice-cream stick. With an adult's help, cut two slits in the barrette. Our pictures show where to put the slits. Make them just wide enough for the stick to fit through. Insert the stick.

More Ideas

Make a set of barrettes for the year's holidays. Use stickers or drawings of valentines, bunnies, ghosts, pumpkins, Pilgrims, Santa, and ideas of your own.

Winged Wonders

Flutter like a butterfly, buzz like a bee, act like an angel, and sail with the swans—or at least pretend to as you make and enjoy these crafts.

You Will Need:

- cardboard tubes
- paint, crayons, markers
- construction paper
- paper plates
- coffee filters
- cardboard or foam board
- waxed paper
- string or yarn
- various items for decoration
- scissors
- glue

1 Choose the winged wonder you want to make. If it's one of ours, read the directions now. You'll see that the materials needed vary quite a bit. Even the types of tubes that will work best differ. For example, you'll need a very sturdy one for the angel, and a long, somewhat flexible one is required for the swan. If you're crafting a design of your own, get your plan set before you begin.

2 Now you're ready to gather all your materials. Then decorate the cardboard tubes. You can paint them—acrylic paint works best, and it may take more than one coat to cover well enough. Another alternative is to cover them with paper or fabric. Sometimes we paint, color, or draw designs on the paper. It's best to do that before gluing the paper to the tube.

To Make the Butterfly

Punch two holes in your long decorated tube (ours is covered with black paper). These holes are for arms and ours are about 3" from the top of the tube. Decorate flexible paper plates. We used eight dessert-sized ones. Overlap and glue them together as shown. Then glue them to the back of the tube. Insert chenille sticks in the arm holes. Add moveable plastic eyes and chenille-stick antennae. Wow!

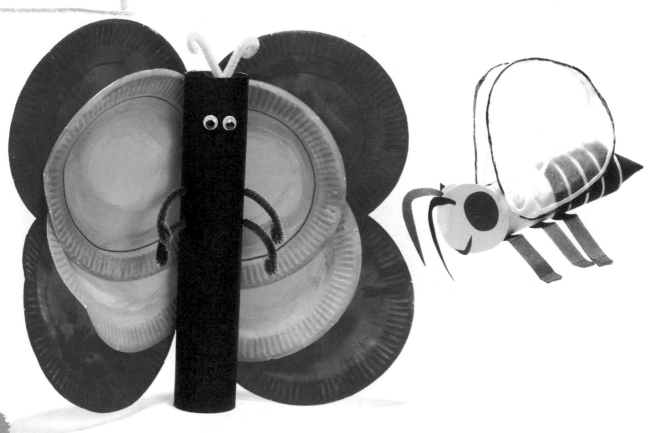

Butterflies, bees, angels, and swans have more in common than wings—they can be crafted from cardboard tubes! These creatures will add beauty to your surroundings.

To Make the Bee

How did you decorate the tube? We covered ours with yellow paper and then added four strips of black construction paper. If you intend to hang your bee, punch holes at each end of the tube now. You'll insert the thread or yarn last. Make a head with facial features and then add antennae, legs, and a cone-shaped stinger. Ours are all from construction paper. Make waxed-paper wings. Outlining them with glue will help them stand up. You can also use glue to show the wing sections. Attach the wings and let your bee buzz away.

To Make the Angel

Did you make the tube angel look special? We did. We painted on a blue dress with a rickrack collar. For her shy face, we used pinkish paper and added details with colored pencils and marker. We cut her hair from yellow paper and wrapped and glued it around her head. Then we added a golden halo made from garland. Her arms are paper. Her cape and wings are made from ripply coffee filters. We colored the edges, folded the filters in half, and then overlapped them as shown. Once the wings are attached, make sure she doesn't fly away!

To Make the Swan

You'll need two tubes, a long flexible one and a shorter sturdy one. Start by attaching the sturdy one to a rectangle of cardboard. Bend your long tube into a Z shape as you can see in our picture. Place the bottom of the Z into the sturdy tube and attach with tape or glue. Paint some flexible paper plates. We overlapped one salad-sized and five dinner-sized plates for each wing. Make a beak from lightweight cardboard, add eyes and pompon details. Sail away!

More Ideas

There are all kinds of winged things you can make using tubes as bodies and creating wings from a variety of materials. Try your hand at an eagle, a turkey, a peacock, a Halloween bat, or a fairy godmother.

Make a host of angels to decorate your holiday mantel or table. Making a variety of sizes will add interest.

Someone you know probably collects butterflies and/or angels. Now you can add to their collection with a hand-crafted one.

45

Tube Frame

What a perfect—and easy—way to present those special photos or original artwork!

You Will Need:

- cardboard tubes
- plastic-foam tray
- scissors
- glue
- various items for decoration

1 Choose the photo you want to showcase and then choose the right-sized tubes. We used bathroom tissue tubes. Decorate and then starting at the top, slit the tubes. Stop at least 1" from the bottom.

2 Paint and/or decorate the tray. We cut ours to make it look like a short table. Glue the tubes in place, placing them just far enough apart for your picture to fit. Insert your picture and make someone happy.

More Ideas

Gluing the photo or artwork to lightweight cardboard will help hold the frame's shape. You may need to enlarge the slits a little. Also, laminating or covering the photo with plastic wrap or stiff, clear plastic will help protect it.

O'Deer

Is it a centerpiece, an ornament, a puppet, or a friend? It can be all these and more.

You Will Need:

- cardboard tube
- construction paper
- twigs
- scissors
- glue
- various items for decoration

1 Cut four sections from the bottom of the tube to form the deer's legs. We added black paper hooves.

2 Add facial features. Be as creative as you dare. We used a Rudolph pompon nose and then added a ribbon with a bell.

3 Punch a hole on each side of the reindeer's head and insert "twig" antlers.

More Ideas

Make a herd of deer. Use them as finger puppets and create a play that you can perform for family and friends.

Hobby Tube Zebra

Don't you know a child who would just love a hobby horse-type toy? Have fun making one—or two! Then enjoy the scene as your little friend rides all around.

You Will Need:

- cardboard tube
- cereal box
- paint, crayons, markers
- construction paper or lightweight cardboard
- ribbon, yarn, or heavy string
- scissors
- glue or tape

More Ideas

Obviously you can make a hobby tube animal of any sort. How about a mustang mare, a long-necked giraffe, a back-packing camel, or a surprising ostrich?

Your hobby-horselike toy doesn't have to be an animal. It can be a cartoon or movie character.

Make small versions of these crafts to hang as wall decorations in a toddler's room. Or how about this for a challenge: Make really tiny ones and hang them from a paper-plate mobile.

1 Decide what toy you want to make. Will you make a zebra or some other toy? Decorate a long wrapping paper tube—ours is 32¨ long. (You can always put shorter tubes together with strong tape.) We began with a 4´ x 32¨ piece of white paper, painted on black stripes, and covered the tube.

2 Make the head from a cereal box. Ask an adult for help in cutting out a wedge. Looking at our picture will show the shape you need. For the neck part of the head, leave the bottom of the box in place and cut out a circle the size of your tube. We covered our box with heavy black paper. (Heavy paper or lightweight cardboard covers the openings well.) Make the paper about ¼¨ longer than the neck.

3 We cut out and glued "stripes" of white paper to the black-paper head. Next we added an eye, pink-lined black ears, and two sections of pink-fringed mane. It's easy to attach the mane if you first cut a piece that is double the shape you want. Fringe on both sides and fold up both sides, leaving a 1¨ flat strip down the middle. Glue that flat strip in place. Our final touches were a pink paper nose and a pink paper-and-ribbon harness.

4 Slide the tube all the way up into the box. If the circle you cut in Step 2 isn't too big, the tube will probably stay in just fine. Otherwise, add glue or tape. Your toy is finally ready to ride!

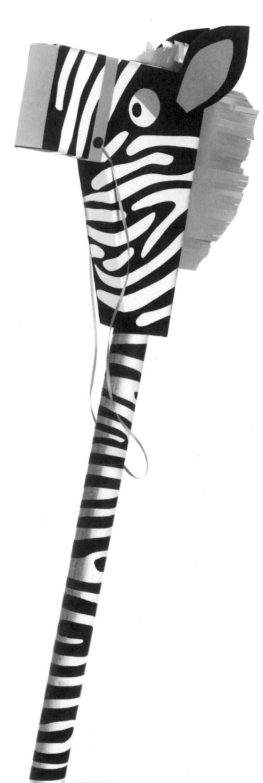

Title Index

Subject Index

Look What You Can Make With
PAPER PLATES

Over 90 Pictured Crafts and Dozens of More Ideas

Edited by Margie Hayes Richmond

Things with Wings

Choose "something with wings" that you want to make. We made an eagle, a bat, a moth, and a butterfly—sections of paper-plate rims make great feathers.

You Will Need:

- flexible paper plates
- cardboard tubes
- construction paper, poster board
- scissors
- tape or glue
- paint, crayons, markers
- glitter
- chenille sticks

To Make the Body and Head

1 Choose the color you want your flying friend to be. We used realistic colors for our eagle and butterfly, but then we let our imaginations take flight with the bat. Wouldn't a red-white-and-blue eagle make a great centerpiece for a Fourth of July or Memorial Day picnic?

2 Get a cardboard tube for each craft you want to make. A paper towel tube is good for taller winged creatures and a bathroom tissue tube works well for smaller flyers. Cover the tube with colored construction paper or with white paper and then paint it. (We found if you paint the tube itself, the glue that holds the tube together shows through.) Just remember to leave time for the paint to dry.

3 Draw a head for your flyer on construction paper or poster board and cut it out. Glue it to the top of the tube. Add features with crayon, marker, paint, cut paper, or chenille sticks. We even used glitter. Be sure to give your winged thing its own personality—we made a fierce eagle and a friendly bat.

You can make a whole flock of flying things. How about attaching strings to hang them from the ceiling or from a painted cardboard ring for a "winged-thing" mobile?

To Make the Eagle

Cut wings from construction paper or poster board. We used two layers to give our eagle a majestic wingspan. To create "feathers" for the wings, use the ripply rims of paper plates. The ripples will add texture and dimension. First color or paint the rims. (We used black, brown, and yellow and colored with a feathery stroke.) Next, cut the colored rims into small sections and glue them on the wings. Glue the wings to the tube body, add eagle feet, and your toy is ready to fly.

To Make the Bat

Cut wings from poster board or construction paper. Color the ripply rim of a paper plate or use a colored plate like we did. Cut the rim into small pieces. Glue the pieces onto the wings. (We used black wings with purple cutouts.) Attach the bat wings to its body, and you've got a great Halloween friend.

To Make the Butterfly

Cut wing shapes from paper plates and decorate. Use the ripply rims for the outer edges of the wings or cut the rims apart to decorate the insect's body. Add antennae and legs made from chenille sticks or pieces of paper plate and glue in place. Attach the wings to the tubes. We liked this idea so much we made a glittery moth, too. Our butterfly's body is horizontal, and the moth is flying upright. Why not brighten someone's day by giving them one of these colorful creations?

More Ideas

You can make a different kind of head for your creature. A small paper cup turned upside down on top of the tube works really well, especially for larger birds, such as eagles or hawks.

Think of all kinds of things with wings. How about a flock of geese or ducks? Their natural coloration is beautiful. Can you make an elegant swan or turn a long wrapping-paper tube into a stand-up angel with paper-plate wings?

Spinning Mix-Ups

Here's a game that makes "making faces" fun. It's easy.

You Will Need:

- 2 dinner-sized paper plates
- 1 dessert-sized paper plate
- pencil
- ruler
- metal fastener
- markers or crayons

1 Mark the centers of all three plates. Cut off the rims of the small and one large plate. Join all three at the center with a metal fastener, putting the smallest plate on top and the largest on the bottom. Draw straight lines through the connected plates so it looks like a pie with four even slices.

2 In each of the four sections, draw a pair of eyes on the top layer, a nose in the middle layer, and a mouth on the bottom. Spin your wheel! See the many different faces you can make.

More Ideas

Buildings, monsters, flowers, even ice-cream sundaes can be fun to mix and spin, too.

Small-Present Package

Make a "package" in which to present a special present.

You Will Need:

- paper bowl
- sturdy paper plate
- pencil
- hole punch
- yarn
- crayons, markers
- felt
- scissors

1 Decorate the bottom of the bowl. Put it in the center of the plate and lightly trace its outline. Ask an adult to help you poke holes 1/4" within the circle you drew. Decorate inside the circle and the rest of the plate.

2 Punch holes (spaced the same as those in the plate) around the edge of the bowl. Use yarn to weave the bowl and plate together face-to-face. Now you can open and close the package.

More Ideas

Hang your package on the wall and you've got a secret safe. Or add a strap to make a purse.

The Great Plate Caper Game

You can use paper plates to make a great game to play with your friends. So gather some together and have lots of fun.

You Will Need:

- sturdy dessert-sized paper plate
- paper cup
- sturdy dinner-sized paper plates (with a "lip" rim)
- scissors
- paint, crayons, markers
- tape or glue
- construction paper
- large paper clip
- metal fastener
- assorted buttons

To Make the Game Board

1 Use the bottom of the dessert-sized plate and draw squares around the border. Number each square in order from 1 to 16. This will be the dial of the game board.

2 To make the handle of the dial, cut off and discard the top half of the paper cup. Then cut several 1/2" slits around the top. Decorate and press the cup upside down against the plate, fanning out the slitted flaps. Tape or glue the flaps to the plate.

3 Paint one of the dinner-sized plates a different color or use a colored paper plate. Set the "dial plate" inside this plate. Draw an arrow on the edge of the larger plate or cut one from paper and glue it on. This will be the game board pointer.

To Make the Spinner

1 Decorate the bottom of a dinner-sized plate. Draw two lines so they divide the bottom into four equal sections (pizza style). Number the sections 1 through 4. Make a hole in the center of the plate.

2 You can use a large paper clip for a spinner. Attach it to the plate with a metal fastener. Make sure the fastener is a little loose so the paper clip will spin.

More Ideas

You can make all kinds of spinners to use in other games. Make more than 4 sections and mark them with a variety of colors, letters, or symbols.

How to Play the Game

Each player places a button on or above one of the numbered sections of the game board.

Players take turns thumping the paper-clip spinner. The number where it stops tells them how many spaces they can turn the dial on the game board. Players can move in either direction, but in only one direction per turn.

The object is to get the button to the game board pointer. The first button to reach the pointer wins.

Paper-Plate Party

You can plan a whole party around paper plates—from creating your own decorations to inventing games and activities. Choose a color scheme or theme for your party and decorate accordingly.

You Will Need:

- a variety of paper plates
- scissors
- paint, crayons, markers, watercolors
- stapler, tape, or glue
- sponge
- straws
- ribbon
- waxed paper
- rubber band

To Make a Party Hat

1 To make the hat brim, draw a circle 1 1/2" in from the edge of a paper plate.

2 Draw your design in the center of the plate, with the bottom of the design touching the circle. We drew a western hat shape.

3 Color or paint your design, then cut away the background area between it and the circle, leaving the bottom of your design attached to the brim. Bend the design part of the hat forward. Add a guest's name.

To Make Goody Boxes

1 Paint both sides of a paper plate. Fold it in half, crease, then unfold. Do the same thing the other way; the creases divide the plate into equal sections.

2 Fold two opposite sides of the paper plate into the center. (The edges should just touch with no overlap.) Crease, then unfold. Do the same thing the other way. This will make a square, which will be the bottom of the box.

3 Beyond each corner of the square is a small rounded triangle. Pull each triangle out, fold down the center, and staple. Do the same thing to all four corners. Decorate the box and fill it with favors or treats.

To Make a Horn

1 Color or paint a flexible dinner-sized plate. Cut one edge off to form a straight side about 6" long. Then roll the paper plate to form a cone. Tape or glue to hold in place. You may still need to trim the straight side evenly for the end. Decorate your horn.

2 Cut a 4" circle of waxed paper and place it over the large end of the cone. Hold in place with a rubber band. We taped a piece of ribbon over the rubber band. Then hum into the other end of the horn and make your own party music.

To Make Personalized Place Cards

1 Fold a small paper plate in half and then open it. Cut out a shape on the top half of the plate. We made a face wearing a western hat. Your shape can be anything that suits your own party theme.

2 Decorate. To sponge paint like we did all our party crafts, just dip a small section of sponge in some watercolor and dab on the plates. When dry, write on a guest's name.

Have a pre-party craft-making get-together. Just gather your paper plates and other crafting materials and invite a couple of friends over a few days before the party date.

To Make a Centerpiece

1 To make the holder part of the centerpiece, color or paint the bottom of a sturdy dinner-sized paper plate. Cut it in half and attach the two halves rim-to-rim with glue or staples.

2 To make a base for your centerpiece, decorate the bottom of a sturdy plate and cut a 4" slit in its center. Slide the bottom of the holder part into the slit. Pour a little glue into the slit if you need more support to make the centerpiece stand up straight.

3 Decide what you want to feature in your centerpiece. To make balloons like ours, cut out and decorate paper balloon shapes. Cut a small slit near the top and bottom of each balloon. Add a guest's name. Insert a straw in the slits and place it in the centerpiece. Everyone can take a straw when the refreshments are served.

More Ideas

Make a card caddy like the one shown on page 8. Just decorate it to fit your party theme and hang it where guests can put in their cards.

Make color-coordinated streamers to hang from the ceiling. Just follow the directions found on page 24.

Make and play the paper-plate games described on pages 14, 15, and 36. Again, you may want to decorate your plates to match your other creations.

Plate Playmates

Hand puppets are great playmates. You can use paper plates to make one or a bunch. And you can make them as playful pals or merry monsters.

You Will Need:

- flexible dinner-sized paper plate
- paint, crayons, markers
- pencil
- bathroom tissue tube
- scissors
- construction and heavy paper
- glue
- tape

1 Fold a flexible paper plate in half and then open it. The bottom of the plate will be your puppet's outer section. Paint or color it. Paint or color the front area of the plate the way you want the inside of the puppet's mouth to look.

2 You can make eyes for your playmate. Just hold the tube upright on a sheet of white paper and trace around its bottom twice. Add a tab to each of the circles you drew and cut them out. Decorate.

3 Cover the cardboard tube with construction paper and cut it in half. Glue the two tubes side-by-side to the top outside half of the plate. These will be your puppet's eye sockets. Glue the tabs of the eyes you made in Step 2 to the inside of the tubes.

4 When completely dry, add features. One of our puppets has paper teeth, tongue, and long eyelashes. And don't you love our frog's dinner? Have fun thinking up cool things for your own playmate.

5 Cut a 3"- by -1" strip of heavy paper, form it into a loop, and tape it securely to the outside of the bottom half of the plate. Be sure your thumb can fit into the loop. Slip your thumb into the paper loop and your index and middle fingers into the back of the eyes and make your puppet come to life.

More Ideas

You can give your playmates hair made from yarn, curly ribbon, or even curly construction paper. To make curly paper strips, just wind them around a pencil and hold for a while. Then unwind.

Make a bull or unicorn; just add horns to your puppet. Add paper flames for a fierce-but-friendly fire-breathing dragon.

Decorate your plate to look like a clam or even a crab. Or how about an oyster shell with a pearl inside?

Invite friends over for a Plate-Playmate-Making Party and then create a play to perform for friends and family.

Angel Chorus

Many people collect angels. Do you?

You Will Need:

- dessert-sized flexible plates
- glue, stapler, or tape
- scissors
- paint, crayons, markers
- chenille sticks
- glitter

1 Cut a plate in half. Curve the half-plate into a cone. Staple, glue, or tape in place. Cut wings from paper-plate rims. Decorate the body and wings.

2 Create a face, hands, and songbook; glue them and the wings to the body. Tape a chenille-stick halo to the back of the angel's head.

More Ideas

Create a glee club. Just leave off the wings and halos and paint the bodies to look like choir robes.

Yarn Art Star

Create a hanging Star of David.

You Will Need:

- flexible dinner-sized paper plate
- yarn
- crayons
- tape
- scissors or hole punch

More Ideas

Try to make geometric shapes with 5, 6, 8, 10, or 12 sides.

1 Punch 6 evenly spaced holes about 1" from the outside edge of the plate. Cut 6 slits about 3" in toward the center. Put slits halfway between holes.

2 To make the small star you'll connect the slits. Begin by taping one end of a long piece of yarn to the back of the plate. String the yarn through a slit and across the plate to the next slit. When the star is complete, tape the back of the slits.

3 You'll connect the holes to form the large Star of David. Finish by taping the other end of the yarn to the plate's back and make a hanger.

Rockin' Crafts

Get ready to rock 'n' roll with a variety of fun things to make. The base of each one is a rocker. And would you believe that each rocker is made from a paper plate?

You Will Need:

- flexible paper plates
- ruler
- pencil
- paint, crayons, markers
- construction paper
- scissors
- small tissue box
- felt, fabric
- drinking straws
- glue
- yarn or chenille sticks
- thin cardboard

To Make the Rocker

1 Lightly fold a plate in half and then unfold it. Using a ruler, draw two straight lines 1 1/2" on either side of the fold. For a broader top area on the rocker, draw your lines farther apart.

2 Fold the paper plate along each of the lines you drew. (Make sure the folds are straight so your craft will rock straight.) Color or paint the rocker.

3 If your craft seems a little head or tail heavy, use a coin or paper clip to balance it. Just tape the "weight" underneath the bottom of the rocker's flat part. This trick will also work if you want your rockin' craft to tip one way more than the other.

20

We've made four very different rockin' creations that will make great gifts, especially for your younger friends or family members.

To Make the Rockin' Cradle

Make and decorate the rocker as described in Steps 1 and 2. We painted our rocker brown and decorated it with yellow scallops cut from paper. To make the bed part, cut the bottom 2" off an empty tissue box and glue felt or other material to its inside bottom. (The cotton that comes in the box when you buy jewelry would make a great soft mattress.) Glue completed bed onto the flat portion of the rocker. You might want to make a blanket and pillow for your cradle from scraps of fabric. You could also make a canopy. Use cut-up drinking straws for bedposts and felt or lacy fabric for the canopy top.

To Make the Rockin' Horse

Follow Steps 1 and 2 to create the rocker. Then make a 1" slit about 1/2" in from the front edge of the rocker top. You will use this slit to insert the head. Make the horse's head from a paper plate or cardboard. Color the head with paint, markers, or crayons. Use yarn, felt, or construction paper to form the features. Make a horse tail by gluing or taping a bundle of cut yarn or twist and bend a bundle of chenille sticks. A combination of yarn and chenille sticks works well, too. Poke a hole toward the back of the rocker top. Make it just large enough to fit in the tail.

To Make the Rockin' Boat

Follow Steps 1 and 2. Paint or color water on the rocker. Create a colorful boat with cut-out colored paper, paint, or markers. We drew a sailboat on cardboard, colored it with markers, and cut it out. Remember to make tabs at the bottom of the boat. Cut a 2" to 3" slit in the center of the top of the rocker and insert the boat's tabs. Bend the ends of tabs and tape them underneath to keep the boat on the "water."

More Ideas

You can make rockin' ducks, turkeys, or just about any one of your favorite animals. Look at the brightly colored parrot we made using a blue paper plate for the rocker.

Try your hand at making a rocking chair. Just make a ladder-style back and arms from heavy paper or thin cardboard.

Cup 'n Platter Warehouse

Here's a pretty storage warehouse for small treasures.

You Will Need:

- sturdy paper platter
- cardboard egg carton
- scissors
- paint, crayons, markers
- ribbon, lace
- glue

1 Paint or color the platter. Cut several cup sections from a cardboard egg carton. Color or paint. Let dry. Decorate the rim of the platter. We glued on lace.

2 Arrange the cup sections on the platter and carefully glue in place. Create a hanger and fill the cups with earrings or other small jewelry items.

More Ideas

Make a workshop organizer for nuts, bolts, and screws or even fishing tackle. Not enough cups? String two or more organizers together.

In Like a Lion, Out Like a Lamb

Make a March weather indicator.

You Will Need:

- paper plates
- paint, crayons, markers
- cotton balls
- construction paper
- scissors
- yarn
- glue
- plastic eyes
- chenille sticks

1 For the lamb, decorate the plate and glue cotton balls around its rim. Create ears, eyes, a nose, and a mouth.

2 For the lion, decorate the other plate. To make the mane, glue loops of brown yarn around the top half of the plate. Create facial features. Make whiskers from chenille sticks.

3 Glue the faces back-to-back.

More Ideas

Make a happy face and a sad face. Hang the plate on your door to let people know how you are feeling. Or make a sunshine/raincloud plate.

22

A Myriad of Mobiles

You can make lots of mobiles. *Lots of*—that's what *myriad* means. Your mobile can be anything. Just choose something you really like or something someone would like as a gift.

You Will Need:

- dinner-sized sturdy paper plates
- ribbon or yarn
- paint
- hole punch
- scissors
- glue
- construction paper
- cotton ball
- napkins

1 To make the crescent-shaped mobile, cut shapes from two sturdy paper plates and paint them. (We made a moon.) Let dry and staple or glue the two pieces together. Punch holes along the inside curve. Punch a hole at the top of the crescent and use ribbon or yarn for a hanger.

2 To make the top part of the full-plate mobile, poke two holes side-by-side and about 1/2" apart in the middle of a plate. Thread yarn through the holes and tie to form a loop. Punch four evenly spaced holes around the edge of the plate. If your mobile does not hang straight, glue a penny to the underside to help balance it.

3 Create the hanging parts of your mobile. For some hanging parts, you'll need to punch a hole at its top and insert a piece of yarn to tie to the mobile top. For types like the ghost, you can tie the yarn directly from the hanging part to the mobile top.

To Make Flowers

Create flower and leaf shapes. Remember you can see both sides, so be sure to decorate fronts and backs.

To Make Ghosts

Put a cotton ball in the middle of a napkin and pull it smoothly around the ball. Tie a long ribbon around the "neck." Glue on eyes. Make pumpkins the same way, trimming off the excess. Then cut out and attach bat shapes.

More Ideas

Make a nighttime mobile by cutting out star shapes in different sizes and covering them with aluminum foil and glitter. Or make trains or boats to hang from your mobile.

23

Sparkling Spirals

You'll find this so easy to do, you'll want to make spirals by the dozens. You can turn spirals into imaginary snakes, spinners to play with, or streamers to decorate for a party.

You Will Need:

- flexible paper plates
- pencil
- scissors
- glitter
- string or yarn
- watercolors, paint, markers
- old newspaper
- colored paper

To Make the Basic Spiral

1 Decide what you want your spiral to be and how many you want to make. Choose your colors and plan the design. Then gather your paper plates and have fun decorating them. Remember to do both sides.

2 With a pencil, lightly draw circular lines on the front of each plate. Make the lines about 1" apart. You can alter the width and length of your spiral by drawing your lines closer together or farther apart.

3 Cut the plate into a spiral by starting at the rim and cutting around and around, following your pencil lines. Punch a hole at what was the center of the paper plate. This will now be the top of your spiral.

To Make a Spinner

To decorate a spinner like the one we show, place two 6" paper plates on old newspaper. With watercolors and a brush, spatter paint on both sides of the plates, letting each side dry first. Of course, you can decorate yours any way you like, using paint, markers, or crayons. A touch of glitter will add sparkle. After you've decorated each plate, cut it into a spiral as described above. Tie a piece of string or yarn through the holes and hang your double spinner where you can watch it blow in the breeze. Or give your spinner even more bounce by hanging it on a piece of elastic instead of string and use it like a yo-yo or spring-type toy.

To Make a Snake

Make your basic spiral and add stripes and eyes. Then glue on fangs and a tongue cut from colored paper. You can make different kinds of realistic snakes. You'll be surprised at what beautiful colors nature gives them. You can also have fun making up totally imaginary snakes as we did. How about a flower-covered one? You'll think of lots of fun and games for your snake. Try wrapping it around your arm like a circus performer or dangling it from a tree branch or vine.

To Make Streamers

Cut very narrow spirals from the colored paper plates. Decorate the spirals with bright colors, glitter, or stickers. (The best way to add glitter is to cover the outside bottom of a *whole* colored paper plate with a glue-and-water mixture. Sprinkle on glitter, let dry, and then cut it into a streamer.) You might make your streamers even more festive by draping or attaching extra ribbon or yarn. Create yarn hangers. You could even add a tassle at the bottom of the yarn. Now you're ready to decorate a room for a party with your colorful streamers—just add a balloon or two.

More Ideas

Make a wind sock. Cut a 6"-by-12" strip from poster board. Roll it into a cylinder that is 6" long and staple the sides together. Attach 6 or 8 decorated spirals. Add yarn or ribbon to the top of the cylinder and hang your "sock" outside where it won't get wet.

Bountiful Baskets

Make a simple basket to fill with goodies or to use as a decoration. We made one for our favorite gardener and one to celebrate Valentine's Day.

You Will Need:

- dinner-sized flexible paper plate
- paint, crayons, markers
- paintbrush
- tissue paper in various colors
- paper doilies
- construction paper
- scissors
- glue
- stapler
- ribbon

1 Use a thick brush and dab paint on the back side of a paper plate or color with crayons. Let dry, then cut the plate in half. Staple or glue the two halves together face-to-face, forming a pocket.

2 Decorate your basket. Follow our directions at right or create your own design. Then punch a hole at each end of the pocket and tie a ribbon through the holes for a hanger.

To Make the Gardener's Basket

To make flowers like ours, cut small squares of tissue paper in a variety of colors. Fold each square in half and then in half again. Hold by the folded corner and twist a few times. Fluff out the loose corners and glue the twisted part to the side of the plate. Cut out and glue on leaves. Fill the basket with packets of flower seeds, cards, gifts, or other treats.

To Make the Valentine Basket

To make our Valentine's Day basket, cut sections from paper doilies and glue to the front of the basket. Add paper hearts on top along with more pieces of paper doily.

More Ideas

Instead of flowers, make tissue-paper fish—just twist so that you form body and tail sections. Fill with small fishing items.

For even more festive baskets, punch several holes at the bottom and tie ribbon bows or streamers in each hole.

Face Plates

You can make lots of faces from plates.

You Will Need:

- dinner-sized flexible paper plate
- scissors
- paint, crayons
- construction paper
- yarn
- glue

1 Cut off about 2/3 of the rim of a paper plate, leaving part of the rim as the Pilgrim's collar and the plate's center part as the face. Paint or color.

2 Using the leftover rim, cut out eyebrows, a mustache, and hair. Paint. Cut a hat and eyes from construction paper. Glue on all cutout pieces. Tape on a yarn loop for a hanger.

More Ideas

Make a Santa. Layering pieces of plate rims will make a great beard. Can you figure out how to make a circus clown or a court jester?

Candle Light

You can make a beautiful holiday wall hanging.

You Will Need:

- platter-sized paper plate
- paint, crayons, markers
- construction paper
- scissors
- tape or glue

1 Create a menorah with candles. Above each candle, except the center one, carefully cut two curved slits to look like the sides of a flame. Make an orange paper "flame" for the center candle.

2 Cut a strip of white paper, about 1" wide and 24" long. Color half of it orange. Thread the strip through the slits. Tape its ends to form a loop.

3 Begin with the white part of the strip showing through the flame shapes. Each day of Hanukkah "light" one more candle by moving the strip.

More Ideas

Draw other holders and change the candles for other holidays.

Ballerinas and Ball Games

What do ballerinas and ball games have in common? A "dome" made from a paper plate. Oh yes, you can also make a bumbershoot—that's an old-fashioned word for umbrella, you know.

You Will Need:

- flexible dinner-sized paper plates
- pencil
- scissors
- stapler
- paint, crayons, markers
- glue
- plastic straw
- metal fastener
- chenille sticks
- glitter
- small paper cup
- plastic-foam ball
- yarn
- cardboard tube

To Make the Basic Dome

1 Put the plate face up and draw a 2" circle in the center. Lightly folding the plate into 4 equal sections will help you find the center. Tracing around a small cup or other circular-shaped object is the easiest way to draw a cirlcle.

2 Cut from the edge of the plate toward the center, stopping when you get to the outside of the circle you just drew. Make another cut, in the same way, about 1/8" from the first cut. After you stop at the edge of the circle, cut back to your first line. Throw away the tiny cutout piece.

3 Repeat this procedure so that when you have completed this step the plate has 4 equal sections with a circle in the center. Overlap the sections and staple the edges. You should have a dome shape with 4 thin triangular slits.

Choose the dome craft you want to make and plan ahead. This is one of those times when you may want to decorate the plate before you make it into a dome.

To Make the Bumbershoot

Decorate your plate. If you paint it, let it dry thoroughly. Use the plate to make your dome as described in Steps 1-3. Then take a straw and make two folds, one about 1 1/4" and the other about 2 1/2" from the top of the straw. Staple the end of the straw to the straight part of the straw. You will have made a triangle with three sides that are about 1 1/4" each. Then make a hole in the middle of the top side of the triangle. Poke a metal fastener through the top center of the dome. Insert the fastener into the straw by pulling and securing the prongs through the hole you made in the straw. Cover the straw by wrapping chenille sticks around it. Insert one chenille stick inside the straw to give it stability and to form a handle. Now give your umbrella a spin!

To Make the Ballerina

The dome will be the ballerina's skirt. Design your own skirt pattern on a plate. We painted ours pink and decorated it with glitter. Make the dome. Then poke a metal fastener through its top center. Bend a straw in half, crease it, then open it. Poke a hole on the straw's crease. Attach the straw to the fastener. Bend down the two parts of the straw and you have legs. For the upper part of the body, decorate a small paper cup. Glue or tape the cup, bottom up, to the top of the skirt. Use a plastic-foam ball to form the head and use yarn for hair. Add some facial features. Attach chenille sticks or paper cutouts for arms and feet. Your ballerina is ready to twirl.

To Make the Toss-n-Scoop Ball Game

Begin by decorating a plate, a small paper cup, and a cardboard tube with paint or markers. When dry, make your dome and glue or tape the bottom of the cup to its top center. After the cup is secure, tape the tube into the base of the cup. Now just turn it over and your scoop is ready for action! Using a foam or yarn ball, toss the ball into the air and catch it in your scoop.

More Ideas

Have a friend make a scoop and play "toss and scoop" together like a game of catch.

Turn your dome upside down to make a candy dish. Creating a base from modeling clay will help it "sit" better. Protect table surfaces by putting a piece of foil on the bottom of the clay.

Decorate your dome to look like an igloo, a greenhouse, or an indoor arena for racquet sports.

Crawling Critters

It's so easy to make your favorite "bug."

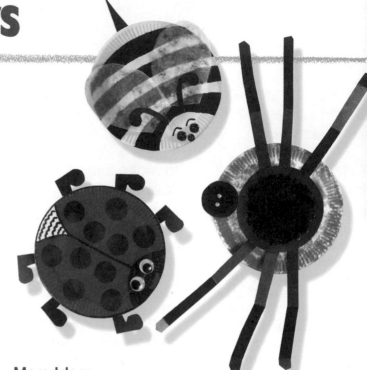

You Will Need:

- paper plates
- yarn or chenille sticks
- paint, crayons, markers
- construction and waxed paper or poster board
- buttons, beads, or plastic eyes
- glue
- scissors

1 Choose the size plate that best suits the critter you want to make. With markers, crayons, or paint, color the front of the plate as your critter's body. Or if you want your critter to have a more rounded body, paint the bottom of the plate.

2 Add a head, legs, and other features with paint, markers, paper cutouts, or chenille sticks. We used small pieces of yarn dipped in glue to add fuzz to our spider and waxed paper for our bee's wings. Add button, bead, or movable plastic eyes.

More Ideas

Can you make a trudging turtle or a rollicking robot from a paper bowl? Or create a totally imaginary critter of your own.

Make several bugs to hang on your wall. Mix them with the flowers from page 47 to make a nature mural.

Everything-in-Its-Place Plates

Make a holder to keep supplies handy.

You Will Need:

- sturdy dinner-sized paper plates
- sturdy lunch-sized paper plate
- paint, crayons, markers
- glue

1 Paint the plates. Cut one plate in half and glue the two sections rim-to-rim, forming a pocket. Do the same with the other plates. Attach the pockets together, back-to-back, making a row that will stand by itself.

2 Decorate the pockets. We gave ours a funny face, but you could add rickrack, lace, or a shoestring around the edges.

More Ideas

Create a watermelon design. Fill with plates, napkins, and plastic utensils. You'll have everything in its place to take on a picnic.

Year-Round Wreath

People love to decorate with wreaths. You see them for all seasons and special occasions. Using a round paper plate is an easy way to begin your own wreath-making.

You Will Need:

- dinner-sized paper plate
- scissors
- construction paper
- glue
- various other materials (nuts, aluminum foil, stickers, glitter, seeds, ribbon, scraps of fabric, cardboard)

1 Cut out the center of the paper plate, leaving a 2" rim. Your circle doesn't have to be perfect because it is the base of the wreath and will be covered up with other materials.

2 Cut out appropriate shapes for the wreath you've chosen to make. Give your wreath extra dimension by covering shapes with foil or fabric and layering them. Add even more pizzazz with ribbons or glitter. Glue the shapes to the paper-plate circle, covering it completely.

3 Poke a hole or two in the top of the paper circle and tie on a piece of ribbon for a hanger. Adjust the length according to where you intend to place the wreath.

A 4th of July Wreath

Cut out star shapes from red, white, and blue construction paper and aluminum foil. Glue the star shapes around the paper plate rim, overlapping them as you go. You may want to decorate with stickers or drawings of patriotic symbols, such as flags, eagles, Uncle Sam, and the Liberty Bell.

An Autumn Wreath

Cut out leaf shapes from red, yellow, orange, and brown construction paper. You can also use leaves that you have pressed; carefully glue them onto the paper plate rim. Decorate with seeds, nuts, or different types of pinecones.

More Ideas

For spring, use flower shapes and decorate with bits of fabric or lace.

For Christmas, use holly-leaf shapes and decorate with red "berries" made from old beads or cut paper.

All in a Row

You can put paper plates "all in a row" to make a caterpillar, a dragon, and even a giraffe. Aren't the ones we made cute? They make great bedroom wall decorations.

You Will Need:

- a variety of paper plates
- paint
- yarn, ribbon, felt
- chenille sticks
- hole punch
- scissors
- construction paper
- poster board
- plastic-foam balls
- thin cardboard

To Make the Body

1 Think about how long you want the body of your creature to be. Then choose the right number and size of plates—perhaps 6 or 8 for the caterpillar, 4 for the giraffe, and 5 for the dragon. We used a variety of sizes and types. We used some colored plates and some that we painted. You can color yours with markers, crayons, or paint. Just remember to let the paint dry.

2 Using a hole punch, make holes in the rims of the plates. Punch only one hole in the plate that will be the head and one hole in the tail plate.

3 Join the plates with yarn, ribbon, or pieces of chenille stick. Arrange your animal's body and attach it to your wall or floor. Or maybe you'll want to make it a character in a play and make it "move" around like a puppet.

Silly snakes and creepy centipedes could be lots of fun to make, too. Or let your own imagination "lead you along" to create an original creature.

To Make the Dragon

Make the body as previously described. Then cut out the head and legs from thin cardboard and glue them in place. To make spikes, cut different-sized triangles from construction paper and glue them along the body, neck, and tail. Smaller spikes can be used for teeth. Add facial features with marker, paint, or glued-on paper cutouts. We made ours a friendly fire-breathing dragon. The "fire" is cutout yellow, gold, and red paper.

To Make the Giraffe

Make the head, neck, and body. Cut a tail and legs from thin cardboard. (You may want to sketch the shapes and then cut them out to be more precise.) Next draw and cut out ears, nose, and horns. Tie or tape a bundle of cut yarn and glue it to the end of the tail. Glue the tail to the body. For a realistic giraffe, use yellow paint with spots made of brown paper or fabric cutouts. Finish by making the eyes, nostrils, and mouth. Punch holes and tie on yarn for a mane.

To Make the Caterpillar

Make the body. Remember, you can make your caterpillar long or short. Use chenille sticks to make antennae. Cut pieces of felt or poster board for legs and eyebrows. Use a small plastic-foam ball cut in half for "bug" eyes.

More Ideas

You can make an alphabet row or number line to decorate a preschooler's room. Decorate each letter or number appropriately—such as an apple on the *A* plate or three little pigs on the *3* plate. In fact, your younger siblings and friends might enjoy helping you make it.

Make a name plate to put above your door. Just put the letters of your name all in a row—one per plate.

Marching Marionette

Creating your own marionette is just the beginning of the fun. Dreaming up adventures for him or her can take you all over the world.

You Will Need:

- paper plate
- scissors
- crayons or markers
- construction paper
- cardboard
- plastic straws
- heavy string

1 Decide what you want your marionette to be. Ours is a sun. Begin with a paper plate—any size will do. You may want to trim the outer edge of the plate to suit your design. We made "rays." You could create hair or a ruffly collar.

2 Draw a face on the plate or create features from yarn, paper cutouts, chenille sticks, cotton balls, or even powder puffs (for big, bushy eyebrows or a mustache).

3 Draw and cut out hands and feet from thin cardboard or construction paper. Punch holes as shown in our picture. Cut a 12"-by-1" strip from heavy cardboard for the guide bar and punch holes in it.

4 Make two pairs of tiny holes in the bottom edge of the plate for attaching legs and two more pairs where the arms will go. Put another pair of holes in the top center of the head. You'll need 5 pairs or 10 holes in all.

5 Cut drinking straws into 2" pieces. Using heavy string or twine, string 3 straw pieces together to form each leg. Tie on feet and attach the legs to the bottom of the plate. String 2 straw pieces together, attach hands, and tie arms to the plate.

6 Attach a 10" string to the ends of each hand and a 5" string to the top of the plate. Tie the arm strings to the ends of the guide bar and the head string to its center. Now you're ready to walk your marionette right through an adventure.

More Ideas

Make a moon and a star to go along with this sun.

Try making some animal marionettes. Wouldn't a monkey be fun? Or how about a wiggly octopus? But watch out for all those arms!

Get some friends to each make a wooden soldier. Then work together to see if you can get them to march in step.

Glimmering "Glass" Garden

You can make your own "stained-glass" decoration.

You Will Need:

- 2 dinner-sized flexible paper plates
- pencil
- scissors
- several colors of tissue paper
- white tissue paper
- glue
- ribbon, rickrack

1 With a pencil, lightly sketch flowers with stems on the front of one paper plate. Carefully cut out the "insides" of the flowers and stems. On the front side of the plate, glue pieces of colored tissue paper over the cutouts.

2 Cut out a 5" circle from the middle of the other plate. Cover the hole with white tissue paper glued to the plate's front.

3 Glue the plates rim-to-rim. Decorate. Attach a hanger and place near a window.

More Ideas

Your picture could be anything—try a lighthouse or an abstract geometric design.

Photo Frames

You can frame your own collage of photographs.

You Will Need:

- sturdy paper plate or platter
- photographs
- scissors
- glue or tape
- hole punch
- yarn or ribbon
- objects to trace around

1 Choose photographs, picking some that can be featured in openings of different sizes and shapes.

2 On the plate, lightly trace around small objects, such as a glass for a circle or a cassette tape holder for a rectangle. Cut out the "inside" of each shape. Decorate your frame and tape your photographs in place. (Make sure the pictures show through the openings.) Create a hanger and display your handiwork.

More Ideas

Make a family tree. Or make a blank frame and give it to new parents to use for baby pictures.

35

Olympic Party Time

You can use paper plates as part of a great Olympic theme party. You can make the Olympic symbol and your own medals. And you can create some Olympics-style games of your own.

You Will Need:

- sturdy dinner-sized paper plates
- flexible dessert-sized plates
- paint, crayons, markers
- scissors
- tape
- ribbon
- glue
- glitter
- coins

To Make the Olympic Symbol

1 For the symbol, cut out the insides of 5 dinner-sized sturdy plates. Put the insides aside and use later for the Number Toss. Paint or color the rings—one each of red, green, blue, gold, and black. Or use paper plates of different colors. If you want these Olympics to be distinctly your own, choose whatever colors you'd like.

2 Make one neat cut in each rim so you can interlock them, as shown on page 37. Then tape the rings back together. Hang your symbol in a prominent spot. It might be fun to make several and hang them throughout the party area.

To Make Olympic Medals

1 Paint small paper plates gold, silver, and bronze. Put glue in the shape of a star and sprinkle on glitter.

2 Tape ribbons on the back of the medals. We used gold paint on the ribbons' edges. You'll probably want to have more than one set of medals. Use them as decorations until you're ready for the medal ceremony.

Olympic Games

THE DISCUS THROW

Begin this event by creating your own Frisbee-like discus from two sturdy paper plates. Color their bottoms and glue or staple them together. Then go outdoors and let the competition begin. The discus that is thrown the greatest distance wins. Consider giving medals for improvement and funny happenings, too.

NUMBER TOSS

Use the leftover insides of the five symbol plates. Decorate and write a different number on each one. Arrange the plates on the floor. Each player has three coins, stands back about 10', and takes a turn tossing the coins. The object is to make the coins land on the "plates." The person who gets the greatest total wins.

More Ideas

AN OLYMPIC PARTY

Decorate the party area with the Olympic symbol and medals. And you can also use the ideas on pages 16 and 17 to decorate.

Serve a cake decorated with Olympic symbols surrounded by your paper-plate medals. Or make the pretend cake described on page 9 and serve Olympic-sized cookies.

Cut rectangles from the center of paper plates to make flags of a variety of countries. Sing "The Star-Spangled Banner" or play the national anthems of other nations. Did you know that some computer software will play these songs? Or let each guest create his or her own personal flag. Take turns telling what each flag symbolizes.

Nesting Plate

Here's a bright "welcome spring" centerpiece.

You Will Need:

- dessert-sized sturdy paper plate
- shredded paper or other nest-building items (twigs, sticks, string)
- glue
- tissue paper

1 Gather some nest-building materials: shredded lightweight paper, some artificial grass, or moss from an old floral or plant arrangement, for example.

2 Cover the inside of the plate with a generous layer of glue. Lay your nest-building materials in place. Let dry.

3 Add more glue to the outer edges of the material and let it partially dry. Then add more nest-building material to make a true nest shape.

4 Add a few twigs, sticks, or string to give your nest a more realistic look.

5 Wad and shape pieces of tissue paper into bird eggs. Glue the eggs in place.

More Ideas

We made a bird out of tissue paper and gave it a paper beak and googly eyes. Can you figure out how to make an eagle or duck nest?

Dino and Crab

Paper plates make great bodies for some exotic creatures.

You Will Need:

- flexible dinner-sized paper plates
- scissors
- stapler
- paint, crayons, markers

1 Paint the bottoms of two paper plates for the bodies. Use them whole or cut out sections. Cut out a head and neck, tails, legs, and claws and paint them.

2 Insert these parts between the body plates and staple them rim-to-rim. Decorate with more paint, crayons, or markers and add facial features.

More Ideas

Your creature can "walk" if you use metal fasteners to attach its legs. Can you make an octopus or a spider?

38

Birds of a Feather

These are birds from a plate. How many different ones can you make?

You Will Need:

- paper plates
- crayons or markers
- scissors
- glue
- stapler
- hole punch
- metal fastener
- yarn

1 Use plates of any size. Draw an outline of a bird's body in the middle of a plate, letting the rim on one side of the plate be the bird's tail and the rim directly opposite it be the bird's beak.

2 Hold a second plate against the first plate bottom-to-bottom. Cut along the outline of the bird you drew. (You'll have two bird bodies.) You'll notice that we even gave our red bird some "feet."

3 Make a set of wings by drawing an outline on a piece of the leftover plate. Hold a second piece against the first back-to-back and cut. You can make several styles of wings like ours.

4 Glue the two bodies together, leaving the tails unglued. Create an eye on each side of the head and attach the wings with glue, staples, or a metal fastener.

5 Find the balance point where your bird will hang as though flying, punch a hole, and string a 20"-24" length of yarn through the hole. Bend the wings away from the bird's body, fluff its tail, and hang your feathered friend where it can "fly."

More Ideas

Color or paint a white plate like a robin to signal the coming of spring, or create eagles to celebrate Independence Day.

Birds like these would look great on the mobile described on page 23.

Ponds and Paths

A paper plate makes a perfect base for all sorts of places. We created a charming duck pond, a wildlife watering hole, an old-fashioned train track, and a scenic bike path.

You Will Need:

- paper plate or platter
- paint, crayons, markers
- poster board
- scissors
- glue or tape
- tissue paper
- old magazines
- bark, sand, rocks, and dried weeds
- yarn

To Make the Base

1 Decide which thing you want your plate to be. The techniques for making the pond, track, bike path, or watering hole will be the same. Only your colors, designs, stand-ups, and materials will differ.

2 Choose any paper plate. Sturdy ones will probably work best. Cut a slit in the plate at each place where you want to put an animal or object. Plan carefully or cut your slits after you make your objects.

To Make the Duck Pond

Color the inside of a paper plate blue to look like water in a pond. Color a section with brown paint mixed with sand around the blue to look like a sandy bank. Color the outer edge green to look like grass. Add gray rocks. Cut out ducks from poster board, leaving a rectangular tab at the bottom. Insert the tabs into the slits you made in the plate. Turn the plate over, fold the tabs, and glue or tape them to the bottom. Add scenery and you've got ducks swimming in a quiet pond.

These crafts can be paper sculptures—perfect for centerpieces or desk decorations. Just think of someone you'd like to surprise and make a sculpture of someplace they really like.

To Make the Watering Hole

Color the plate with shades of green, brown, and yellow to look like the ground of the African plain. Use blue for the watering hole. You should have already cut slits where you want to place your animals, bushes, and trees. Draw and cut out African animals or cut some from old magazines as we did. Put a tab on the bottom of each one. Draw and cut out trees and bushes with tabs. Arrange your animals, trees, and bushes on the plate, putting the tabs into the slits and taping them underneath the plate.

To Make the Train Track

Color the plate to look like the "ground." (Gray paint mixed with sand works well.) You can use yarn or markers and crayons to create the tracks. Remember to cut slits where you want your train to be. Draw and cut out a steam engine, cars, and a caboose. Make a tab on the bottom of each one. Put the tabs into the slits and attach them to the plate. We added a station, water tower, and a tree. Have fun creating your own scenery.

To Make the Bike Path

Color the plate to look like the ground of the countryside. We colored a rock wall with gray paint mixed with sand. Add a stream if you like. Draw and color a bike path. Add pictures of trees, bushes, and people on bicycles cut from old magazines—or draw your own on poster board. Put a tab on the bottom of each one. Be sure the slits are where you want your scenery and bikers to be. Put the tabs into the slits and attach them to the plate. We added pieces of bark and dried weeds along the path.

More Ideas

Think of other kinds of tracks you can make. How about horse or car racing? Look in old magazines for pictures of crowds of people and see if you can figure out how to attach a grandstand full of people to the edge of your track.

You can even make a track like the ones on the campus of your local high school. Can you show a stick figure jumping hurdles?

How about creating a frozen pond filled with gliding skaters or a lake full of sail boats?

Hats Galore

Heads are round, hats are round, plates are round. You could go round and round all day making hats. Here are some ideas.

You Will Need:

- dinner-sized paper plates
- paper bowl
- scissors
- poster board
- glue
- paint, crayons, markers
- string or yarn
- ribbon
- button

To Make a Party Hat

Cut a large circle from poster board. Cut it in half and shape one half into a cone. Cut a section of rim from a paper plate to use as the hat's brim. Make notches or tabs along the inner edge of the brim so you can glue it to the cone. Looking at our picture will help you. Create a decoration special to you. We drew and cut out a clown. Glue your decoration to the cone. Add tie-on strings.

You can make small party hats for dolls or to use as party favors by forming a cone from half of a flexible paper plate. Decorate with sparkles and tassels.

To Make the Hat Wall Hanging

Glue a soup bowl upside down in the center of the front of a dinner-sized plate. Paint or color your hat anyway you choose. Can you make it look like straw? Glue ribbon around the area where the plate and bowl are glued together and add decorations. Make a yarn hanger and find a special place to hang your hat.

Make a wall-hanging hat to suit all seasons just by creating different decorations. How about robins for spring, flowers for summer, leaves for fall, and snowflakes for winter?

To Make a Cap

Cut a brim from the center of a paper plate or from a section of the rim. Make tabs where the brim will attach to the cap part. Fold tabs up and glue to the inside of an upside-down paper bowl. Decorate with crayons, paint, or markers. Glue a button to the top.

More Ideas

Make a cap for each of your favorite sports teams. Hang them on the wall of your room.

Or make lots of caps. Write a person's name on each and use them as place cards. This would be a great idea for an end-of-season sports banquet.

Bunny Basket

Create a cuddly dish.

You Will Need:

- flexible paper plates
- crayons, markers
- paper clips
- hole punch
- scissors
- yarn
- construction paper
- metal fasteners
- cotton balls
- plastic "grass"

1 Color both sides of 3 plates. Fold 2 of the plates in half. Place one part of each folded plate on top of the third plate. Hold in place with paper clips. Punch holes around the rim, then lace the plates together with yarn. The vertical part of each plate will be the bunny's body.

2 Cut ears from a plate's rim, color, and attach them with metal fasteners. Glue on a nose and a cotton ball for a tail. Add eyes and yarn whiskers. Open the bunny up and stuff with grass and treats.

More Ideas

Instead of ears, add the neck and head of a swan. Or make antlers and a red nose for you-know-who.

Paper-Plate Christmas Tree

Make an ornament.

You Will Need:

- dinner-sized flexible paper plate
- scissors
- construction paper
- paint
- glitter, sequins, small beads
- glue
- yarn or ribbon

1 Cut the rim off a paper plate. Cut the rim into sections, going from large to small. The smallest section should have a pointed top.

2 Paint the sections green and glue them in place to form a tree as shown in the picture.

3 Decorate your tree with glitter, sequins, small beads, or cut-paper ornaments.

More Ideas

Create a wintertime mural. Make a forest of trees and decorate with snow made from white paper cutouts.

Amusement Park Plates

You can make a pretend amusement park for your action figures or dolls. We'll give you brief directions for making a few rides. You'll probably think of other park attractions to make.

You Will Need:

- paper plates
- cardboard tubes
- paint, crayons, markers
- hole punch
- poster board
- tape
- glue
- yarn, string
- detergent bottle caps
- wooden dowel
- plastic straws
- chenille sticks

To Make Spinning Swings

1 Decorate both sides of two sturdy dinner-sized paper plates and a cardboard tube. (We used a 7" tube.) Glue the tube to the front side of one of the plates. This will be the swing's top. Punch two holes in the edge of the plate about 1/2" apart. Punch other pairs of holes evenly around the plate's edge.

2 Draw and cut out seats from poster board. Attach them to the top plate with yarn or string. We taped one end of the yarn to the back of the seat, threaded the other end through one of the pairs of holes in the top, and then tied it underneath.

3 Make the swing's bottom by gluing the tube to the middle of the other plate. Finish off your swing with decorative detergent bottle caps on top and bottom.

To Make the Twirling Spaceship Ride

1 Make two flying saucers as described on page 8. We colored ours with crayons and markers. You may choose to paint yours or use colored plates. Find a long cardboard tube and decorate it. We used an 18" wrapping paper tube.

2 Cut a hole the size of the tube in the middle of the bottom layer of each spaceship. Put glue on each end of the tube and stick the tube's ends into the holes. Let the materials dry thoroughly before proceeding.

3 Poke a small hole on each side of the tube halfway between the spaceships. Insert an 18" wooden dowel. You can balance the ends of the dowel on two level surfaces or just hold it and give the spaceships a spin.

To Make a Monster Slide

1 Follow the basic directions for the spiral on page 25. Alter the shape and decorations to suit your design.

2 Decorate a cardboard tube. Glue the bottom of the tube to a poster board circle to help the tube stand more steadily. Attach the top of your spiral to the top of the tube and let it loosely wind around the tube to form the slide.

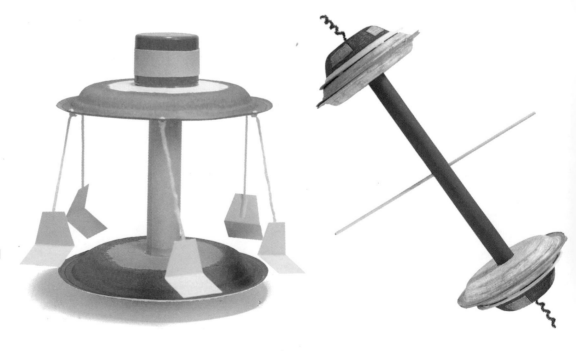

44

Sometimes boys and girls celebrate birthdays with a group of friends at an amusement park. Wouldn't a craft-making, amusement-park party be fun, too?

To Make the Merry-Go-Round

1 Decorate the bottom of two plates and a cardboard tube cut to 8". Securely attach the tube to the front side of the top plate with glue or tape.

2 Use 4 or 5 straws to make merry-go-round poles that are 8" long. Determine where you want the poles to be, spacing them evenly. Secure the poles to the plates by threading a chenille stick so that it sticks out the ends of the straw. Then bend the chenille sticks to form top and bottom tabs. Tape, glue, or staple the tabs to the top plate.

3 Attach the tube and the straw tabs to the bottom plate with glue, tape, or staples. Glue detergent bottle caps to the top and bottom of the carousel. Cut out or create a picture for each straw pole. Animals or vehicles would work well. Tape the pictures to the straws facing out.

More Ideas

Create some paper dolls or make stick-figure people from chenille sticks. Tape or glue them to the slide, swings, and merry-go-round.

Create a script for a play or movie that takes place in an amusement park. Use these craft creations as props and scenery. Work with some friends and together give an amusing performance.

Balloon Bat

Here's a great make-it, play-it idea.

You Will Need:

- large paper plate
- paint, crayons, markers
- colored glue
- glue
- jumbo craft sticks or tongue depressors
- balloon

1 Decorate a plate with whatever materials you like. We used several shades of colored glue on ours.

2 Glue one stick to the middle of the back of the plate. For a longer handle, glue another stick to the first stick with about a 1" overlap.

3 Blow up a balloon to about softball size and see how many times you can bounce the balloon off the bat.

More Ideas

Make two bats and play pretend tennis with a friend.

Jigsaw Plate

You can make a puzzle for yourself or one to give to a friend who's about to go on a long car trip.

You Will Need:

- sturdy dinner-sized paper plates
- pencil
- markers or crayons
- scissors

1 Decorate your plate. Color a realistic scene or create an abstract design like ours. Carefully cut the plate apart into puzzle-shaped pieces. You might want to lightly sketch outlines of the pieces before you begin cutting.

2 Use a second plate as a base on which to reassemble your puzzle. You may want to draw the shapes of the pieces on the base plate if it is going to be for younger children. Store your puzzle in a plastic bag.

More Ideas

Cut the puzzle pieces into geometric shapes. Or write a message on the puzzle and give it to a secret pal to put together.

Paper-Plate Garden

You can make a flower garden from paper plates. We'll show you three, and you'll probably have some great ideas of your own. Can you think of how you might use layers or sections of paper plates to make a rose or a zinnia?

You Will Need:

- a variety of paper plates
- scissors
- paint, crayons
- chenille sticks
- brown tissue paper
- glue
- construction paper
- pencil
- ruler
- metal fastener

The Folding Flower

Take a flexible paper plate and trim away part of its edges so that the plate is wavy all around. Paint the plate to show a center and petals. Cut slits at intervals all the way around, or try a fringed or jagged cut. (Space between cuts can vary.) Fold and shape segments to look like petals. You could fold some petals up and some back, or try to curl petals with a pencil. Bend a chenille stick to form stem and leaves, then tape it to the back of the flower.

The Sunflower

Paint or color a paper plate or use a bright-yellow colored one. Glue crumpled pieces of brown tissue paper on the plate to make the flower's center. Use cut-out pieces of a paper plate or construction paper to make the stem and leaves. Glue the leaves and stem to the flower.

More Ideas

Instead of making the center of the sunflower, glue on a circular-shaped photo of someone special. Straws, sticks, or tongue depressors can also be used to make stems.

The Blooming Tulip

Mark a pencil point on the edge of a plate. On the opposite side of the plate mark 2 points about 4" apart. Use a ruler to draw two lines, starting at the two points and meeting at the opposite point. Then cut on the lines. You'll have three pieces. Next cut a V in the tip of the cone-shaped piece. Paint the pieces your favorite tulip color or use colored paper plates. Connect the 3 parts of the bloom with a metal fastener as shown below. To make a stem, cut a 1" strip from the center of a paper plate. Use the leftover pieces for leaves and attach to the stem.

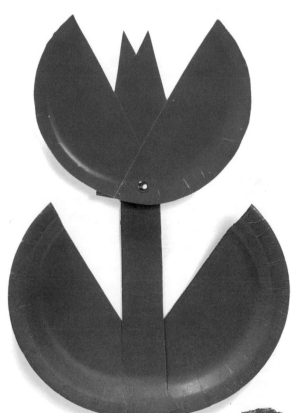

Title Index

Subject Index

Look What You Can Make With
EGG CARTONS

Over 90 Pictured Crafts and Dozens of Other Ideas

Edited by Betsy Ochester

Look What You Can Make With

Egg Cartons

Edited by Betsy Ochester
Photographs by Hank Schneider

Boyds Mills Press

Craft Coordinator:
Betsy Ochester

Contributors:

Patricia Barley
Katherine Bartow
Anne Bell
Frances M. Callahan
Marie E. Cecchini
Mary Colacurcio
Sandra Csippan
Kathy Everett

Vicki Felix
Marguerite Harrington
Carmen Horn
Helen Jeffries
Tama Kain
Garnett Kooker
Lee Lindeman
Betsy Ochester

James W. Perrin, Jr.
Sylvia W. Sproat
Matthew Stockton
Debora Sullivan
Sharon Dunn Umnik
Francis Wales
D. A. Woodliff

Copyright © 2000 by Boyds Mills Press
All rights reserved

Published by Bell Books
Boyds Mills Press, Inc.
A Highlights Company
815 Church Street
Honesdale, Pennsylvania 18431
Printed in China

U.S. Cataloging-in-Publication Data
    (Library of Congress Standards)

Look what you can make with egg cartons : over 90 pictured crafts and dozens of other ideas /
edited by Betsy Ochester ; photographs by Hank Schneider. --1st ed.
[48] p. : col. ill. ; cm.
Summary: Toys, games, and other ideas all from egg cartons.
ISBN: 1-56397-906-3
1. Box craft. 2. Handicraft. I. Ochester, Betsy. II. Schneider, Hank, ill. III. Title.
745.54 --21 2000   AC CIP
00-100007

First edition, 2000
Books in this series originally designed by Lorianne Siomades
The text of this book is set in 10pt Avant Garde Demi, titles 43pt Gill Sans Extra Bold

10 9 8 7 6 5 4 3

Getting Started

This book is filled with fun, easy-to-make crafts, and each one begins with an egg carton. You'll find a wide variety of things to make, including toys, games, and gifts.

Directions

Before you start each craft, read the directions and look closely at the photograph, but remember—it's up to you to make the craft your own. If we decorate a craft with markers, but you want to use glitter paint and stickers, go for it. Feel free to stray from our directions and invent new crafts.

Work Area

It's a good idea to keep your work area covered. Old newspapers, brown paper (from grocery bags), or old sheets work well. Also, protect your clothes by wearing a smock. A big, old shirt does the job and gives you room to move. Finally, remember to clean up when you've finished.

Materials

You'll need a lot of egg cartons, so start saving now. Ask friends and relatives to help. Keep your craft-making supplies together, and before making each craft, check the "You Will Need" list to make sure you have everything. In this list, we'll often specify whether we used plastic-foam or cardboard egg cartons. For some crafts, however, either type will work. Also, since you'll need scissors and glue, tape, or a stapler for almost every craft, we don't list these supplies.

Other Stuff

When we show several similar crafts, we'll often list numbered directions that apply to all of the crafts, then specific directions for each craft.

Important egg-carton terms: In our directions, we refer to the parts of the carton that hold the eggs as "cups" or "egg cups." The bottom of the cup is the part on which the egg sits. A "peak" refers to the cone shape that is in between the cups.

Here's a painting tip: Poster paint won't stick to plastic-foam egg cartons (though it works great for cardboard cartons). Try mixing liquid soap with the paint. It works for us.

That's about all. So, find a bunch of egg cartons, select a craft that you like, and have some fun. Before you know it, you'll be showing everyone what you made with egg cartons.

Critter Keepers

Need a place to store small treasures? These adorable animals can help!

You Will Need:

- felt
- egg cartons
- markers
- toothpicks
- plastic wiggle eyes
- foam paper
- plastic-foam balls
- construction paper
- chenille sticks

To Make the Basic Container

1 Cut a piece of felt big enough to cover the lid of an egg carton. It should be at least 7 inches by 15 inches in size. Glue the felt to the lid, tucking in the edges as you would gift wrap and gluing them securely. Let the glue dry.

2 Follow the directions for the animal you want to make.

To Make the Hedgehog

For the quills, use markers to color wooden toothpicks. Dip the end of each quill into glue, then poke it into the top of the lid. Glue on wiggle eyes, and a nose and mouth cut from foam paper.

To Make the Frog

For the eyes, glue two plastic-foam balls to the top of the carton and glue a black paper circle to each. Cut out a tongue shape from red foam paper and add detail with marker. Glue the tongue in place on the inside of the lid.

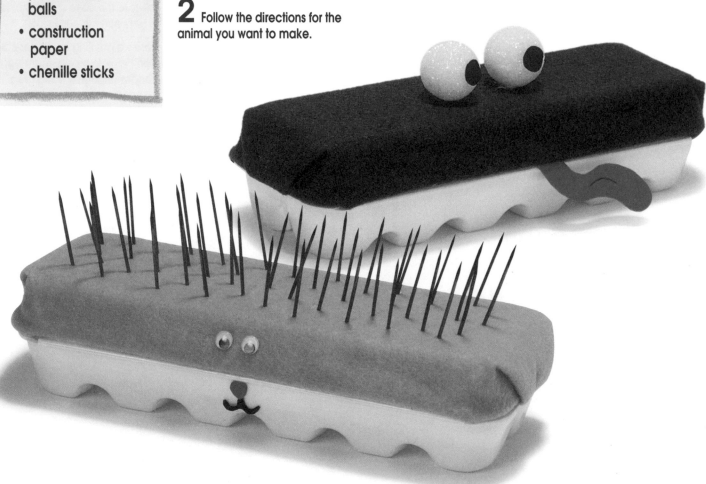

Make the creatures shown here, or create your own—just about any animal can be a critter keeper.

To Make the Lobster

To make the eyes, poke a piece of white chenille stick into each of two plastic-foam balls. Use a toothpick to poke two holes in the top of the egg carton. Insert the chenille sticks into the holes with a little glue. Cut claws from foam paper, and glue them to the inside of the lid. Glue on wiggle eyes and a foam-paper mouth.

To Make the Blue Whale

Fold a piece of blue felt in half. Cut a tail shape from the felt, using the fold as the top of the tail. Place two chenille sticks between the felt pieces, leaving about 1 inch of each stick poking out from the bottom of the tail. Glue the pieces of felt together. When the glue is dry, bend into a curved shape. Poke the two ends of the chenille sticks into the back of the carton, bend them, and add glue to secure. Glue on wiggle eyes and features cut from foam paper.

More Ideas

Use a critter keeper as a desk organizer to hold paper clips, erasers, and rubber bands. Or place one on a bathroom counter to store cotton balls and swabs.

For Halloween, make a monster critter keeper. Fill it with candy and give it to a friend for an extra-special treat.

Great-Shape Necklace

Make your own fashion statement with this unique necklace.

You Will Need:

- plastic-foam egg carton
- markers
- drinking straws
- string or yarn
- needle

1 Cut shapes from the lid of the egg carton and color them with markers. Cut out small pieces of the drinking straws. Cut a piece of string or yarn long enough to fit over your head. Thread one end of the string onto the needle.

2 String a shape and then a section of straw onto the string, leaving an inch of string at the bottom. Continue stringing the shapes and straws until you almost have reached the end of the string. Tie the two ends of the string together.

More Ideas

Necklaces are just the beginning of the egg-carton jewelry you can make. String together bracelets for your wrists and ankles. Create a ring by poking a few shapes onto a piece of chenille stick, and wrapping it around your finger. Or design a decorative belt by stringing shapes onto a strong piece of twine.

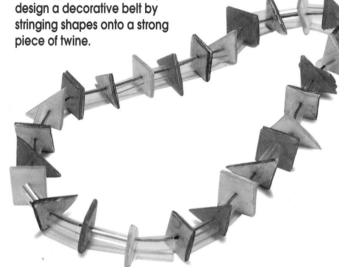

Ladybug Pin

This colorful friend will brighten your shirt, jacket, or backpack.

You Will Need:

- egg carton
- markers or paint
- cotton balls
- poster board
- black yarn
- safety pin

1 Cut one cup from the egg carton. Trim it into a ladybug shape. Color the cup with a red marker or paint. Draw on a black head, spots, and a line to separate the wings.

2 Glue cotton balls to the inside of the cup. Attach a piece of poster board with glue to the bottom of the cup and cotton balls. Let the glue dry, then trim around the edges of the poster board with scissors. Glue legs, made from short pieces of yarn, to the poster board. Tape or glue a safety pin to the bottom of the ladybug.

More Ideas

Make matching ladybug pins. Give one to a friend, and keep one for yourself.

Instead of a safety pin, glue a piece of magnetic strip to the ladybug to make a refrigerator magnet.

6

Fun Fliers

Recycle your family's egg cartons into your own fleet of planes. Then zoom into the wild blue yonder!

You Will Need:

- plastic-foam egg cartons
- straight pins
- paint
- markers
- stickers

To Make the Planes

1 On the lid of a plastic-foam egg carton, draw the body, wings, and tail of the airplane you want to make. (Look at the pictures to determine the shapes of these pieces.) Cut out the shapes.

2 Carefully cut slits into the plane's body for the wings and the tail. Insert the wings and the tailpiece into the slits.

3 Follow the instructions for the plane you want to make.

To Make the Biplane

Make a short slit beneath the bottom wing. Insert a small rectangle cut from the lid and bend it to form a stand for the plane. Cut a propeller from the lid and attach it to the front of the plane with a straight pin. Color the plane with markers or paint.

To Make the Jet

For engines, cut small oval pieces from the egg carton and glue them under the wings. Decorate the plane with paint or markers.

To Make the Blue Plane

Attach a propeller as described for the biplane. Cut small circles from the egg carton lid for wheels, and glue them in place. Decorate the plane with paint, markers, and stickers.

More Ideas

Make a runway for your planes by cutting strips from the lid of an egg carton and gluing them together. Use a small box to create a hangar to park your planes when they're on the ground.

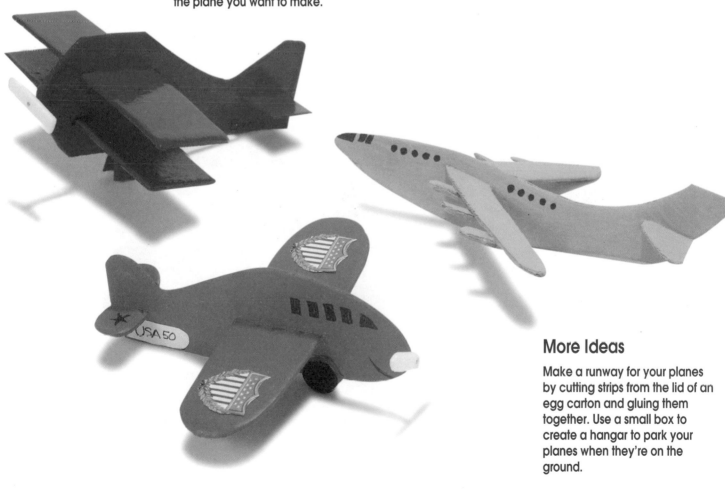

Design Your Own Doll Furniture

This doll furniture is beautiful and easy to make, too.

You Will Need:

- cardboard egg cartons
- paint
- clear nail polish (optional)
- ruler

1 Cut the lids from two egg cartons. Follow the directions for the piece of furniture you want to make.

2 Paint the pieces as you wish. We chose flowers and dots as decorations. You might decide to make a striped couch or polka-dotted chairs. If you want to give your furniture a glazed finish, add a coat of clear nail polish.

To Make the Kitchen Table

Cut a flat circle from the lid. Make legs by cutting three strips from the top of the lid that each extend about ¾ of an inch into the side of the lid. Overlap these three legs, and glue the ¾-inch ends to the bottom of the table.

To Make the Straight Chairs

Cut a piece from the side and bottom of the lid. For legs, cut two strips from the side of the lid that each extend about ¾ of an inch into the top of the lid. Overlap these two strips, and glue the ¾-inch ends to the bottom of the chair. Trim the legs so the chair stands evenly.

You'll want to create enough to fill an entire dollhouse!

To Make the Couch

Cut off the end of a lid for the seat. For the legs, cut off an inch-wide lid section next to your previous cut. Glue the legs to the bottom of the seat.

To Make the Armchairs

For the seat, cut off a corner of a lid. Trim it into an armchair shape. Add legs as for the straight chair.

To Make the Coffee Table

Cut a strip from the middle of the lid, including the sides. Cut legs into the sides of the strip.

To Make the Couch Pillow

Glue the ends of two egg-carton cups together to form a pillow shape.

More Ideas

Make an egg-carton tea set for your larger dolls. Cut out individual egg cups for teacups. Add chenille-stick handles. A square of four egg cups can be a caddy to carry your tea cups. Cut round pieces from the lid for saucers. Add a creamer and a sugar bowl made from egg cups. Decorate with paint and markers. Invite all your dolls and stuffed animals for tea!

Colossal Castle

Be the king or queen—and the architect—of your own castle. Ask friends and family to start saving egg cartons now—this kingdom calls for a royal number of cartons.

You Will Need:

- seventeen cardboard egg cartons
- large pieces of construction paper
- paint
- large piece of cardboard
- poster board
- craft sticks
- one plastic-foam egg carton
- toothpicks
- markers

1 To make each of the towers, cut four lids from cardboard cartons. Cut off the short ends from two of the lids. Fit the four lids together, with the two trimmed lids inside the other two, to form a rectangle. Staple or glue the lids together. Cover each tower with construction paper. Cut out four four-cup sections from the cartons, paint them, and glue one on top of each tower.

2 To make each wall, cut a cardboard egg-carton bottom in half. Glue the two halves together by overlapping three cups. Make "feet" for each wall to stand on by cutting slits at the bottom of two cups and inserting the bottom edge of the wall into the slits. Paint each wall.

3 Cover the large piece of cardboard with green poster board. Glue the towers and walls in place onto the poster board.

4 Cut a gate from poster board and glue the sides to the two front towers. Make a bridge by cutting off two-thirds of a lid, and gluing four cups to it for supports. Paint craft sticks and glue them to the top of the bridge. Glue the bridge in front of the castle.

5 Glue on a moat cut from blue poster board. Make a "moat monster" from scraps cut from a plastic-foam egg carton (our monster's head is half of the lid's raised peak). Add flags made from paper and toothpicks. Draw on windows with a marker.

More Ideas

Make trees for your castle by gluing a stack of egg-carton cups on top of one another, and painting them green. Make finger-puppet dolls to inhabit your kingdom. (To make a basic doll shape, see pages 24-25.) Color one silver for a knight, and give one an aluminum foil crown for a king or queen.

Egg-Carton Greetings

Instead of buying cards from a store, create your own original works of art.

You Will Need:

- egg carton
- paper
- ink pads

1 Cut off parts of the egg carton that have unusual shapes or patterns to use as stamps.

2 Cut a piece of paper to the size you'd like and fold it in half.

3 Press your egg carton parts onto ink pads. Then press them on the front of the card to create a design. Let your creativity shine! You can make abstract designs or realistic drawings. Write a message inside the card.

More Ideas

Use your egg carton pieces to design wrapping paper. Spread out a large sheet of paper, and stamp away. To make special stationery, stamp shapes around the edges of writing paper.

Pumpkin-Patch Pals

This spirited trio will add spice to your Halloween decorating.

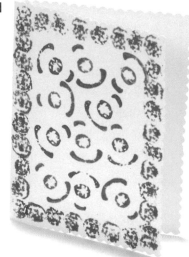

You Will Need:

- cardboard egg carton
- paint
- construction paper

1 Cut six cups from the egg carton. Glue them together in pairs to make three pumpkins. Paint them orange.

2 Cut a section of three peaks from the egg carton for the base. Trim two peaks different heights. Paint the base black.

3 Glue the pumpkins to the base. Attach cut-paper features to the pumpkins. Place your jack-o'-lanterns on a windowsill or table.

More Ideas

Make lots of egg-carton jack-o'-lanterns, without the base, and hand them out with candy to trick-or-treaters.

Halloween Hangers

These spooky mobiles will bring fleets of ghastly ghosts, batty bats, and "boo-tiful" black cats to your Halloween party. They'll also bring lots of smiles to your guests.

You Will Need:

- plastic-foam egg cartons
- hole punch
- yarn
- cardboard egg carton
- paint
- construction paper
- beads
- markers
- thread
- tree branch

To Make the Ghost Mobile

To make the top, cut the bottom section of a white plastic-foam egg carton in half. Poke a hole in each of the four corner cups. Thread a piece of yarn through each hole and knot the yarn. Join the four pieces of yarn in one knot for a hanger. With a hole punch, make holes to hang the ghosts.

For each ghost, cut five cups from a white plastic-foam egg carton. Poke a hole in the bottom of each cup. Tie a knot at the end of a piece of yarn, and thread a bead onto the yarn. Then thread on one egg cup, then two beads, then another egg cup. Continue in this way until you have put on five cups. Then tie a knot at the top of the ghost's head, and tie the end of the yarn to the top section. Draw on faces with a marker.

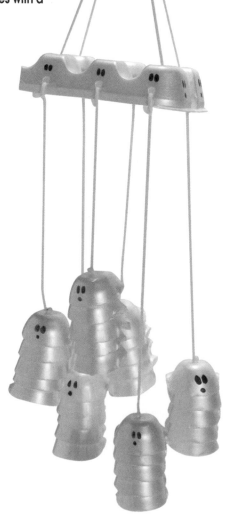

To Make the Black Cat Mobile

For the top, cut the lid of a plastic-foam egg carton in half, then cut out a square from the middle of that half. Use the hole punch to make holes in each corner and one hole for each cat. Tie a piece of yarn to each corner hole, and join these four pieces in a knot for a hanger.

For each cat, cut one cup from a cardboard egg carton and trim it into the shape of a cat's head, leaving on pointy ears. Paint the heads black. Glue on paper whiskers and eyes. Poke a hole in the top of each cat's head, and tie a piece of yarn to it. Cover the back of each head with a circle of black paper. Tie each cat to a hole in the top section.

To Make the Bat Mobile

For each bat, cut two cups from a plastic-foam egg carton. Make wings and ears from black paper, and glue them between the cups. Add hole-punch eyes and a mouth. Glue or tape a piece of thread to each bat and tie them to a fallen tree branch. Tie three pieces of yarn to the branch, and gather the pieces in a knot for a hanger.

More Ideas

Egg cartons can be turned into all kinds of mobiles—not just Halloween ones. Make an Easter-egg mobile by gluing pairs of egg-carton cups together to make egg shapes. Paint the "eggs" bright colors and tie them to a hanger. Pairs of cups can also be decorated to make a solar-system mobile, an insect mobile, and a baseball mobile. Can you come up with other ideas?

Windowsill Menorah

This Hanukkah decoration can be used year after year.

You Will Need:

- egg carton
- tissue paper
- ruler
- corrugated cardboard
- aluminum foil
- craft sticks
- marker
- construction paper

1 Cut out two rows of egg-carton cups: one row of six and one of three. Stuff each cup with a piece of crumpled tissue paper.

2 Measure and cut a 3-inch-by-19-inch rectangle from the cardboard. Glue the cups, with the stuffed side down, in one straight row, to the cardboard. When the glue has dried, cover the entire menorah with aluminum foil. Crunch the foil around each cup and tape it to the bottom of the cardboard.

3 Color nine craft sticks with a marker. Cut out nine "flames" from construction paper. Glue a flame to the top of each stick. Cut a small slit at the top of each egg cup. Using a little glue, slide the craft sticks into the slits, placing the middle stick slightly higher than the rest.

More Ideas

Instead of gluing the flames to t[ ] sticks, use a loop of tape and "light" a new candle for each night of Hanukkah.

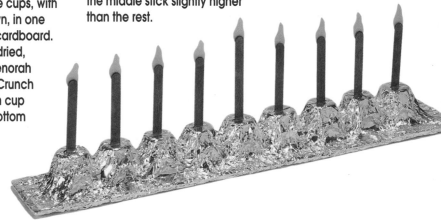

Egg-Carton Carolers

Add a festive note to any holiday gathering with this charming chorus.

You Will Need:

- gift wrap
- egg carton
- hole punch
- construction paper
- yarn
- marker

2 With a hole punch, make eyes and mouths from construction paper. Glue them to the twelve egg sections. Cut bow ties from construction paper, and glue them in place. Make hair by gluing strands of yarn to the top of each head. Draw on noses.

3 Write the name of your favorite Christmas carol on a strip of paper. Add musical notes, and glue the paper to the front of the carton.

More Ideas

Place a small cassette player behind the carolers, and play a tape of Christmas music.

Make choruses for other occasions, such as a birthday or anniversary.

1 Glue gift wrap to the top of the egg carton, tucking the edges inside the carton. Turn the carton over.

Dump Truck

Haul loads around your bedroom with this working dump truck.

You Will Need:

- plastic-foam egg cartons
- construction paper
- ruler
- drinking straw
- chenille stick
- markers

3 For the bed of the truck, cut off a little less than half of a lid. Cut a 3¾-inch-long piece from a drinking straw. Tape this to the bottom of the bed, about ¾ of an inch from the bed's back end. Place the bed on the body, fitting the straw into the notches you made in step 1. Insert a chenille stick through the straw. Twist the stick's ends together under the bumpers to fasten the bed of the truck to the body. This will allow your truck to "dump."

4 To make the tires, cut the tips from four egg-carton cups and glue them to the wheels. Decorate the truck with markers and paper. We made a paper license plate and glued it over the chenille stick.

More Ideas

Create train cars from the lids and bottoms of egg cartons. Connect the cars with short pieces of chenille sticks. Make a track with strips cut from carton lids.

1 For the bottom of the truck, cut a six-cup section from an egg carton, leaving on a small part of the seventh and eighth cups for back bumpers. Cut off the bottoms of the two middle cups; the other four cups will be the truck's wheels. Turn the piece over so that the four "wheels" are facing down. At the top of the body, cut a notch between each of the rear wheels and their "bumper." The two notches should be directly across from each other. Cut a piece of paper to fit over the six-cup section and glue it on top of the body, making sure it doesn't cover the notches.

2 For the truck's cab, cut a two-cup section from the end of an egg carton. Glue it in place on the body.

Cruising Cartons

You're the captain! Build one of these boats, or design your own floatable fleet.

You Will Need:

- plastic-foam egg cartons
- ruler
- craft sticks
- craft spoons
- permanent markers
- paint
- toothpick

To Make the Rowboat

Remove the lid from an egg carton and cut it in half. Turn this half-lid section over so the flat part is facing down. This will be your boat. With scissors, make a 3-inch-long slit on each side of the boat at the spot where the side meets the floor. Then make cuts on the boat floor from the middle of the front of the boat to the far end of each slit. This will leave a triangle shape on the boat's floor. Bend the two sides in to meet the point of the triangle, and tape securely in place.

To add a seat, cut two small slits on opposite sides of the boat. Insert a craft stick. Make oars by cutting slits on opposite sides of the boat and inserting craft spoons. Color your boat with permanent markers.

To Make the Barge

Remove the lid from an egg carton and turn it upside down to form the bottom of the boat. Cut a four-cup section from the carton and glue it onto the lid. Paint craft sticks and glue them onto the rest of the lid. Add life preservers cut from the bottoms of egg cups. Glue on a smokestack made from the raised peak in a carton's lid. Color the boat with permanent markers.

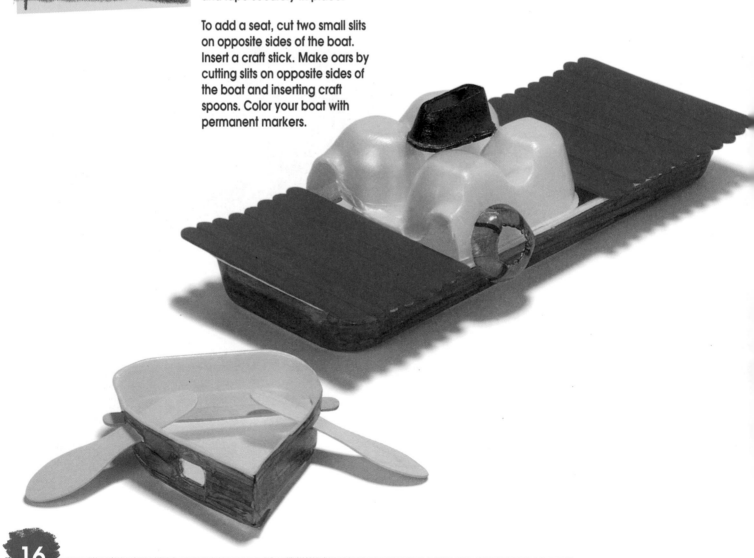

Then take your vessels sailing in a pond, stream, sink, or bathtub.

To Make the Cruise Ship

To make the bottom level of the ship, turn an egg carton over so the cup section is facing up. To form the second level, cut the lid from another carton in half and turn it upside down. Cut flat pieces from another lid and glue them across the top and back of the half-lid to enclose it. Glue the second level to the bottom level.

Next, cut a section of four cups from the end of a carton and glue that on top of the second level. Glue on a smokestack made from the raised peak in a carton's lid. Make a flag by cutting a triangle from a carton and taping it to a toothpick. Color the ship with permanent markers.

More Ideas

Take bath toys for rides on the barge and rowboat. Store soap in the bottom of the cruise ship.

Beautiful Bouquet

Long after ordinary flowers would wilt, these bright blossoms will keep their beauty. Display them as a cheery centerpiece for family meals.

You Will Need:

- cardboard egg cartons
- plastic-foam egg cartons
- chenille sticks
- paint
- old water or soda bottle
- small pebbles
- gift wrap

To Make the Daffodils

For the petal section, cut one cup from a cardboard egg carton and trim the edges. For the flower's center, use a peak cut from the carton.

To Make the Tulips

Cut one cardboard egg cup for the petal section. Bend a short piece of black chenille stick for a stamen.

To Make the Tiger Lily

For the petal section, cut a tall peak from a cardboard carton, leaving on four small triangular shapes from the carton's bottom. Make a stamen as described for the tulips.

To Make the Daisies

For each daisy, cut two cups from a plastic-foam carton. Cut the sides of each cup into petals. The stem will be attached to one of the petal sections. The second petal section will be the flower's center.

To Make Basic Flowers

1 Make the petal sections and the flower centers or stamens, following the instructions for the flowers you want to make. Color them with paint or markers.

2 To make a stem, poke two small holes in the bottom of a petal section. Thread a green chenille stick up through one hole, then bend the stick and poke an inch of it down through the second hole. Twist the inch around the stem to secure it. Glue on the flower center or stamen.

3 Arrange your flowers in a vase made from an old bottle that's weighted down with small pebbles and wrapped in gift paper.

More Ideas

Add a little spray of perfume to make scented flowers. Tie a flower to a wrapped present as a special touch. Make a wreath by tying flowers to a piece of painted cardboard cut in an "O" shape. Design a daisy-chain necklace by stringing together lots of egg-carton daisies.

Useful Bulletin Board

You won't get bored with this handy bulletin board.
Create an ever-changing display of photos, notes, and other keepsakes.

You Will Need:

- three plastic-foam egg cartons
- hole punch
- yarn
- pushpins

1 Remove the bottoms from the three cartons. Fasten them together using several pieces of tape placed on the inside.

2 Punch two holes at the top. Tie a piece of yarn through the holes to make a hanger. Use pushpins to mount your items.

More Ideas

Create "thoughts for the day." Write down each thought on a separate piece of paper, and pin a new one to your board each morning.

Use your bulletin board to keep track of homework assignments, or as an art gallery for your drawings.

Frame It!

Egg carton lids make "egg-cellent" frames
to display photos of family and friends.

You Will Need:

- cardboard egg carton
- index cards or paper plate
- ruler
- paint
- markers
- construction paper
- ribbon

1 Cut the lid from the egg carton. From the index cards or paper plate, cut circles about 1¾ inch in diameter. Glue the circles to the lid's peaks.

2 Decorate your frame with paint, markers, and construction paper. Add a ribbon hanger. Tape or glue small photos to the white circles.

More Ideas

To make a larger frame, use a lid from a carton that holds two dozen eggs.

Frames filled with pictures of you and your family make special presents for grandparents and aunts and uncles.

Egg-Carton Creatures

These cute critters are fun to play with and to make. Keep several in your room and share some with friends. Everyone's going to want some of these friendly creatures!

You Will Need:

- cardboard egg cartons
- yarn
- toothpick
- one raw egg
- paint
- plastic wiggle eyes
- construction paper
- chenille sticks
- sequins
- plastic-foam egg carton
- markers
- poster board

To Make the Bird on a Nest

Cut a cup from a cardboard egg carton and spread glue around the outside of it. Wrap brown yarn around the cup. With a toothpick, poke a hole in the end of an egg. Carefully enlarge the hole until you're left with about half of the shell. Remove the egg and rinse the shell with water. Glue pieces of yellow yarn inside the nest for straw. Paint the eggshell, and glue it inside the nest. Add wiggle eyes and a paper beak.

To Make the Snail

Cut out two cardboard egg-carton cups and glue them together. Paint the cups. Roll one end of a chenille stick into an oval for the snail's head. Curl the other end of the stick into a flat oval for the bottom of the snail. Glue the chenille-stick body onto the cups. Twist a small piece of chenille stick to the head for antennae. Glue on wiggle eyes.

To Make the Dog

Remove two cups from a cardboard egg carton and trim them so that one has legs and the other has pointy ears. Glue them together as shown. Paint the body. Poke a small hole in the back. With glue, insert a chenille-stick tail. Glue on sequin eyes and a paper nose.

To Make the Octopus

Cut out two cardboard egg-carton cups and glue them together. Paint the cups. Attach eight yarn tentacles with glue. Cut eyes and a mouth from paper, and glue them in place.

To Make the Camel

From a cardboard egg carton, cut a connected two-cup section for the body and a peak for the head. To make the back of the head, trace the bottom of the peak onto a flat piece of lid. Draw on ears and cut out the shape. Paint all these pieces. Poke a hole into the front of the body. With glue, insert a piece of chenille stick for the neck. Glue the other end to the inside of the head. Glue on the back of the head. Attach chenille-stick legs and wiggle eyes with glue.

To Make the Monster

Cut two cups from a plastic-foam egg carton. Cut teeth along the edges of both, and staple or glue the cups together at the back. Color with markers. Glue on poster-board feet and wiggle eyes.

More Ideas

Practically any animal can be made from egg cartons. Look at pictures of animals and think of how to create them using egg cups. You might try a horse, a zebra, a bear, a cat, a bee, a centipede, or a penguin.

Tidy Garden Starter

Make this useful seed starter several weeks before it's warm enough to garden outside. Then give it as a gift to your favorite green thumb.

You Will Need:

- toothpicks
- a dozen eggs
- potting soil
- flower or vegetable seeds
- plastic-foam egg carton
- paper
- markers

1 With a toothpick, poke a hole in one end of each egg. Carefully enlarge the hole and remove the top part of the shell. Remove the eggs and rinse the shells. Poke a small drainage hole in the bottom of each shell. Fill each with potting soil. Plant a seed in each shell.

2 Cut the bottom half from the egg carton, and place the planted shells into the cups. Use flags made from toothpicks and paper to label each shell. Decorate the carton with markers.

3 When the seeds have sprouted and the weather is warm enough, the entire shell with sprout can be planted outdoors.

More Ideas

The bottom of a plastic-foam carton also makes a great bird feeder. Punch a hole at each corner. Tie yarn to each hole, then tie the other ends of the yarn together to make a hanger. Fill the cups with birdseed and hang outside.

Cat Jingle Toy

Cats will have hours of fun batting at this jingly toy.

You Will Need:

- cardboard egg carton
- yarn
- two jingle bells
- masking tape
- tissue paper

1 Cut two cups from the egg carton and trim the tops flat. Poke a hole in the bottom of one cup. Push one end of a piece of yarn through the hole, and tie a knot inside the cup. Place a jingle bell inside the cups and tape them together with masking tape.

2 Cut small squares of tissue paper. Spread a thin layer of glue over the toy, and place the tissue paper pieces onto the glue. Smooth another layer of glue on top of the paper. Slide the second jingle bell onto the yarn and down to the top of the toy. Tie a knot above the bell. Tie a loop at the end of the yarn.

More Ideas

Make a couple of these toys and give them as gifts to friends with cats.

Magnet School

We went fishing for magnets and landed this cool school. They'll "perch" on your refrigerator and keep track of important messages, notes, and pictures.

You Will Need:

- cardboard egg carton
- markers or paint
- crepe paper or tissue paper
- plastic wiggle eyes
- magnet strips

More Ideas

These fish are so simple to make, you might want to create a school big enough to swim all the way around your fridge.

Add decorations to make your magnets look like specific types of fish, such as catfish, sunfish, or swordfish. Make a magnetic eel by gluing together a chain of cups.

1 Cut out one egg-carton cup for each fish you want to make. Trim each cup to look like the ones in the picture.

2 Color the cups with markers or paint. Cut out fins from crepe paper or tissue paper and glue to the inside top and bottom of each cup.

3 Glue a wiggle eye to one side of each fish. Glue a piece of magnet strip to the opposite side. Use a marker to draw on a mouth.

Finger Puppets and Theater

There are countless ways
To put on great plays.
These puppets are one way we know
To produce a fabulous show!

You Will Need:

- cardboard egg cartons
- paint
- toothpicks
- construction paper
- ribbon
- poster board
- plastic-foam ball
- markers
- plastic-foam egg carton
- yarn
- plastic wiggle eyes
- chopsticks or dowels
- craft sticks
- craft feathers
- foam paper

To Make the Rabbit

Cut one cup from a cardboard egg carton and paint it white. Paint six toothpicks for whiskers. Poke three holes on each side of the cup. Place the whiskers in the holes with glue. Cut eyes, nose, and mouth from construction paper and glue in place. Glue on a ribbon bow. Cut a small strip of poster board. Glue it in a loop to the back of the rabbit's head, leaving enough room so two fingers will fit inside. Your fingers will be the rabbit's ears.

To Make the Rainy-Day Puppet

Cut two peaks from a cardboard egg carton. Cut the top from one peak to make the hat. The taller peak will be the body. Paint the body and hat. Glue a plastic-foam ball to the top of the body. Glue the hat to the plastic-foam ball. Add paper eyes and mouth. Draw on coat buttons and pockets with a marker. To make the umbrella, cut a cup from the plastic-foam egg carton, color it with a marker, and push it onto the end of a toothpick. Poke the other end into the side of the body using a drop of glue.

To Make the Lion

Cut a peak from a cardboard egg carton, trimming it flat around the edges. Glue on feet and ears cut from the carton. Paint the lion's body. Attach a yarn tail and mane with glue. Add wiggle eyes and a paper nose. Draw on a mouth.

To Make the Rooster

Cut a tall peak from a cardboard egg carton, leaving on thin strips for legs. With scissors, trim feet at the bottom of the legs. Paint the rooster. Poke a small hole in the back of rooster near the bottom. Insert a few feathers, using a drop of glue. Glue on a foam-paper comb, beak, and wattle. Add wiggle eyes.

To Make the Theater

Cut the lid from the plastic-foam egg carton. Poke a chopstick or dowel into each side of the lid. Glue on a stage of craft sticks. Add paper curtains and signs.

More Ideas

Write an original play using these puppets as characters, or create your own finger-puppet cast. Hand out invitations to your friends and family. Then, on with the show!

Whirlybird

Go soaring with this nifty helicopter. The propellers turn, but it's up to you to make the chopping noises!

You Will Need:

- plastic-foam egg carton
- ruler
- drinking straw
- metal paper fasteners
- toothpicks
- markers

1 Cut two cups from the egg carton. Glue them together to form the cockpit. Let dry, then carefully cut a small hole (slightly smaller than the width of a drinking straw) in the middle of both the cockpit's roof and floor.

2 From the carton's lid, cut the raised peak, and then cut a small V-shaped notch in the top of it. Make the notch large enough for a drinking straw. Glue it to the top of the cockpit, lining up the two straw holes.

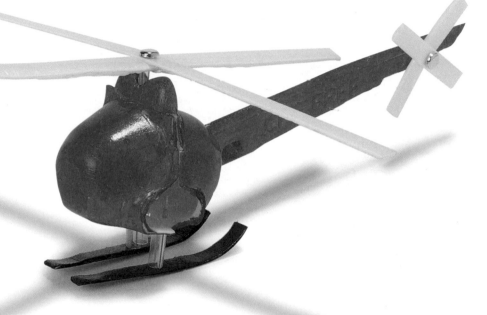

3 Cut two 9½-inch strips from the egg carton lid for propellers. Glue these in an X shape. Let dry, then poke a small hole in the middle of the X. Cut a 3-inch piece of straw. Near one end of the straw, cut two small slits across from one another. Insert a metal paper fastener through the hole in the propellers and into the piece of straw, putting the legs of the metal fastener through the slits you made in the straw and bending them up to secure. Then insert the straw through the holes in the cockpit to put the propellers in place.

4 Cut a 7-inch tailpiece from the side of the egg carton. Cut a slit in the back of the cockpit and insert the tailpiece. For tail propellers, cut two short strips from the lid, glue them in an X shape, and attach with a metal paper fastener.

5 To make landing gear, cut two strips from the side of the carton. Cut a toothpick in half, and poke one half into each strip, using a bit of glue. Place a ¾-inch piece of straw on each toothpick. Using a little glue, stick the ends of the toothpicks into the bottom of the cockpit.

6 Decorate with markers. You may need to glue a small piece of clay in the nose of the helicopter to make it balance.

More Ideas

Tie a piece of fishing line around your helicopter and hang it in your bedroom.

Frosty Ring Toss

"Snow" doubt about it: this game is fun to play by yourself or with friends.

You Will Need:

- cardboard
- construction paper
- poster board
- cardboard egg carton
- paint
- plastic lids from small coffee cans
- glitter
- markers

1 Cut a large circle from the cardboard and cover it with white paper. Cut a hat shape from black paper or poster board. Glue it in place.

2 Cut six cups from the carton and trim their edges nearly flat. Paint five cups black and one cup red. Glue these to the white circle to create a snowman's face. Cut six small circles from white paper. Write a number on each circle, and glue to the cups as shown in the picture.

3 To make the rings, cut the center from the coffee can lids. Cover the rings with glue and sprinkle with glitter to look like snow. To play, set the snowman board on the floor. Stand at a distance, toss the rings, and add up your score.

More Ideas

When playing this game with others, see who can be the first to score 100 points.

"Bee" Mine, Valentine!

Friends and family will love to get this special Valentine's Day card from you.

You Will Need:

- egg carton
- brown yarn
- chenille sticks
- waxed paper
- cardboard
- construction paper
- markers

1 Cut one cup from the egg carton. Cover it with glue. Wind brown yarn around the cup to make it look like a hive.

2 Wrap a yellow chenille stick around your finger or a pencil to make a bee shape. Wrap a black chenille stick around the yellow bee to make stripes. Glue the bee to the hive. Cut wings from waxed paper, and glue them in place. Glue on paper eyes.

3 Cut a large heart from cardboard and cover it with paper. Glue the hive to the center of the heart. Write a Valentine greeting.

More Ideas

Using the hive and bee, make a birthday card with the message, "Have a happy BEE-day!"

Bunches of Baskets

A handmade basket filled with jellybeans or gumdrops makes a wonderful Easter present.

You Will Need:

- plastic-foam egg cartons
- pompons
- construction paper
- ribbon
- cardboard egg cartons
- paint
- chenille sticks
- sequins, paper stars, and other decorations

To Make the Bunny Basket

Cut the bottoms from two plastic-foam egg cartons. Cut one in half the long way so you have a row of six cups. Glue this row, upside down, over half of the other carton bottom, leaving the other half open for your basket.

Decorate the row of egg shapes with pompon noses and paper whiskers, eyes, and heart shapes for feet. Make ears from paper and glue one pair to the back of each bunny head. On every other bunny, glue a bow of ribbon. Cut little hats from a cardboard egg carton's peaks. Paint them black and glue each to a circle of black paper. Glue the hats to the remaining bunny heads.

To Make the Two-Cup Basket

Cut a two-cup section from a cardboard egg carton and trim the top edges. Paint the basket. Poke two small holes on opposite sides of the basket. Twist two 8-inch pieces of chenille stick together to form a handle. Push the ends of the handle into the holes, and twist the ends around the rest of the handle to secure.

To Make the One-Cup Mini Baskets

Cut individual cups from a cardboard egg carton and trim the top edges. Paint the cups. Cut 5-inch strips from construction paper and glue to the inside of the cups for handles. Decorate the cups however you'd like. We used sequins and paper cutouts, but glitter and ribbon work well, too.

Isn't there "some-bunny" you know who would like one?

To Make the Four-Cup Basket

Cut a square, four-cup section from a plastic-foam egg carton. Poke two small holes on opposite sides of the basket. Twist two chenille sticks together to form a handle. Attach the handle in the same manner as for the Two-Cup Basket. Make a decoration for the handle by cutting petal shapes into two egg cups. Glue the two cups together, alternating the petals, to make a flower. Poke two holes in the center of the flower. Push a small piece of chenille stick through the holes, and use it to secure the flower to the handle.

More Ideas

Make mini-baskets for any occasion. Fill them with peanuts or candy, and they make great party favors. Decorate some with pictures of your favorite things and use them to hold desk supplies. Paint one in a friend's favorite colors and give it as a jewelry holder.

Four-cup baskets make great "organizer" gifts. Decorate one to match a friend or family member's tastes, then give it as a garden-seed sorter, pocket-change collector, or nail-and-screw caddy.

Collection Display Case

Show off stamps, coins, or other collections in this "see-through" storage container.

You Will Need:

- ruler
- egg carton
- paint
- hole punch
- chenille sticks

1 Mark a ¼-inch border all the way around the top of the egg carton. Carefully cut out the center of the lid, leaving the border. Paint the carton.

2 Use the hole punch to make two holes at each side of the lid. To make the handles, insert the ends of an 8-inch piece of chenille stick into each set of holes. Then twist the ends together to secure.

3 To make the front fastener, punch a hole in the center of the front side of the lid. Punch a corresponding hole on the inside flap. Make a small loop from chenille stick and slide its ends through the holes. Tape the ends to the inside of the carton. Slide another piece of chenille stick through the loop.

More Ideas

Use the display case to wrap a gift. Place a small, wrapped present in the case. It will be two gifts in one.

Paddle Game

Sharpen your hand-to-eye coordination skills with this fun "whack-it-back" game.

You Will Need:

- cardboard egg carton
- craft feathers
- masking tape
- markers
- two small paper plates
- crayons
- paper towel tube

1 To make the shuttlecock, cut out one egg-carton cup and glue feathers around the outside edge. After the glue dries, cover the bottom of the feathers with masking tape. Use markers to color the masking tape and egg cup.

2 To make the paddles, color the two plates with crayons or markers. Cut two 1-inch rings from the tube, and glue one to the back of each plate for handles.

3 To play with a friend, use the paddles to tap the shuttlecock back and forth. To play alone, tap the shuttlecock up in the air with your paddle.

More Ideas

Make four or five paddles and play with a group of friends standing in a circle.

Al Gator

Be a 'gator creator! Make your own Al or Allie Gator. Or create a whole family.

You Will Need:

- cardboard egg cartons
- white paper
- light cardboard
- paint

1 For Al's body, cut the row of peaks from an egg carton, leaving slight extensions at both sides of the second and fourth peaks. Al's legs will be attached to these extensions.

2 To make each of Al's legs, cut out a piece from the bottom of an egg carton. The piece should stretch from the top of one peak over to and including a strip of the side of the carton. Once you've cut four legs in this manner, cut claws into each leg. Fit the top of the peak section of each leg over the extensions you left on in step 1. Glue the legs in place. (Looking at our picture should help you see what we mean.)

3 Cut Al's head from a piece of carton that includes the bottom of two egg cups (these are his eyes) and extends up to include half of the peak in between (this is his nose). Glue his head to the front of his body. Attach white paper teeth with glue.

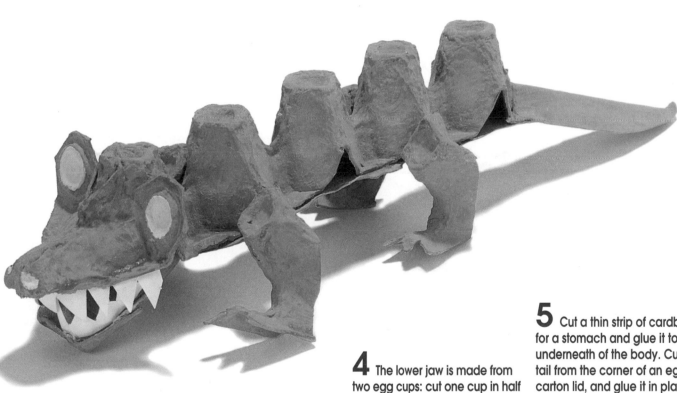

4 The lower jaw is made from two egg cups: cut one cup in half for the front of the lower jaw; cut out half of one side of the other cup for the back of the lower jaw. Overlap these two pieces, with the bottoms of the two cups facing in opposite directions, and glue together. Add paper teeth. Glue the lower jaw in place beneath the upper jaw.

5 Cut a thin strip of cardboard for a stomach and glue it to the underneath of the body. Cut a tail from the corner of an egg carton lid, and glue it in place. Paint Al.

More Ideas

Wrap bracelets and necklaces around the peaks on Al's back to use him as a jewelry holder. Or place Al on a desk and use his peaks to hold rubber bands.

Masks and More!

Disguise yourself with these masks and costume starters.

You Will Need:

- cardboard egg carton
- masking tape
- paint
- pompon
- plastic-foam egg cartons
- markers
- glitter
- craft stick
- construction paper
- paper towel tube
- plastic wrap
- chenille sticks

To Make the Noses

For each nose, cut a cup from a cardboard egg carton and trim it into the shape shown in the picture. Decorate the nose as described below. To wear it, put a loop of masking tape in the craft nose so it sticks to your nose. (If this doesn't work for you, punch holes in opposite sides of the nose and tie on a string that fits around your head.)

To make the tiger, pig, and Martian noses, paint the cups, then add details with paint or marker. To make the mouse nose, leave the cup gray (or paint a cup gray if it came from a colored carton). Glue on a pink pompon.

To Make the Stick Mask

Cut the lid from a plastic-foam egg carton. Draw a mask design, including eyeholes, onto the lid and cut it out. Color the mask with markers. Outline the edges with glue and sprinkle on glitter. Tape a craft stick to the back of the mask as a handle.

To Make the Tube Mask

Remove the lid from a plastic-foam egg carton. Hold it to your face and place two fingers where your eyes are. Remove it from your face, leaving your fingers there. Draw eyeholes, then cut them out. Decorate the lid with construction paper cutouts. Cover a paper towel tube with paper and add cut-paper decorations. Glue it to the back of the mask for a handle.

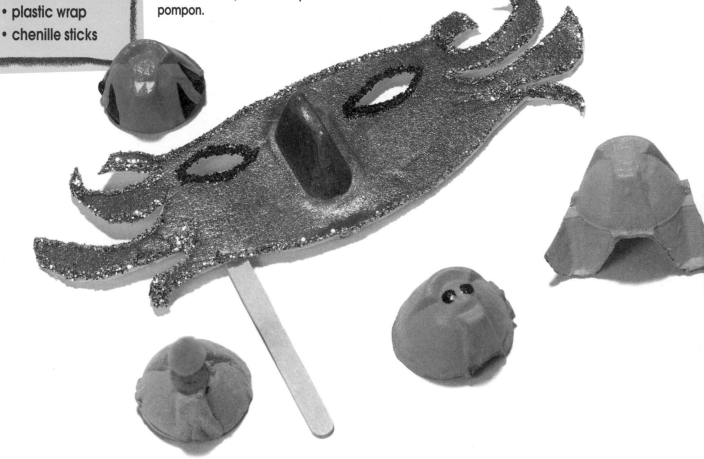

Use one by itself, or create a costume to go with it. Your friends will wonder, "Who is that masked kid?"

To Make the Groovy Glasses

To make the frames, cut a two-cup section from a plastic-foam egg carton. Cut the bottoms from the cups to make eyeholes. Color a piece of plastic wrap with a marker and cut out two circles for lenses. Glue the lenses to the inside of the frames. Color the frames with a marker. Poke holes at opposite sides of the frames. Insert the end of a chenille stick into each hole and twist it around the frame to secure. Try your glasses on, bending the chenille sticks over your ears. Trim the sticks to fit your head.

More Ideas

Throw a "mask"-erade party where you and your guests each make a costume starter. Or give noses out as party favors and have your guests design costumes to go with them.

Make an elephant's trunk by gluing a stack of gray egg cups together. Poke holes in the sides of the bottom cup on the stack. Tie on a string to wear it around your head.

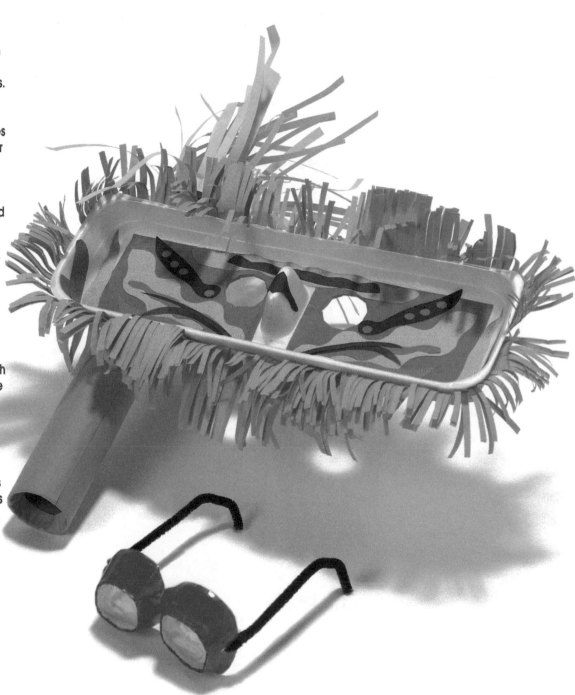

No-Snow Snowman

Here's a snowman you can build without getting your hands cold. And this wintry friend will stick around even when the temperature soars.

You Will Need:

- plastic-foam egg carton
- twig
- white paper towels or napkins
- poster board
- buttons
- construction paper or foam paper
- marker
- fabric scrap

1 Cut two rows of three cups from a white egg carton. (If you use a color other than white, you'll need to add extra layers of ripped paper in step 2.) Place a thin twig in between the two pieces, between the first and second cups. Tape the cups together to form the body, making sure the twig "arms" are secure.

2 In a small bowl, combine equal amounts of glue and water. Tear small pieces of the paper towels or napkins and dip them into the glue mixture. Use these pieces to cover the entire surface of the snowman. Cut a 4-inch square from the poster board and cover it in the same manner. Let the snowman and the square base dry.

3 Glue the snowman to the square base. Decorate him with buttons, paper eyes, and marker. Tie a small strip of fabric around his neck for a scarf.

More Ideas

Create other figures in this way. Make a clown by covering the body with pieces of multicolored tissue paper and decorating it with pompon buttons, a red nose, and yarn hair.

Make an ant by laying the body on its side and covering it with black tissue paper pieces. Add chenille-stick legs and antennae, and paper eyes.

3-D Apple

This apple decoration makes an "egg-stra" nice gift for a teacher.

You Will Need:

- plastic-foam egg carton
- paint or markers
- string or ribbon

1 On the lid of a plastic-foam egg carton, draw two apples of the same size. Draw a stem on only one apple. Cut out the apple shapes.

2 Cut a slit in each shape in the following manner: The shape with the stem should be slit from the bottom to the center of the apple. Slit the other piece from the top down to the center. Fit the apple together by sliding the slits into one another. Spread some glue around the slits.

3 Color the apple with paint or markers. Poke a hole in the stem, and attach a loop of string or ribbon for a hanger.

More Ideas

All kinds of fruit can be made in this manner. Create enough 3-D fruit to fill an entire fruit bowl and use it as a centerpiece. Or make 3-D fruits and vegetables to use as part of a Thanksgiving cornucopia decoration.

Sunflower Magnet

Add some sunshine to your family's day with this cheerful magnet.

You Will Need:

- egg carton
- marker
- glitter
- cardboard
- felt or construction paper
- sunflower seeds
- magnet strips

1 Cut two cups from an egg carton and trim their sides to look like petals. Use a marker to color your flowers. Trace around each flower petal with glue and sprinkle with gold glitter.

2 Cut out a cardboard circle larger than the bottom of an egg cup. Cut out leaves from felt or paper and glue them to the circle. Glue one flower section to the center of the leaves. Then glue the second flower section inside the first, alternating flower petals.

3 Cover the flower center with glue, then set sunflower seeds into the glue. Attach magnet strips to the back.

More Ideas

Make a garden of flower magnets. Try some of the flower patterns on page 18 or design your own colorful flowers.

Deck the Halls

Make your Christmas season merry and bright with these festive decorations.

You Will Need:

- cardboard egg cartons
- ribbon
- paint
- glitter
- lightweight cardboard
- ruler
- buttons
- chenille sticks
- jingle bells
- wooden and plastic beads
- plastic-foam egg carton

To Make the Glittery Ornaments

For each ornament, cut two cups from a cardboard egg carton. For round ornaments, trim each cup's edges flat. Tie a piece of ribbon into a loop, place the knot inside the cups, and glue the cups together. For the arched ornament, trim the two cups as in the picture. Poke a hole in the bottom of one cup, insert a loop of ribbon, and tape its ends to the inside of the cup. Glue the two cups together by their tips. Decorate your ornaments with paint and glitter.

To Make the Candy Cane

Cut 20 cups from cardboard egg cartons. Paint ten white and ten red. Measure across the bottom of one cup. Cut nineteen circles from cardboard that are about ¼-inch wider than the cup's bottom. These are spacers to hold the cups apart. Poke a hole in the bottom of each cup and in the center of each circle. Twist a button onto the end of a chenille stick. Thread on a white cup, spacer, red cup, spacer, white cup, and so on until only the last ¾-inch of chenille stick is showing. Twist a jingle bell onto the end. Gently bend into a cane shape. Add a ribbon hanger.

You'll find ornaments to spruce up a tree, and bells to jingle on a door. Once you start crafting them, you'll want to make more and more.

To Make the Angel Ornaments

For each angel, paint a face and hair onto a wooden bead. Fold a 7-inch piece of chenille stick in half. Thread the wooden bead onto the chenille stick, forming the fold of the stick into a small "halo" above the head. Thread a two-hole button on beneath the head, then tie on a piece of ribbon. Cut a cup from a white plastic-foam carton for the skirt. Poke a hole in the top of the cup, and thread it on next. Thread on a small bead and push it tightly against the skirt. Spread the ends of the chenille stick apart. Thread a bead onto each end, and bend the ends up to keep the beads from sliding off. Tie a ribbon hanger to the top.

To Make the Silver Bells

For the bells, cut peaks from a cardboard egg carton and trim the edges. Cover them inside and out with silver paint. Sprinkle them with glitter and let dry. Tie a piece of ribbon to a jingle bell and make a knot about an inch above the bell. Poke a small hole in the top of an egg-carton bell, and pull the ribbon through the hole until the knot is against the inside of the bell. Tie a knot in the ribbon on top of the bell. Repeat this for each silver bell. Gather all the ribbons together, and tie a knot for a hanger.

More Ideas

Make a long chain to wrap around the tree by threading individual painted egg cups onto a piece of string. Add glitter or other decorative touches.

Create a wreath by threading a chain of cups onto a string and tying the two ends of the string together to form a circle. Add a bow, and glue on small pinecones.

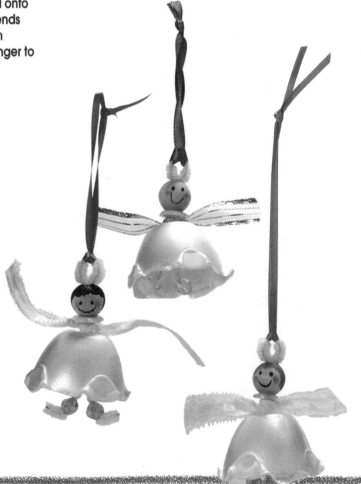

Compact Binoculars

Enjoy the sights with your own pair of binoculars.

You Will Need:

- plastic-foam egg carton
- yarn
- hole punch
- construction paper
- marker
- paint
- toothpaste cap

1 Cut the end from an egg carton, so that you have a two-cup piece and the lid above it. Glue the lid portion and the cup portion shut. Glue a piece of yarn around the seam.

2 Cut eyeholes from the bottom of the two egg cups. In the lid directly opposite these holes, cut holes of the same size. With the hole punch, make a hole on each side of the binoculars. Tie a piece of yarn to the holes to make a strap.

3 Glue on a piece of black paper to cover the bottom of the binoculars. Color the binoculars with a marker. Add details cut from paper. Glue a painted toothpaste cap to the top.

More Ideas

Instead of the yarn strap, glue a craft stick to one side to make opera glasses.

Egg-Carton Carryall

Transport pencils, notepads, and much more in this super shoulder bag.

You Will Need:

- plastic-foam egg carton
- hole punch
- ribbon
- felt
- ruler

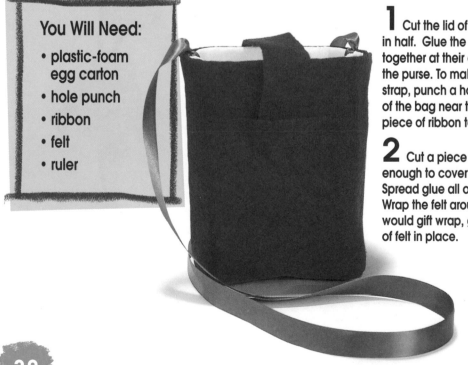

1 Cut the lid of the egg carton in half. Glue the two halves together at their edges to form the purse. To make the shoulder strap, punch a hole on each side of the bag near the top. Tie a piece of ribbon to these holes.

2 Cut a piece of felt big enough to cover the purse. Spread glue all over the purse. Wrap the felt around it as you would gift wrap, gluing the folds of felt in place.

3 Cut a 7-inch strip of felt for the bag's latch. Glue the bottom of the latch onto the back of the bag. Cut a small strip of felt that is about 1½ inches longer than the latch is wide. Glue both ends of this strip to the front of the bag as a fastener in which to tuck the latch.

More Ideas

Make a longer shoulder bag by cutting only a short end off of each of two lids, and gluing them together. Or make a mini-bag by using two small sections from one lid.

Carton Crawlers

These caterpillars won't turn into butterflies, but they will turn any space into a more pleasant one.

You Will Need:

- cardboard egg cartons
- paint
- chenille stick
- plastic wiggle eyes
- yarn
- construction paper

To Make the Straight Caterpillar

Cut a row of six cups from an egg carton to make the body of the caterpillar. To make legs, cut a small section from both sides of each cup. Paint the caterpillar and let it dry. To make antennae, poke two small holes in the top of the caterpillar's head. Poke a piece of chenille stick into each hole, using glue. Curl the ends of the antennae. Glue on wiggle eyes.

To Make the Wiggly Caterpillar

Cut the twelve cups from an egg carton. Paint each cup inside and out. Poke a small hole in the bottom of each cup. Tie a knot at one end of a piece of yarn—this will be the caterpillar's nose. String the other end of the yarn through the holes in the cups. When the twelve cups are strung together, knot the other end. Add eyes cut from construction paper.

More Ideas

Make caterpillars of all sizes. String together cups from two or three egg cartons to make a super-long wiggly caterpillar. Or cut a three-cup section to make a small straight caterpillar.

Cut out a giant construction-paper leaf for your caterpillars to "nibble" on.

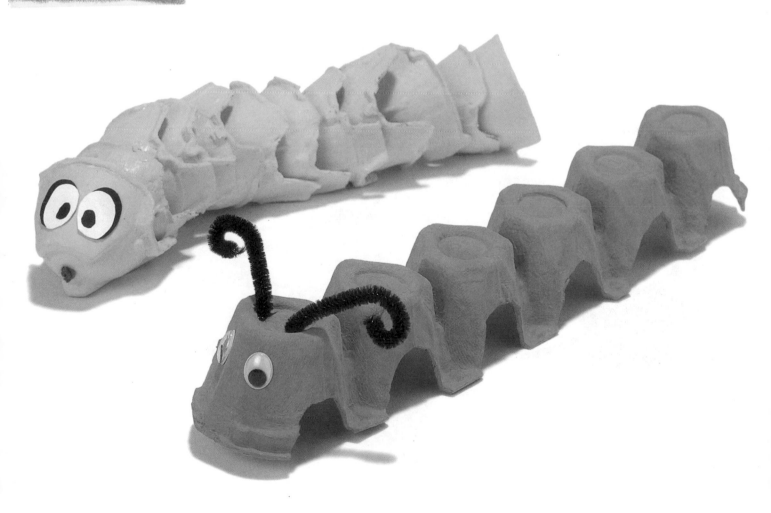

Perfect Party Favors

Make your guests feel special with handmade party favors and place cards.

You Will Need:

- cardboard egg cartons
- paint
- sequins
- construction paper
- yarn
- ruler
- aluminum foil
- chenille sticks
- thin ribbon
- plastic wiggle eyes
- toothpick
- markers
- thin cardboard
- glitter

To Make the Rabbit and Cat Trinket Cups

For each trinket cup, cut one egg cup from a carton and trim it into the shape in the picture. Paint the cup. Add details with sequins, paper, yarn, and paint. Fill with small candies.

To Make the Mini Treasure Box

Cut two cups from an egg carton and trim the edges flat. Paint the outsides of the cups. Press a 3-inch square of aluminum foil into each cup. Trim the excess. Glue a piece of chenille stick or other trim to the edge of each cup. Lay a 14-inch piece of ribbon on a flat surface. Spread glue on the middle 4 inches of the ribbon, leaving 5 unglued inches on each end. Put one cup on top of the other, and place them at one end of the glued section of ribbon. Wrap the long end of the ribbon up and over the top of the box. Tie to close.

To Make the Flower Nut Cup

Cut one cup from an egg carton. Scallop the edges with scissors, and paint the cup. For a base, draw and cut out a section of leaves from paper. Then cut a flower with long petals. Glue the leaf section and the flower together. Glue the cup to the middle of the flower. Fill with peanuts.

Or use some to turn a family meal into a festive occasion.

To Make the Spider Place Card

Cut one cup from an egg carton and paint it black. Poke four evenly spaced holes on each side of the cup. Insert a chenille stick into each hole, using a bit of glue. Bend each stick into a leg shape. Glue a black paper circle to the bottom of the cup. Add wiggle eyes. Make a sign by folding a piece of paper over a toothpick and gluing shut. Write your guest's name on the sign. Glue the toothpick in place on one of the spider's front legs.

To Make the Graduation-Cap Place Card

Cut one cup from an egg carton. Cut a square from a piece of cardboard. Paint both pieces black and glue the square to the bottom of the cup to form a cap. Glue a piece of yarn to the middle of the cap's top, and tie and fringe its end to form a tassel. Cover the glued end of yarn with a small square of black paper. Write a message with a silver marker. Use as a place card, or turn it over to fill with nuts or candy.

To Make the Hanukkah Place Card

Cut one cup from an egg carton, leaving on the side "legs" as shown. Paint it blue. From a piece of cardboard, cut a Star of David. Trace the star onto blue paper and cut it out. Glue the two stars together. Decorate the star with glitter, and write a guest's name. Cut a small slit in the top of the cup and insert a point of the star. Make one for each guest.

More Ideas

There's no end to the party favors you can create from egg cartons. Most round objects can be made from egg cups. For example, make soccer ball, basketball, and hockey puck favors for a sports-themed party. Or throw a summer party, and make small egg-cup suns with construction-paper rays.

Fourth of July Wreath

Reach for the stars with this patriotic Independence Day wreath.

You Will Need:

- plastic-foam egg carton
- tissue paper
- foil stars or construction paper
- ribbon
- yarn

1 Remove the lid from the egg carton and discard. Cut the cup section of the carton in half the long way, so you have two six-cup rows.

2 Staple the two six-cup sections together, end to end, with the open part of the cups facing out. This will make a circle. Add some glue or staples between each cup to help hold them together.

3 Crumple a piece of tissue paper into a ball, and glue the ball into an egg cup. Fill each of the twelve cups in this manner.

4 Decorate the outside of the cups with foil stars or stars cut from construction paper. Glue a ribbon to the bottom of the wreath. Tie a yarn hanger to the top, and hang on a door or wall.

More Ideas

Design egg-carton wreaths for other occasions. Welcome the first day of autumn with a wreath made with yellow, red, and orange tissue paper, and decorated with cutouts of fall leaves. Make a get-well wreath to cheer up a friend who is under the weather. Use brightly colored tissue paper and glue on flowers and suns from construction paper. Or try making a Superbowl wreath using tissue paper of your favorite team's colors, and cutouts of footballs and helmets.

Turtle Paperweight

This trusty turtle will hold down the loose papers on your desk.

You Will Need:

- egg carton
- small pebbles
- small piece of cardboard
- craft sticks
- paint
- marker

1 Cut one cup from an egg carton to make the turtle's shell. Fill the cup with small pebbles. Glue a piece of cardboard to the bottom of the cup. When the glue is dry, trim the edges to match the turtle's shape.

2 Cut a head, a pointy tail, and legs from craft sticks. Glue them in place on the bottom of the turtle. Paint the turtle. Draw on eyes with a marker.

More Ideas

Keep your paperweight on the kitchen counter to hold down recipe cards, or place it near a phone to keep track of messages.

Thread Caddy

Here's a great gift for anyone you know who likes to sew.

You Will Need:

- egg carton
- markers
- felt
- toothpick or knitting needle
- small spools of thread

1 Decorate the lid of a clean egg carton with markers and scraps of felt. (We used an eighteen-count egg carton, but a carton for a dozen eggs will work well, too.) With a toothpick or knitting needle, poke a hole in the lid over each of the egg cups.

2 Place a small spool of thread into each of the cups, then poke the ends of the thread up through the holes. You may need to use a sewing needle to guide the ends of the thread through the holes.

3 Close the lid, and pull up pieces of thread as you need them.

More Ideas

An egg carton also makes a perfect button box. Decorate the outside of a clean carton with markers and old buttons, and use the compartments inside to store buttons.

Game Time!

Egg cartons can be the starting point for all sorts of games. Here are four of our favorites. If you're game, try inventing some of your own. Have fun, and let the games begin!

You Will Need:

- cardboard egg cartons
- paint
- construction paper
- markers
- plastic-foam egg cartons
- marbles
- twelve buttons of four different colors
- a die
- various items for decoration: chenille sticks, plastic wiggle eyes, waxed paper, and toothpicks

To Make the Memory-Match Game

Cut the twelve cups from a cardboard egg carton and paint them. Cut out twelve 1-inch circles from paper. Draw a picture on each one, making six pairs of pictures that are the same (for example, draw two kites, two stars, and so on). Glue one picture into each cup.

To play, place all the cups face-down. Each player turns over two cups and looks at the pictures. If they match, the player keeps the pair. If not, the cups are returned to the face-down position. It is then the next player's turn. The game continues until all the cups are matched up. The player with the most pairs wins. For a more challenging game, add another twelve cups.

To Make the Marble-Pitch Game

Decorate the lid of an egg carton with construction paper. Remove the front flap from the carton. Cut twelve circles from paper and number them 1 to 12. Glue these, in random order, inside the cups of the carton. To play the game, set the open carton on the floor with the lid propped against the wall or another solid surface. Place a piece of tape on the floor at least 5 feet from the carton. Each player gets six marbles. Players take turns standing behind the tape and pitching the marbles toward the cups. To score, add up the numbers in the cups where marbles landed. The first player with 100 points wins.

To Make the Beehive Game

Cut a row of six cups from a cardboard egg carton. Paint them yellow to look like a beehive. We decorated our hive with the bee described on page 27. To play, place the hive on the floor against a wall. Place a piece of tape about 3 feet from the hive. Each player gets five marbles, which represent bees. Players take turns sitting behind the tape and rolling marbles one at a time toward the six openings of the hive. Each time a marble remains in a hive, the player gets one point. The first to reach 20 points wins.

44

To Make "Eggsasperation"

Cut the bottom sections from four egg cartons. From a fifth carton, cut a square of four cups. Cut four circles from different colors of paper and glue them inside the cups of the four-square section. If you'd like, make a sign from toothpicks and paper. Set the game up as shown in the picture.

Two to four people can play this game. Each player chooses one of the four egg cartons, which corresponds to one of the cups in the four-square section. Each player gets three buttons (or other markers) of the same color, which are placed in the top right-hand cup of the player's egg carton for the start of the game. The object of the game is to be the first player to move all three buttons around the board and into "home," which is their cup of the four-square section. A player moves around the board by going down the first six cups, up the next six, and then clockwise on to the next carton and so on.

To begin, the first player rolls the die and moves the number of "spaces" shown. Special rules: If you roll a 2, you get an extra turn; if you roll a 3, you must move one of your buttons—you choose which one—to the cup directly next to it in the same carton (this will either advance you or set you back, depending on where you are); if you land on one of your opponent's buttons you send that button back to that player's very beginning cup.

Once you've moved a button up, down, and around the four cartons, you head for "home." You must roll the exact number needed in order to get home.

More Ideas

Hold a game party. Set up each of these games in a different part of a room. Have your friends take turns playing the various games. Give prizes to the winners—some of the crafts in this book would make excellent prizes!

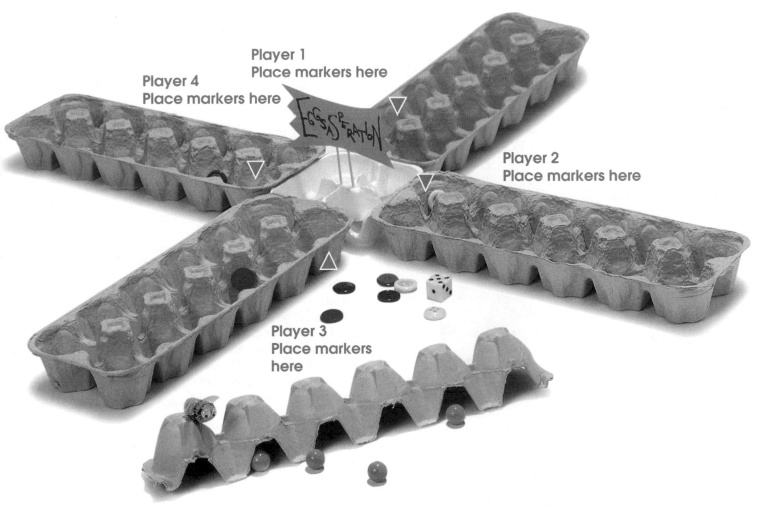

Player 1
Place markers here

Player 4
Place markers here

Player 2
Place markers here

Player 3
Place markers here

Pilgrim Heads

Invite this cheery duo to your Thanksgiving dinner table.

You Will Need:

- cardboard egg carton
- paint
- construction paper
- yarn

1 Cut six cups from the egg carton. For each head, glue two cups together. Glue the bottom of each head to another cup for shoulders. When the glue is dry, paint the heads and shoulders.

2 Cut eyes and mouths from paper, and glue in place. Glue on a yarn bow and a white paper triangle. Attach yarn hair with glue. Top your pilgrims with egg-carton hats. The bonnet is trimmed from a cup, and the man's hat is a peak glued to a circle cut from the lid.

More Ideas

Create some egg-carton turkeys to keep your pilgrim heads company. Make the turkey bodies by gluing two cups together. Add paper eyes and a beak, cardboard legs, and a few tail feathers.

"Egg-ceptional" Totem Pole

Totem poles traditionally tell stories. Design one that tells a story unique to your family.

You Will Need:

- cardboard egg carton
- paint
- markers
- lightweight cardboard
- corrugated cardboard

1 Cut out eight cups from the egg carton and trim their edges flat. Glue pairs of cups together. Paint each pair.

2 Decorate each pair of cups with paint and markers. You might want to give one figure a pair of wings, as we did. To do so, cut small slits in the side of one cup and, using a little glue, insert wings cut from lightweight cardboard.

3 Glue the sections into a stack. Cut a square of corrugated cardboard for a base. Paint it, then glue your totem pole to its center.

More Ideas

Use stacked pairs of cups to make dolls. Decorate the head (the top pair of cups) with yarn hair and paper eyes and mouth. Add fabric scraps for a skirt and shirt, and chenille sticks for arms.

Treat Tree

This sweet tree is two crafts in one—it's a colorful Christmas decoration and a handy candy holder.

You Will Need:

- three cardboard egg cartons
- ruler
- paint
- 14-inch-by-17-inch piece of cardboard
- Christmas gift wrap
- heavy white paper
- chenille sticks
- small box (from crackers or cookies)
- aluminum foil
- ribbon or yarn

1 Cut the bottoms from three egg cartons and lay them side by side. With a ruler, draw a triangular tree shape extending from the top middle of the uppermost of the three cartons, down to the bottom of the third carton. (Looking at our picture should help you see what we mean.) Cut out the tree shape and glue the pieces together. Paint the tree green.

2 Wrap the piece of cardboard with gift wrap, taping the folded edges of the gift wrap to the back. From white paper, cut a triangle that's slightly larger than the tree. Glue it to the wrapped cardboard, leaving room for a trunk.

3 Shape chenille sticks to the tree and tape their ends at the back of the tree. Glue the tree onto the white triangle you made in step 2.

4 Cut off the bottom section of the small box and trim it into a tree-trunk shape, leaving the bottom of the box intact. Paint it brown. Fit it to the bottom of the tree and glue in place.

5 Crumple a small square of aluminum foil. Unfold it and cut out a star shape. Glue the star to the top of the tree. Poke a hole at either side of the tree top. Tie a loop of ribbon or yarn through the holes to make a wall hanger.

6 Hang up your tree and fill its trunk with candy.

More Ideas

To make your tree even more festive, glue glitter to the end of each branch.

Make a forest of trees, decorating each one differently. Fill each tree with a different kind of goody.

Title Index

Subject Index

Look What You Can Make With
CRAFT STICKS

Over 80 Pictured Crafts and Dozens of Other Ideas

Edited by Kelly Milner Halls

Look What You Can Make With

Craft Sticks

Edited by Kelly Milner Halls
Photographs by Hank Schneider

Boyds Mills Press

Craft Coordinator:
Kelly Milner Halls

Craft Makers:
Rebecca Ent
Kelly Milner Halls
Kerry O'Neill

Contributors:

Arlene Macksoud Aissis
Beatrice Bachrach
Katherine Corliss Bartow
Linda Bloomgren
Marie E. Cecchini
Jeanne Corrigan
Clara Flammang
Donna M. Graham
Kelly Milner Halls
Ann E. Hamilton
Edna Harrington

Olive Howie
Helen Jeffries
Tama Kain
Susan Lucci
Carol McCall
June Rose Mobly
Jerry Mundy
Marianne Myers
Joan O'Donnell
Kerry O'Neill
Jane K. Priewe

Bertha W. Reeser
Janet Roelle
Kathy Ross
Dorothea V. Shull
Bernice P. Smith
Cheryl Stees
Sharon Dunn Umnik
Agnes Choate Wonson

Copyright © 2001 by Boyds Mills Press
All rights reserved

Published by Bell Books
Boyds Mills Press, Inc.
A Highlights Company
815 Church Street
Honesdale, Pennsylvania 18431
Printed in China

Publisher Cataloging-in-Publication Data

Look what you can make with craft sticks : over 80 pictured crafts and
dozens of other ideas / edited by Kelly Milner Halls ; photographs by
Hank Schneider.—1st ed.
[48] p. : col. photos. ;   cm.
Includes index.
Summary: Toys, games, and other things to make from craft sticks.
ISBN: 1-56397-997-7
1. Handicraft. 2. Wood crafts. I. Halls, Kelly Milner.
II. Schneider, Hank. III. Title.
745.51 21 2001 AC CIP
2001091965

First edition, 2001
Books in this series originally designed by Lorianne Siomades
The text of this book is set in 10-point Avant Garde Demi, titles 43-point Gill Sans Extra Bold

Visit our Web site at www.boydsmillspress.com

10 9 8 7 6 5 4 3 2 1

Getting Started

This book is filled with fun, easy-to-make crafts, and each one begins with a craft stick. You'll find a wide variety of things to make, including toys, games, and gifts.

Directions

Before you start each craft, read the directions and look closely at the photograph, but remember—it's up to you to make the craft your own. If we decorate a craft with markers but you want to use glitter paint and stickers, go for it. Feel free to stray from our directions and invent new crafts.

Work Area

It's a good idea to keep your work area covered. Old newspapers, brown paper (from grocery bags), or old sheets work well. Also, protect your clothes by wearing a smock. A big old shirt does the job and gives you room to move. Finally, remember to clean up when you've finished.

Materials

You'll need a lot of craft sticks, so start saving now. Ask friends and relatives to help. Keep your craft-making supplies together, and before making each craft, check the "You Will Need" list to make sure you have everything. You can use either non-toxic acrylic paint or poster paint. A few projects in this book call for tongue depressors. You can find those in craft-supply stores or the craft section of discount department stores. Also, since you'll need scissors, glue, tape, or a stapler for almost every craft, we don't list these supplies.

Other Stuff

When we show several similar crafts, we'll often list numbered directions that apply to all of the crafts, then specific directions for each craft. Plus, you'll find other ways to jazz up your projects in the "More Ideas" section that appears with every craft. You'll also think of new ideas of your own once you get rolling. So browse through these pages, choose a craft, and have some creative fun. Before you know it, you'll be showing everyone what you made with craft sticks.

Sail-Away Vessels

"Stick" to this simple plan, and shove off to sea.

You Will Need:

- plastic foam
- craft sticks and tongue depressors
- yarn and other trims
- paint and paintbrush
- construction paper

To Make the Rowboat

Cut a triangle shape from plastic foam. Cut tongue depressors to fit each side of the triangle. Glue in place. Break a craft stick in half, and glue each piece to a side of the boat in the back. Lay two craft-stick pieces on top to make seats. Poke a hole in two plastic-foam pieces. Glue to the sides for oarlocks. Add decorative trims.

To Make the Raft

Apply glue to one side of four craft sticks. Lay them about 1 inch apart. Line twelve craft sticks side by side across the four sticks. Leave enough space between the sixth and seventh sticks to insert one stick. Glue two craft sticks together to form a mast. Glue the mast between the sixth and seventh sticks. Let dry overnight, then paint it and let dry. Cut a piece of construction paper for a sail. Draw a design on it. Cut a tiny slit in the top and bottom of the sail. Thread the sail onto the mast. Add details with decorative trims.

More Ideas

Glue paper to an empty matchbox to make a storage box for your raft.

Cover your sail with clear self-adhesive paper to protect it.

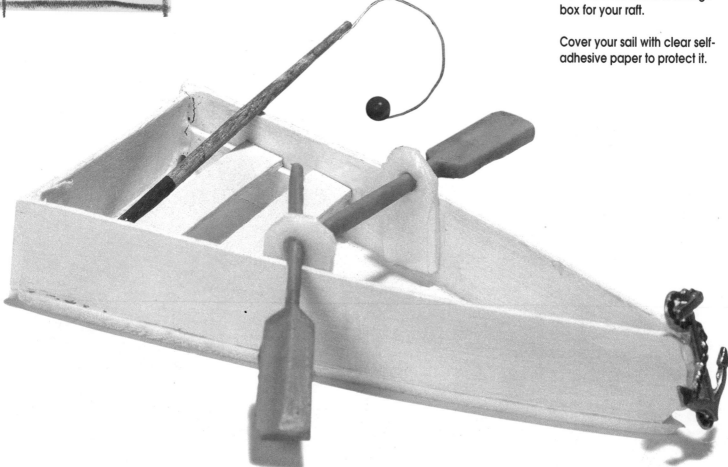

Stick-to-It Puzzle

Turn your favorite picture into a puzzle.

You Will Need:
- photograph, old magazine, or poster
- craft sticks

1 Cut your favorite photo, cartoon, or phrase from a poster or a magazine. (Ask permission first.)

2 Turn the picture upside down. Cover the back with glue.

3 Lay your craft sticks touching side to side on the glue side of your picture. Number each stick.

4 Allow the glue to dry overnight. Ask an adult to cut the sticks apart with a sharp knife to make the puzzle pieces.

More Ideas

For a real challenge, make a puzzle without numbering the sticks.

Make two puzzles, then give one to a friend. See who can solve the puzzle first.

Court Jester

This lovable pal will entertain your kingdom.

You Will Need:
- two craft sticks
- construction paper
- plastic wiggle eye
- cardboard-box scraps
- paint and paintbrush

1 Glue two craft sticks together to make an X shape.

2 Cut two construction-paper hearts to form the body. Glue them together with the X sandwiched in between.

3 Cut a smaller paper heart for the head. Glue a plastic wiggle eye and a paper smile on the face. Add small paper hearts, if you like.

4 Cut four ½-inch hearts from cardboard-box scraps. Cut small slits into, but not through, the center of the hearts. Paint them, if you wish, and let dry. Press the craft-stick ends into the slits. Glue to secure.

More Ideas

Can you make a king and queen using the same X base?

Stick Pals

Make new friends who can come out to play anytime.

You Will Need:

- craft sticks and tongue depressors
- construction paper
- yarn
- old doll's clothes
- fabric and netting
- embroidery thread
- pompons

To Make the Girl and Boy

Overlap two crafts sticks to form a leg. Glue two craft-stick legs to the bottom of a single craft-stick body. Add two craft-stick arms just below the other end of the body. Add a paper head, and glue on yarn hair. Dress them in old doll's clothes and shoes.

To Make the Ballerina

Use a tongue depressor for the body. Add craft-stick arms and legs. Glue on a paper head and yarn hair. Wrap yarn around the body, and glue the ends. Add a fabric-and-netting tutu with a bow of embroidery thread. Add chenille sticks to the legs and pompons to the feet and shoulders.

More Ideas

Use the craft-stick furniture on pages 8 and 9 to furnish your stick pals' backyard.

Petite Picnic Set

"Stick" with these instructions to build some outdoor furniture for your pretend playmates.

To Make the Lounge Chair

Cut a piece of poster board about 6½ inches long by 3 inches wide. Cut craft sticks to fit the width of the poster board, and glue them in place. Cut a second piece of poster board 4 inches long by 3 inches wide. Cut craft sticks 3½ inches long, and glue them to the poster board, leaving a ½-inch tab. Glue the tab underneath the seat. Add glue to the front where the seat and back meet. Glue small pieces of craft sticks to two 3-inch-long pieces of poster board to make arms. Add small pieces of craft sticks underneath, and glue to the seat and back. Add legs.

To Make the Table

Cut a piece of plastic foam 4 inches wide by 6 inches long. Cover one side with glue, and apply seventeen craft sticks one at a time. Break 1 inch off eight craft sticks. Glue two sticks side by side, making four pairs, and let dry. Poke one end of each leg into the plastic-foam base at an angle. Glue in place. Glue a strip of plastic foam where the legs cross. Paint and let dry.

To Make the Benches

Cut two pieces of plastic foam about 1½ inches wide by 4 inches long. Glue four craft sticks side by side to each piece. Glue the seat to two thread spools. Paint and let dry.

More Ideas

Make an umbrella: Glue a circle of colorful paper on the end of a craft stick. Glue the other end to the center of an empty thread spool.

Something Fishy

Net these fantasy fish just for fun.

1 Paint craft sticks in the same or different colors. Let dry. Glue two sticks together at one end, fanning the opposite ends out.

2 Glue three sticks underneath the top stick and parallel with the bottom stick. Add three dots of glue, 1 inch apart, to the top of those sticks. Place three sticks into the glue, forming a crisscross pattern.

3 Place one more stick across the entire pattern.

4 Glue on a plastic wiggle eye. Add yarn for a hanger.

More Ideas

Make a bed of seaweed. Paint a craft stick green. Curl green chenille sticks around a pencil, then glue one end of each chenille stick to the craft stick. Hang your fish above the seaweed.

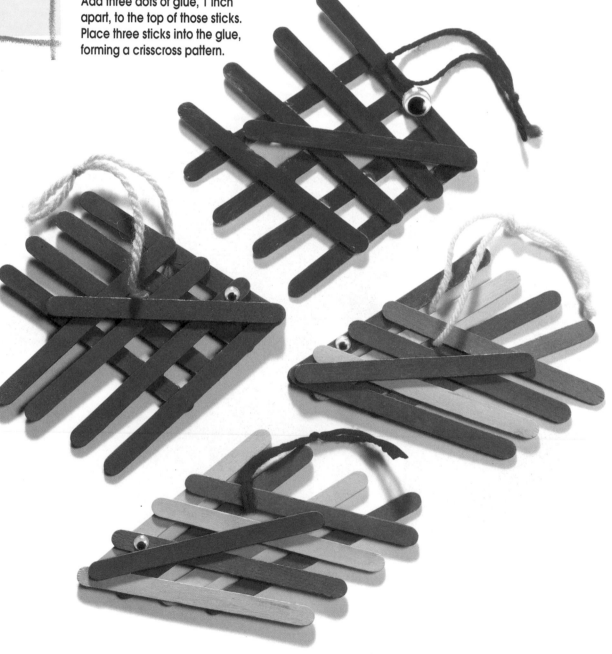

"Some Bunny Loves You" Card

Send some "bunny" your love with this cheery holiday greeting.

You Will Need:

- construction paper
- markers
- chenille sticks
- two craft sticks
- small pompon

1 Fold a piece of construction paper in half. Write a message inside the folded paper.

2 Cut an oval from a piece of white construction paper, and draw a bunny face.

3 Cut six small pieces of chenille stick.

4 Glue the face on the front of the card. Glue craft-stick ears. Glue the chenille-stick pieces on as whiskers and the tiny pompon for the bunny's nose.

More Ideas

Draw a sun face, and use the craft sticks as the sun's rays.

Glue the tree shape from page 17 to poster board to make a special Christmas card.

Star-Studded Rainbow

Dazzle your friends with this unusual decoration.

You Will Need:

- black felt
- eight craft sticks
- rainbow yarn
- craft rhinestones

1 Cut a 5-inch star shape from black felt.

2 Tightly wrap each of the eight craft sticks with rainbow yarn, stopping near each end. Tie the yarn in a half-knot and cut the end, leaving a tiny tail.

3 Glue each yarn-covered stick to the felt star, pointing toward the center of the circle.

4 Decorate the ends of the sticks with star or other shaped rhinestones. Let dry. Glue a piece of yarn to the back.

More Ideas

Wrap each craft stick in a different color in "rainbow" order: red, orange, yellow, green, blue, indigo, and violet.

Picture This

Surround your photos with these unique frames.

You Will Need:

- craft sticks and tongue depressors
- paint and paintbrush
- photographs
- construction paper
- thin cardboard
- craft rhinestones
- yarn
- poster board
- black marker

To Make the Triangle-Topped Frame

Place nine craft sticks as shown in the picture. Glue two sticks across them horizontally as shown. Glue one stick vertically over each end stick of the frame. Glue another craft stick over each horizontal stick. For a stand, bend a stick about an inch from its end. Glue the short end to the back. Paint and decorate the frame, and slide a photo through the side.

To Make the Blackboard Frame

Cut a 4$\frac{1}{2}$-by-5-inch piece of black construction paper. Glue craft sticks around it. Add a construction-paper apple and chalk. Glue a photo in the middle. Fold a 5-inch-by-8$\frac{1}{2}$-inch piece of cardboard in half. Glue one half to the back of the frame.

To Make the All-Star Frame

Paint four craft sticks. Let dry. Squeeze glue underneath two craft sticks. Glue them to the top and bottom edges of your photograph. Put a dot of glue on each end of the two craft sticks already in place. Add the last two craft sticks to complete the frame. Decorate with rhinestones, then add a yarn hanger to the back.

To Make the Harvest Frame

Glue four tongue depressors together. Create two ears of corn from poster board. Add details with a black marker, and glue the corn to the frame. Glue a piece of poster board and a yarn hanger to the back. Glue a photo to the front.

More Ideas

Don't have star-shaped rhinestones handy? Any decoration will do. Even beans or uncooked popcorn adds color and texture to your picture frame.

Funny Bunny Hanger

Hop to it! Display this bunny on your doorknob.

You Will Need:

- five craft sticks
- construction paper
- markers
- thin ribbon

1 Glue three craft sticks together at the ends to form a square without a top. Glue two craft sticks as crosspieces about 1 inch apart as shown.

2 Cut a bunny from construction paper. Cut a grassy strip of green construction paper. Cut two small Easter eggs from different-colored paper.

3 Draw a face on your bunny, and decorate your eggs with markers. Glue the grass strip to the bottom craft stick, then glue the bunny over the grass. Add the eggs.

4 Glue ribbon to the top fence posts.

More Ideas

Make a squirrel shape and draw some acorns to add on the fence. Or glue on some small fallen pinecones.

Easy Easel

Show your favorite photo or artwork with pride.

You Will Need:

- five craft sticks
- markers
- chenille stick
- sequins, pompons, and other trims

1 Decorate each craft stick with markers.

2 Glue two craft sticks with the plain sides together. This will be the easel's tray.

3 Cut a 2-inch piece of chenille stick. Glue half of the piece to the back of a decorated craft stick near the tip. Let the remaining half stick out.

4 Glue the last two craft sticks together in a V shape. Let dry.

5 Glue the edge of the easel tray across the front of the V shape. Let dry. Glue the end of the chenille stick to the point of the V. Let dry. Bend the chenille stick so the easel can stand. Decorate with trims.

More Ideas

Create an easel twice as big by gluing two craft sticks together at each step.

14

Plant Projects

Help your greenery grow.

You Will Need:

- clean empty milk carton
- craft sticks
- construction paper or felt
- potted plant, such as ivy

To Make the Plant Caddy

Cut away the top half of a clean milk carton so it's a little shorter than the length of a craft stick. Glue craft sticks side by side around the carton. Let dry. Decorate with construction paper or felt. Place a small plant in the caddy.

To Make the Craft-Stick Trellis

Glue two craft sticks together, end to end, to form one long stick. Center and glue another craft stick across the top of the long stick about 1 inch from the tip. Center and glue another craft stick across the long stick about 1½ inches down from the first. Repeat with a third craft stick about an inch down from the second stick. Glue one craft stick on the left side and one on the right, forming a V shape. Let dry. Stick the trellis into the dirt behind a small ivy plant.

More Ideas

For a special look, paint the caddy and trellis after the glue has dried, and seal it with clear varnish. Add tiny ribbon flowers.

Christmas Tree Trims

Decorate for the holidays.

You Will Need:

- construction paper
- craft sticks
- glitter
- string or yarn
- plastic wiggle eyes
- paint and paintbrush
- sequins or paper stars

To Make the Glitter Snowflake

Cut a 4-inch-by-4-inch piece of construction paper. Fold the paper in half three times to form a small square. Cut tiny notches out of the edges of the small square, being careful not to cut all of the folds away. Unfold the square to reveal your snowflake. Glue craft sticks around the snowflake to form a frame. Apply a fine layer of glue to the ornament, then add glitter. Let dry, then add a string or yarn hanger.

To Make Rudolph

Glue two craft sticks together to form a V shape. Glue the third stick across the open end of the V. Cut a red nose from construction paper, and glue it to the bottom of the V. Add two plastic wiggle eyes just under the third stick. Decorate Rudolph's forehead with green paper cut to look like ivy. Add a few red paper berries. Glue ribbon or yarn to Rudolph's ears.

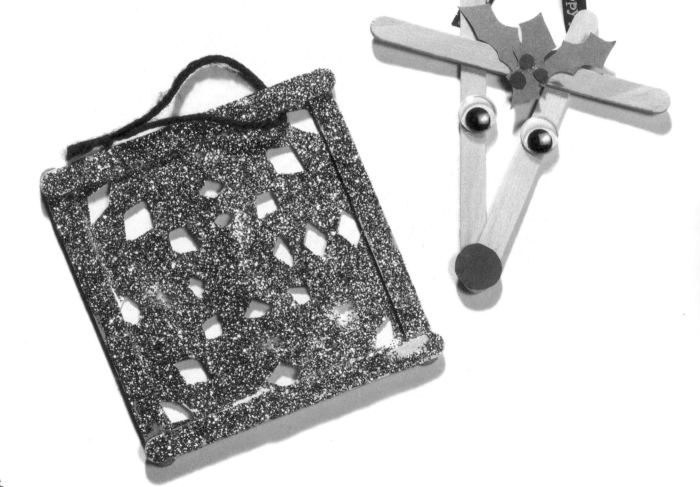

To Make the Tree Ornament

Paint two sticks brown. Paint seven sticks green. Let dry. Glue the two brown sticks together at one end to form a long tree trunk. Glue the remaining green sticks to form staggered branches. Decorate with sequins or paper stars. Add string or yarn for a hanger.

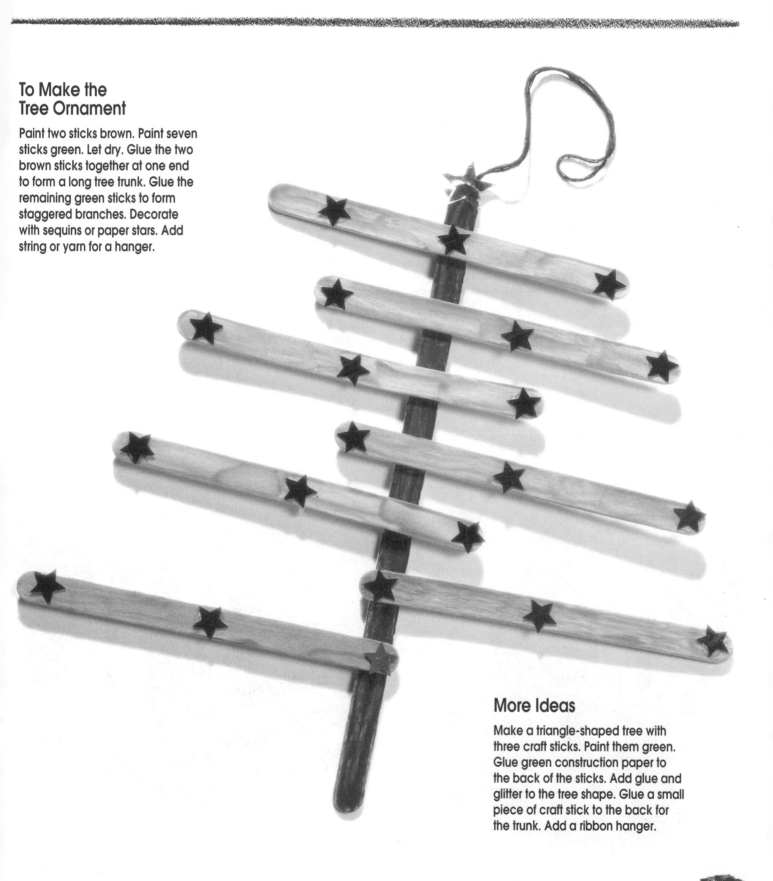

More Ideas

Make a triangle-shaped tree with three craft sticks. Paint them green. Glue green construction paper to the back of the sticks. Add glue and glitter to the tree shape. Glue a small piece of craft stick to the back for the trunk. Add a ribbon hanger.

Beautiful Baskets

These craft-stick baskets will come in handy whatever the season.

You Will Need:

- craft sticks
- plastic-foam tray
- glitter
- plastic berry basket
- cardboard
- poster board

To Make the Egg Basket

Paint eight craft sticks and let dry. Cut eight egg shapes from a plastic-foam tray. Decorate the eggs with glitter, and let dry. Glue each egg to the end of a craft stick. Let dry. Weave the craft sticks in and out of the sides of a berry basket. Add a dab of glue at each cross point to be sure the sticks stay put.

To Make the Handle Basket

Cut two squares of cardboard as wide and as tall as a craft stick. Cut tabs $1/4$ inch long and the width of a craft stick apart into two sides of each square. Fold back every other tab. Use a dot of glue to attach one end of a craft stick to each folded tab on one square. Glue the other end of each stick to the folded tabs on the other square. Tape a piece of cardboard to fit the bottom. Add a poster-board handle.

More Ideas

Add seasonal grasses or tissue paper to make this basket a great gift idea. Tuck a small present inside.

Wooden Bracelet

Wrap this around your wrist with pride.

You Will Need:

- tongue depressor
- bowl of warm water
- clean empty frozen-juice container
- rubber bands
- poster paint and paintbrush
- sequins
- clear nail polish

1 Soak the wooden tongue depressor in warm water for about an hour, until you can gently bend it around a frozen-juice container. Place rubber bands on top of the tongue depressor to hold it in place. Let dry for one day.

2 Remove the tongue depressor, cover it with poster paint, and let dry.

3 Glue on sequins or other trims. Let dry.

4 Cover with clear nail polish.

More Ideas

Use this as a headband for a doll.

Stick-with-a-Heart Bouquet

Express your affection with this pretty heart design.

You Will Need:

- construction paper
- craft stick
- ribbon

3 Arrange the four large hearts to make a heart bouquet at one end of the craft stick, and glue in place. Add the two green hearts to make heart-shaped leaves. Add the small purple heart in the middle of the craft stick.

4 Add a small ribbon bow. Write a message on the center large heart, if you wish.

More Ideas

Cut construction-paper tulips or pansies to make a flower bouquet.

1 Cut four hearts—two pink and two red—about 2½ inches wide by 2½ inches high.

2 Cut two 1-inch hearts from green paper. Cut a slightly smaller heart from purple paper.

Fan-tastic Keepsakes

Give one as a Mother's Day gift, or make one for someone special.

You Will Need:

- poster board or construction paper
- markers
- stickers
- sequins, glitter, and other trims
- craft sticks or tongue depressors
- yarn or ribbon
- coffee filter
- water
- food coloring

To Make the Personalized Fan

Cut your poster board or construction paper in the fan shape shown. Write a message on the fan. Decorate with stickers, sequins, or other trims. Glue craft sticks or tongue depressors together at the base, then fan them out in the width of your paper fan. Add a fine line of glue to each of the craft sticks. Glue the paper fan on top. Let dry, then add a yarn or ribbon tassel or bow to the base.

To Make the Rainbow Fan

Color six craft sticks and let dry. Spread the sticks out in a fan shape, and glue the ends together. Spray a coffee filter with water, then color with a few drops of food coloring. Let dry. Fold the filter in half, then in half again. Trim the pointed sections into a curve. Unfold the filter once, then cut the folds at either end to create two sections. Glue a section to each side of the fan. Add sequins and other trims.

More Ideas

Personalize your fan for that special someone. Is the fan for your teacher? Use apple stickers to dress it up. Is it for your grandmother? She probably loves flowers. Is it for your soccer coach? Soccer-ball stickers should do the trick.

Greeting Card Stitch-Up

Share your fondest wishes with this special card.

You Will Need:

- three craft sticks
- hole punch
- old greeting card
- thin ribbon or yarn

1 Spread glue on one craft stick. Place two craft sticks, side by side, on the first stick.

2 Punch holes about ½ inch apart around the outside of a closed greeting card.

3 Put glue on both sides of the top half of the stick handle. Place the glued half of the handle inside the card. Let dry.

4 Using thin ribbon or yarn, "sew" the front and back of the card together through the punched holes. Start on one side of the stick handle, leaving a 6-inch length of ribbon at the beginning and end. At the last hole, tie the two loose ends of the ribbon together in a bow.

More Ideas

Stick each card in the bottom of a large plastic-foam cup to make a festive display.

Use the card as a fan.

Stair-Step Swirl

Stack your sticks into this whirly wonder.

You Will Need:

- paint and paintbrush
- craft sticks
- thin ribbon

1 Paint eight sticks in one color, eight sticks in a second color, and eight sticks in a third color—front and back. Let dry.

2 Select one craft stick of each color. Put a dab of glue at the center of one craft stick. Form an X with the second stick at the glue point. Close the X until the sticks just slightly overlap.

3 Repeat the process with each of the remaining sticks, making a pattern with your colors.

4 Before you put the last stick in place, slip a length of ribbon in between the last two sticks. Knot the ribbon, and let dry.

More Ideas

Make a wider swirl. Glue two sticks together with the tips overlapping. Then arrange a set of these as you would for the smaller swirl.

Bug Magnets

Cheer up your kitchen with these colorful critters.

You Will Need:

- colored poster board
- paint and paintbrush
- craft sticks
- chenille sticks
- large and small pompons
- plastic wiggle eyes
- magnetic strip

1 Cut a butterfly, dragonfly, or ladybug shape from poster board.

2 Paint one craft stick, if you wish, and glue it to the middle of the shape.

3 Bend a chenille stick into a V, and glue to the end of the craft stick to form the bug's antennae. Add a pompon to make the head.

4 Add plastic wiggle eyes, if you wish. Decorate the wings. Let dry. Glue a magnetic strip to the back of the craft-stick body.

More Ideas

Instead of adding a magnet, glue one of your insects to the top of a flat rock to make a paperweight.

Crafty Desk Set

Set those sticks to hold homework helpers.

To Make the Notepad Holder

Lay three craft sticks about 1 inch apart, and spread glue on top of each. Center eleven craft sticks side by side on top of the three craft sticks. Place two craft sticks side by side, and glue a third stick on top of the pair. Glue to one end of the craft-stick base. Do the same to the two opposite sides. Lay two tongue depressors as shown, and glue in place. Add beads or other trims.

To Make the Paper Clip Holder

Break or cut craft sticks to the height of a small can. Glue in place. Add beads or other trims.

To Make the Pencil Holder

Squeeze a thick line of glue at the top, bottom, and middle of the can, 2 to 3 inches at a time. Place the craft sticks into the glued sections, covering almost all of the can except ¼ inch. Cover the gap with a thick line of glue. Add beads or other trims. Let dry.

More Ideas

Paint the craft sticks to match
your room color.

Draw a picture on the sticks with
markers.

Easy Stick-Puppet Zoo

This wild and woolly group is easy to tame.

You Will Need:

- pre-pressed foam animal shapes
- craft sticks

More Ideas

Cut out the bottom of a shoe box, leaving a 2-inch frame in place to create a puppet theater. Decorate the stage with rain forest drawings or magazine pictures glued to the outside of the box.

You can find foam shapes of every type and style—from sea creatures to dinosaurs to letters of the alphabet—in craft stores. Create life under the sea or a prehistoric land.

1 Select as many pre-pressed foam shapes as you would like.

2 Count out as many craft sticks as you have shapes.

3 Add a spot of glue to the tip of each craft stick. Place the animal shapes on the glue, being careful to keep the tip of the stick in the center of the animal's body.

Craft-Stick Gobbler

Colorful "feathers" make this turkey a hit on Thanksgiving Day.

You Will Need:

- paint and paintbrush
- 2-inch and 3-inch plastic-foam balls
- craft sticks
- chenille sticks
- felt

1 Paint the 2-inch plastic-foam ball for the head and let dry. For the body, cut the 3-inch ball in half. Paint one half, and let dry.

2 Insert about 1 inch of a craft stick into the center of the head. Poke the other end into the body. Wrap a chenille stick around the stick.

3 Cut a 3-inch piece of chenille stick. Fold it in half, and push the folded end into the face. Add a chenille-stick wattle and felt eyes.

4 Paint craft sticks, and let dry. Put glue on one end of each stick, and insert the sticks in the body.

More Ideas

Make a baby turkey using smaller plastic-foam balls and pieces of craft sticks for the feathers.

How about making a peacock? Paint the craft sticks green and blue.

Spirit Eye

Weave yarn and sticks into something eye-catching in minutes.

You Will Need:

- two craft sticks
- yarn

1 Glue two craft sticks together in an X shape.

2 Beginning at the center of the X, wrap the yarn once around one stick half. Then move to the next and repeat. When you get to the stick half you started with, go around again without overlapping the original yarn loop. Continue in this way. Keep your yarn tight at all times.

3 When the spaces between the sticks are filled in with yarn, knot the yarn and loop it to form a hanger. Glue to secure.

More Ideas

Weave several spirit eyes, and give them as gifts.

Mobiles and Wind Chimes

Use recyclables to make these crafts dance in the breeze.

You Will Need:

- craft sticks
- metallic chenille sticks
- decorative trims
- embroidery thread
- old compact discs (CDs)
- yarn
- sixteen frozen-juice can lids

To Make the Juice Jingle Wind Chime

Glue two craft sticks together to form an X. Tie a piece of yarn at the X for a hanger. Cut four 1-foot pieces of yarn. Glue one of the juice-can lids to the end of a piece of yarn, another one almost at the center, and the last one near the top, leaving about 3 inches of yarn. Repeat this three more times. Tie each piece of yarn to one of the sticks. Cut a piece of yarn about 1½ feet long. Glue four lids onto the yarn, leaving about 2½ inches at the top. Tie the yarn to the center of the sticks.

To Make the Stick and Sparkle Mobile

Wrap six craft sticks in colorful metallic chenille sticks. Add decorative trims, if you wish. Glue a 3½ -inch piece of embroidery thread to one end of each craft stick. Glue the other ends to an old CD. Tie three pieces of embroidery thread together. Knot each loose end, then glue each knot to the center of the CD. Hang the mobile in a sunny place.

To Make the CD Mobile

Make the base as described in the Juice Jingle Wind Chime. Cut four 1 1/2 -foot pieces of yarn. Glue two old CDs to each piece. Tie each piece of yarn to one of the sticks. Cut a piece of yarn about 2 feet long. Glue three CDs to the yarn. Tie the yarn to the center of the stick base.

More Ideas

Add cutout pictures of your favorite animals to the juice-can lids.

Make a mobile with baseball cards, tiny cars, or any other small collectible.

Flip-and-Match Game

How good is your memory? Try to match these silly sticks and find out.

You Will Need:

- paint and paintbrush
- twenty craft sticks
- two pairs each of ten different kinds of tiny stickers
- plastic bag

1 Paint the craft sticks.

2 Apply one sticker to each stick.

3 Store the game in a plastic bag.

How to Play

Place the sticks sticker-side down. Take turns trying to find the matching sticks. Whoever has the most matches at the end of the game wins.

More Ideas

Add pairs of sticks to the game to make it more challenging.

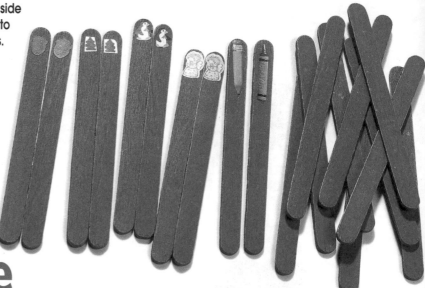

Nativity Scene

Create the joy of the Christmas season.

You Will Need:

- paint and paintbrush
- five craft sticks
- pencil
- construction paper
- old Christmas card
- thin cardboard

1 Paint five craft sticks, and let dry. Glue them together in a stable shape.

2 Trace around the stable onto construction paper. Cut out the tracing, and glue it to the back of the stable.

3 Cut out a Nativity scene from an old Christmas card. Glue it in the stable.

4 Cut a triangle from thin cardboard. Fold the edges forward, and glue the center to the back of the stable to make it stand up.

More Ideas

Make the roof of the stable come to a point to make a house, and glue a photo of your family inside.

Dream Catcher

Hang this near your bed to capture your dreams.

You Will Need:

- paint and paintbrush
- six craft sticks
- plastic vegetable bag
- thin ribbon
- three craft feathers
- craft rhinestones

1 Paint each craft stick, front and back, in your favorite color. Let dry.

2 Glue the sticks to form a hexagon.

3 Cut a hexagon shape from the vegetable bag, and glue it to the back of the stick hexagon.

4 Glue three thin ribbons to the hexagon. Glue a feather to one end of each ribbon. Decorate the dream catcher with rhinestones.

5 Add ribbon to the top for a hanger.

More Ideas

Make a dream catcher for family members to hang over their beds.

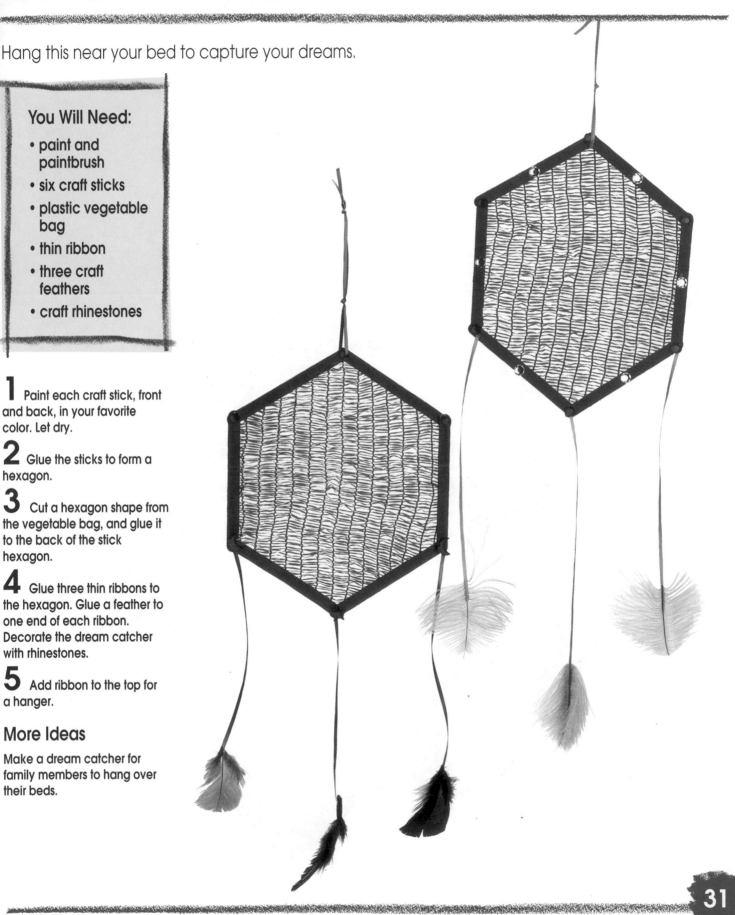

Craft-Stick Wreaths

Make these wreaths for any season.

You Will Need:

- paint and paintbrush
- sixteen craft sticks
- construction paper
- ribbon
- yarn

1 Paint the crafts sticks, and let dry.

2 Glue the sticks together in pairs to form X shapes. Arrange the Xs in a wreath shape, and glue them together, end to end.

3 Glue cut-paper shapes to the wreath.

4 Add a wide bow at the top. Tie yarn on the back for a hanger.

More Ideas

Use a cardboard ring as a wreath base. Glue craft sticks around the cardboard. Decorate with paper cutouts.

Bookmark Buddies

Make these book pals to help you keep your place.

You Will Need:

- paint and paintbrush
- craft stick or tongue depressor
- markers
- chenille stick
- large or small pompon
- plastic wiggle eyes

1 Paint the craft stick or tongue depressor. Let dry, then decorate with markers or paint.

2 Bend a 2-inch piece of chenille stick in half to form a V. Glue the V to one end of the craft stick, pointing up.

3 Glue on a pompon head and plastic wiggle eyes. Let dry.

More Ideas

Decorate a potted houseplant with a craft-stick worm poking out of the dirt.

If your pompon head is large enough, you can glue the chenille-stick V to the pompon.

QUICK REACTION

It's simply my reaction
Who cares
what it's abo...
I reach for sat...
with my tongue...
I stick it out.

NOT FORGOT

I forgot to take the trash out;
    you didn't tell me that's my job.
I forgot to bring my money;
    you never know when you'll get robbed.
I forgot that game ar ...

The Joys of Snowboarding

I laugh out loud
As I float through powder,
Float through the fluffy snow.

I do a front flip
And laugh even louder.
Big air—the way to go!

Down to the lift
Then up again,
Making this board behave

As I speed down the hill
In graceful arcs,
Surfing the winter wave.

The Snowboarder

Snow, soft, white
In the morning light
Takeoff! And I'm in flight.

Down the hill
In the vivid chill
Bumps, jumps, and nary a spill.

Ribbon-Weave Trivet

In and out, slow and steady, and you'll create this "hot" gift for your favorite cook.

You Will Need:

- thirteen craft sticks
- fabric ribbon

1 Glue four sticks together to form a square frame.

2 Glue nine sticks side by side on top of the square frame. Leave a small space between each stick. Let dry.

3 Cut several pieces of ribbon about 10 inches long.

4 Weave the first ribbon in and out of the sticks. Leave at least 2 inches of ribbon dangling on each side of the square. Weave the second ribbon next to the first, using the opposite pattern. If you went under the first slat with the first ribbon, go OVER the first slat with the second ribbon. Repeat until the trivet is covered.

5 Glue the loose ends of the ribbons underneath the trivet.

More Ideas

Use different widths of ribbon to create different designs.

Teacher's-Pet Remembrance

Tell your favorite teacher you care.

You Will Need:

- four craft sticks
- stiff black felt
- white gel pen or fabric paint
- red and green construction paper
- ribbon or yarn

1 Glue four craft sticks together to make a square.

2 Cut a square of black felt a bit smaller than the craft-stick square.

3 Write your message on the felt with a white gel pen or white fabric paint. Let dry. Glue the felt square to the back of the craft-stick square.

4 Cut four apple shapes from red construction paper, and glue to each corner of the frame. Add green leaves.

5 Glue a ribbon hanger to the back.

More Ideas

Write your message on paper before you write it on the felt, so you know exactly what you want to say and how you want to write it.

Cut out baseballs or footballs, glue them to the frame, and give it to your dad or grandfather on Father's Day.

Finger Puppet Frolic

These puppets make it easy to put the finger on fun.

You Will Need:

- construction paper
- markers
- craft sticks
- plastic wiggle eyes
- chenille sticks, pompons, and other trims

To Make the Sheep

Cut a sheep shape from construction paper. Draw a face with markers. Break two craft sticks to form two sheep legs and a crosspiece. Color the legs black. Glue the legs to the back of the sheep, and glue the crosspiece just above the legs. Cut a strip of paper, and roll it to form a finger slot. Glue it on the back of the crosspiece. Add a plastic wiggle eye.

To Make the Frog, Bear, Rabbit, and Penguin

Cut out the animal shapes from construction paper. Add decorative trims. Glue a craft stick vertically to the back. Cut a strip of paper, and roll it to form a finger slot. Glue it on the craft stick.

More Ideas

Create "habitats" for your animals. Make fences from drinking straws and a heavy-cardboard base for the sheep, a construction-paper pond for the frog, green pompon bushes for the bear, and papier-mâché icebergs for the penguin.

Stick Tic-tac-toe

Customize your own game of *X*s and *O*s.

You Will Need:

- paint and paintbrush
- four craft sticks
- construction paper
- markers
- clear self-adhesive paper
- plastic bag

1 Paint the craft sticks your favorite color. Let dry.

2 Lay two sticks parallel about 1½ inches apart. Lay the other two sticks on top of the two parallel sticks to form a crisscross pattern. Glue in place.

3 Cut ten circles out of construction paper. Mark five with *X*s and five with *O*s.

4 Cut a 10-inch piece of self-adhesive paper. Cut it in half. Peel the backing off of one piece. Lay the circles on the sticky side. Place the other half of the self-adhesive paper over the top of the circles, sticky side against sticky side.

5 Cut the circles out of the plastic to form ten game pieces. Store your game in a plastic bag.

More Ideas

Make a larger grid by overlapping craft sticks at the tips. Lay the grid on a table. Give each box a point value. Toss clean milk caps into the grid. Add up the points.

Sunflower Place Card

Add some sun to your company dinner table.

You Will Need:

- construction paper
- colored pencil or pen
- two tongue depressors
- craft stick

1 Cut a small piece of construction paper, and write a guest's name on it. Glue it to a tongue depressor.

2 Glue the other tongue depressor to the first one as shown. Let dry.

3 Cut a sunflower shape from construction paper.

4 Paint a craft-stick half green. Glue one end to the back of the sunflower. Glue the other end to the place card.

More Ideas

Instead of a sunflower, make turkeys for your Thanksgiving Day table.

Mystery Masks

Shield your identity with these terrific masks.

You Will Need:

- poster board
- craft sticks
- craft feathers
- craft rhinestones
- glitter
- markers

To Make the Basic Mask

1 Cut a mask shape from poster board.

2 Measure the eyeholes, then cut them out.

3 Glue a craft stick to the mask on the back. Glue a second craft stick to the end of the first to form a long handle.

To Make the Sparkly Mask

Glue a feather to the front of the mask, being careful not to block the eyehole. Decorate with rhinestones and glitter. Let dry.

To Make the Totem Pole Mask

Decorate the mask with markers. Add feathers.

More Ideas

What kind of character would you like to be ? A cat? A dog? A robot? You decide, then use your imagination to decorate your mask.

Stick-Puppet Personalities

Use your imagination to create one-of-a-kind characters.

You Will Need:

- plastic drinking straws
- craft sticks and tongue depressors
- markers
- felt
- straw
- construction paper
- colored pencils
- yarn

To Make the Scarecrow

Cut three plastic drinking straws in half. Glue three pieces to a tongue depressor vertically for the body and three horizontally for the arms. Draw a face on felt, and glue in place. Fold a piece of felt in half, and cut out a coat shape. Cut a slit in the fold, and slip the coat over the head. Glue in place, and stuff pieces of straw at the hands and feet. Add details.

To Make the King and Queen

Glue two tongue depressors together to make the body. Add construction-paper clothing to the front and back. Glue pieces of craft sticks for hands. Add a head and crown to the front and back. Draw faces with colored pencil. Glue on yarn hair.

More Ideas

Make a castle from cardboard tubes.

Make a farm field from three or four plastic-foam trays stacked and glued together. Paint the top brown. Add rows of green chenille-stick "crops." Stick your scarecrow in the field.

Star Banners

Let your colors proudly wave with this star decoration.

You Will Need:

- paint and paintbrush
- four craft sticks
- tissue paper or poster board
- eight craft rhinestones or construction paper
- yarn or ribbon

More Ideas

Make these banners your own. Decorate them with glitter, stickers, beads—it's up to you.

1 Paint four craft sticks in the same or different colors.

2 Glue the sticks together to form an eight-pointed star.

3 Add tissue-paper or poster-board streamers to the lower half of the star points. Glue a rhinestone or a paper star on the end of each point.

4 Add a yarn or ribbon hanger.

Pressed-Flower Window Wonder

Capture the colors of spring all year long.

You Will Need:

- white paper
- small wild flowers
- heavy book
- clear self-adhesive paper
- eight craft sticks
- ribbon or yarn

1 Fold a sheet of plain white paper. Place brightly colored wild flowers inside the folded paper. Put the paper between the pages of a heavy book. (It will take about ten days for the flowers to dry.)

2 Arrange the dried flowers on the sticky side of a 5-inch-by-5-inch piece of clear self-adhesive paper. Place another 5-inch piece of self-adhesive paper on top of the first.

3 Glue four craft sticks together to make a square. Let dry.

4 Glue the flower square to the craft-stick square. Glue four more craft sticks on top of the square.

5 Add a ribbon hanger to the back.

More Ideas

Instead of a square window, make another shape to hold your flowers.

Mirror, Mirror on the Doll

Get a grip on this smiling face—and your own.

You Will Need:

- construction paper
- poster board
- aluminum foil
- craft stick
- markers
- yarn or synthetic hair

1 Cut construction paper and poster board into an oval shape exactly the same size—about 2½ inches wide by 3½ inches long.

2 Cover the poster-board oval with aluminum foil on one side. Wrap the foil to the back of the oval.

3 Glue the craft stick to the back of the "mirror" so that most of it sticks out at the bottom.

4 Draw a silly face on one side of the construction-paper oval. Glue the face to the back of the "mirror" so the craft stick handle is sandwiched in between.

5 Add yarn or synthetic hair to the paper face. Decorate the mirror handle.

More Ideas

Make your mirror into a clown face. Or how about a cat? Just vary the colors and shapes of your mirror.

Wood Plaques

Make these decorative panels for any occasion.

You Will Need:

- craft sticks
- old magazine or catalog
- yarn
- construction paper
- markers
- red, white, and blue sticker stars or sequins
- chenille stick

To Make the Basic Plaque

1 Apply glue on the back of two craft sticks. Lay them about 3 inches apart.

2 Place about ten craft sticks side by side across the two sticks, with no spaces showing. Let dry.

To Make the Cow Plaque

Cut out your favorite cow picture from a magazine or a catalog. Glue it to the plaque. Add a yarn hanger.

To Make the Election Day Plaque

Write "vote" in big, bold letters across a piece of white construction paper, using red and blue markers. Outline the letters in black, if you like. Glue the paper to the front of the plaque. Decorate the ends of the sticks with red, white, and blue sticker stars or sequins. Add other trims. Let dry. Glue a chenille stick bent into a V shape to the back of the sign as a hanger.

More Ideas

Make a nameplate for your room, and hang it on the doorknob.

Star of David Garland

Make the Hanukkah or Passover holiday even more festive.

You Will Need:

- crafts sticks
- glitter
- embroidery thread

1 Make Star of David shapes from craft sticks.

2 Add glue and glitter on each star.

3 Tie them together with embroidery thread. Add thread at each end to hang.

More Ideas

Arrange the stars in a circle to create a sparkly centerpiece for your holiday table.

Personal Magnet Banner

Show the world what you like best.

You Will Need:

- craft sticks
- old magazines or catalogs
- stickers or other trims
- magnetic strip

1 Cover three craft sticks with glue, and lay them side by side. Lay four craft sticks side by side over the glued sticks. (Half of each stick will be in contact with the glued sticks.)

2 Cut letters from an old magazine or catalog to spell out your name or the name of the person you want to describe. Glue the letters in place. Add stickers or other trims.

3 From the same magazine, cut out three tiny pictures that you like or that remind you of the person named on the banner.

4 Glue the pictures to the sticks. Glue a magnetic strip to the back.

More Ideas

Create a Personal Magnet Banner as big as the plaque on page 44. Add your favorite pictures.

Sled Ornament

Remember good times with this winter decoration.

1 Line up five sticks side by side as shown in the picture.

2 Spread glue across the back of the remaining stick. Place it across the five sticks about 1 inch from the tip of the center stick. Let dry.

3 Decorate your sled with felt or other trims. Write your name or the name of a friend or family member on the center stick. Use glitter markers, or paint the sticks in your favorite color.

4 Add a ribbon hanger.

More Ideas

Add runners by stacking and gluing three sticks underneath the sled on both sides.

Title Index

Subject Index

Look What You Can Make With
NEWSPAPERS, MAGAZINES, AND GREETING CARDS

Over 80 Pictured Crafts and Dozens of Other Ideas

Edited by Kathy Ross

Look What You Can Make With

Newspapers, Magazines, and Greeting Cards

Edited by Kathy Ross
Photographs by Hank Schneider

Boyds Mills Press

Craft Coordinator:

Kathy Ross

Craft Makers:

Kerry O'Neill
Kathy Ross

Contributors:

Debra Boyles
Doris D. Breiholz
Joyce T. Buckner
Tera Burgundy
Betty Burt
Frances M. Callahan
Blanche Campbell
Catherine Carmody
Marie E. Cecchini
Patricia Coon
Mary Curtis
B. J. Deike
Donna Dowdy

Helen Kitchell Evans
Clara Flammang
Kelly McCumber Freihofer
Norah Grubmeyer
Nan Hathaway
Deborah L. Hogshead
Jerry Holcomb
Carmen Horn
Olive Howie
Tama Kain
Lillian Koslover
Elizabeth Searle Lamb
Lee Lindeman

Lory MacRae
Carol McCall
R. C. McIntyre
Beth Mehall
Ouida Johnston Moore
Kathy Ross
Sally E. Stuart
Sherry Timberman
Marion Ullmark
Carol E. Vogel
Francis Wales
Mary Zook

Copyright © 2001 by Boyds Mills Press
All rights reserved

Published by Bell Books
Boyds Mills Press, Inc.
A Highlights Company
815 Church Street
Honesdale, Pennsylvania 18431
Printed in China

U.S. Cataloging-in-Publication Data
  (Library of Congress Standards)

Look what you can make with newspapers, magazines, and greeting cards: over
80 pictured crafts and dozens of other ideas / edited by Kathy Ross ;
photographs by Hank Schneider. — 1st ed.
[48] p. : col. photos. ; cm.
Includes index.
Summary: Toys, games, and other things to make from newspapers, magazines, and
greeting cards.
ISBN: 1-56397-566-1
1. Paper work — Juvenile literature. 2. Cutout craft — Juvenile
literature.
[1. Paper work. 2. Cutout craft.] I. Schneider, Hank. II. Title.
745.54 21 2001 AC CIP
2001092561

First edition, 2001
Books in this series originally designed by Lorianne Siomades
The text of this book is set in 10-point Avant Garde Demi, titles 43-point Gill Sans Extra Bold

Visit our Web site at www.boydsmillspress.com

10 9 8 7 6 5 4 3 2 1

Getting Started

This book is filled with fun, easy-to-make crafts, and each one begins with old newspapers, magazines, or greeting cards. You'll find a wide variety of things to make, including toys, games, and gifts.

Directions

Before you start each craft, read the directions and look closely at the photograph, but remember—it's up to you to make the craft your own. If we decorate a craft with markers but you want to use glitter paint and stickers, go for it. Feel free to stray from our directions and invent new crafts.

Work Area

It's a good idea to keep your work area covered. Old newspapers, brown paper (from grocery bags), or old sheets work well. If you're creating papier-mâché, you might want to use an extra-thick covering of newspaper for your work area. (Papier-mâché is messy.) Also, protect your clothes by wearing a smock. A big old shirt does the job and gives you room to move. Finally, remember to clean up when you've finished.

Materials

You'll need a lot of old magazines, greeting cards, envelopes, calendars, and newspapers, so start saving now. Ask friends and relatives to help. Keep your craft-making supplies together, and before making each craft, check the "You Will Need" list to make sure you have everything. In this list we will often specify a certain kind of printed paper. For some crafts, however, more than one kind of paper will work. Look at the type of paper used for the craft pictured, and see what you might have on hand that is similar. Also, since you'll need scissors, glue, tape, or a stapler for almost every craft, we don't list these supplies.

Other Stuff

When we show several similar crafts, we'll often list numbered directions that apply to all of the crafts, then specific directions for each craft. When you start a craft made from printed paper, make sure that the magazines, catalogs, greeting cards, calendars, and newspapers you will use are no longer wanted by the original owner.

That's about all. So choose a craft that you like, check your paper stash to find what you need, and have some fun. Before you know it, you'll be showing everyone what you made with newspapers, magazines, and greeting cards.

Papier-mâché Banks

Save your coins in one of these characters.

You Will Need:

- newspaper
- measuring cup
- water
- flour
- mixing bowl
- round balloon
- plastic-foam egg carton
- masking tape
- paint and paintbrush
- pompons, yarn, buttons, and other trims
- old compact disc (CD)
- felt
- chenille stick
- large and small paper cups
- paper plate
- sponge
- plastic wiggle eyes
- cardboard ring
- paper

This project is extra-messy, so use lots of newspaper to cover your work area.

To Make the Basic Bank

1 Tear lots of newspaper into strips.

2 Mix 1 cup of water with 1 cup of flour to make a paste.

3 Blow up the balloon to the size you want your bank to be and knot it.

4 Dip the newspaper strips in the paste, and lay them on the balloon. Cover the balloon with three to four layers of strips. Leave the knot of the balloon uncovered. Let the project dry completely on the egg carton.

5 When the paper ball is dry, pop the balloon and remove it. Cover the hole with masking tape to close it.

To Make the Mouse Bank

Paint the ball in your favorite mouse color. Glue a pompon over the area where the balloon was removed to make the nose. Cut a coin slot in the top of the mouse. Glue the mouse to the CD to keep it from rolling to the side. Cut round eyes and ears from felt, and glue them to the head. Wrap the chenille stick around your finger to make a spiral tail. Glue it to the back of the mouse. Secure the tail with masking tape over the glue. Paint the masking tape. Decorate the body with felt.

To Make the Fish Bank

Tape the small paper cup over the covered hole to form the nose. Cut fins and a tail from a paper plate. Tape them in place. Cut a 1-inch ring from the rim of a large paper cup. Glue and tape the bottom of the fish to the ring to make a stand. Cut a coin slot in the top. Paint the fish. When it's dry, add a light speckled layer of paint in another color by dabbing it over the fish with a sponge. Use the sequins to give the fins and tail some sparkle. We glued buttons under the plastic wiggle eyes.

To Make the Clown Bank

Paint the papier-mâché ball, and let it dry. Cover the cardboard ring with felt or paper to make a collar. Cut a coin slot in the back of the head. Glue the ball to the collar with the covered hole down in the ring. Add a bow tie or other decorations, if you wish. Glue on yarn hair. Glue a cup hat on top of the hair. Decorate the hat. Use trims to give the clown a face. This clown has a felt smile, a pompon nose, and eyes made from felt, buttons, and sticker stars.

More Ideas

Other characters are easy to make. Try a bear, or a porcupine with chenille-stick quills. Make different-shaped fish to turn your room into a tropical sea.

Newspaper Dolls

Make a fashionable friend or two to play with.

You Will Need:

- newspaper
- paper towel
- masking tape
- paint and paintbrush
- yarn
- plastic wiggle eyes
- beads, buttons, and other trims
- fabric scraps
- ribbon
- chenille stick
- paper baking cup
- artificial flowers

1 Crumple half of a single sheet of newspaper into a ball for the head. Cover the ball with a paper towel, and hold it in place with masking tape.

2 To make the body, fold a single sheet of newspaper in half from top to bottom. Then roll the sheet from the fold to the end. Secure the newspaper roll with glue. Do the same thing with another sheet.

3 Glue the two rolls together in an X with the top of the X slightly shorter than the bottom. Secure the two rolls in the center with masking tape while the glue dries. Attach the head by taping the excess paper towel to the center of the X. Bend the arms down, and glue them at the fold.

4 Paint the doll, and let it dry.

5 Use the yarn to make hair. Paint on shoes and a face, or use plastic wiggle eyes and other trims. Cut a rectangle of fabric to form both the front and the back of the dress. Cut a slit in the center. Slip the head through the slit. Tie the dress at the waist with ribbon.

To Make the Basket

Glue the ends of a chenille stick to each side of a paper baking cup. Glue artificial flowers in the basket. Glue the basket to the doll's arm.

More Ideas

Cut the toe from an old sock to make a hat. Roll the cut edge to make a brim, and glue a pompon on the top.

String some beads for the doll to make a necklace and a bracelet.

Switch-Plate Decoration

Make every light switch bright.

1 Glue the front and back of the greeting card together.

2 Remove the switch plate from the wall, and trace around it on the card. Don't forget to trace around the rectangle for the switch.

3 Cut out the new cover from the card.

4 Attach the cover to the switch plate with a small roll of masking tape.

More Ideas

Save special cards to make covers for each season.

Flowery Card

Send this card to someone you love.

1 Cut out the letters that spell "Mom" or another name from the cardboard.

2 Cut out pictures of flowers from magazines or catalogs.

3 Glue the pictures on the letters. Trim around the edges.

4 Glue the letters to a folded piece of cardboard. Write a message inside.

More Ideas

Make a card for your sister or aunt using pictures of flowers she likes best.

Neat Note Holders

Display your messages in style.

You Will Need:

- greeting cards and magazines
- thin cardboard
- spring-type clothespins
- thin ribbon

To Make the Note Holder

Select a picture from a greeting card or a magazine, and carefully cut it out. If necessary, glue the picture to thin cardboard to make it stiff. Glue the picture to one side of a spring-type clothespin with the bottom of the picture at the handle end of the clothespin. Stick a note in the clothespin.

To Make the Line of Birds Note Holder

Glue a picture of a bird to a clothespin with the feet of the bird touching the tip of the pinching end of the clothespin. Slip flower pictures from cards or magazines behind each bird, and glue them in place. Tie a length of ribbon from wall to wall, and clamp the birds across the ribbon.

More Ideas

Glue a magnetic strip on the back of the clothespin, and stick a note holder to the refrigerator.

Make note holders for dinner guests, and put a place card in the holder at the table.

Hang birthday or other greeting
cards from your Line of Birds
Note Holder.

Papier-mâché Mouse

This little critter has a body made of newspaper.

You Will Need:

- newspaper
- measuring cup
- water
- flour
- mixing bowl
- plastic-foam egg carton
- paint and paintbrush
- beads, pompons, thread, ribbon

This project is extra-messy, so use lots of newspaper to cover your work area.

1 Tear the newspaper into strips.

2 Mix 1 cup of water with 1 cup of flour to make a paste.

3 Wad a piece of newspaper to make a mouse base. Twist one end of the base to make the tail.

4 Dip the strips of newspaper into the paste, and wrap them around the base, shaping the mouse as you wrap. Cover the base with several layers of strips. Add folded strips at the head for ears. Cover the ears with more layers of pasted newspaper. Let the mouse dry on the egg carton overnight or until completely hard.

5 Paint the mouse. Add a face using trims. This mouse has tiny bead eyes, a tiny pompon nose, thread whiskers, and a ribbon bow on the tail. How will you decorate yours?

More Ideas

You can use this technique to make other animals. How about a sleeping dog or cat, or maybe a bird?

For some extra painting fun, add something decorative to the animal, such as a small painted flower on the side.

Covered Gift Box

Make this little gift box for someone special.

You Will Need:

- toothpick box
- magazine or calendar picture
- pencil

1 Carefully take the toothpick box apart at the places where it is glued. Flatten the box out.

2 Place the flattened box upside down on an interesting or colorful part of the picture. Trace around the box, and cut the shape out.

3 Glue the cut picture to the outside of the box.

4 Reassemble the box and reglue the edges.

More Ideas

Add a sticky-back Velcro closure to the box so you can use it to store tiny toys.

Car Carrier

Stash all your small vehicles in one place.

You Will Need:

- half-gallon milk carton
- magazines
- hole punch
- yarn or chenille stick
- colored plastic tape

More Ideas

Make a carrier for any kind of small item. Once you decide what your carrier will hold, look for pictures of those objects to cut and paste.

1 Cut the top off the milk carton and discard it.

2 Cut out lots of pictures of vehicles from old magazines.

3 Glue the pictures all over the outside of the milk carton.

4 Punch a hole on the opposite sides of the carrier. Attach yarn or a chenille stick through each hole to make a handle.

5 You can cover the top edge of the carrier with colored plastic tape to give it a more finished look.

Greeting Card Mobiles

Display your holiday cards in a special way.

You Will Need:

- ribbon
- greeting cards
- yarn
- wire
  coat hanger
- hole punch
- craft beads
- jingle bells

To Make the Greeting Card Mobile

Cut different lengths of ribbon. Cut one large picture from a card, cutting through the back panel. Glue the card together with the two ends of one ribbon in between to form a hanger and the other ribbons hanging down from the bottom. Cut around the pictures, including the back panel, of other greeting cards. Glue the front and back of each card together with a ribbon in between. Hang the cards at different heights so they do not cover each other. Trim off any excess ribbon sticking out from the bottoms.

To Make the Valentine Mobile

Tie pieces of yarn across the hanger. Punch a hole in the center of the top and bottom of each card. String the valentines onto the yarn. String beads in between some of the cards. Tie off the end of each piece of yarn with a bead or a jingle bell. Arrange the cards along the yarn so they are evenly spaced. Use tape on the back of any cards that slip on the yarn. Slide some beads over the hook. Secure the top bead with glue. Cut two cards the same size. Glue the two cards, back to back, over the hook. Tie a bow at the top.

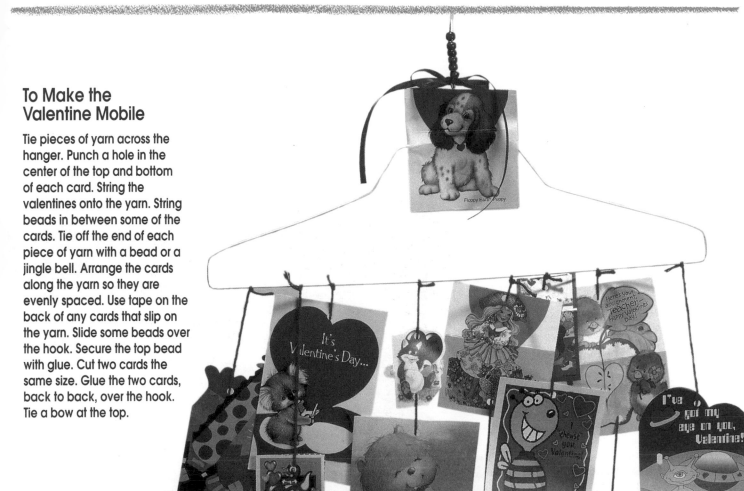

More Ideas

Instead of a wire hanger, make a base from two craft sticks. Glue the sticks in the center to form an X, then hang ribbon or yarn from the ends.

Newspaper Nelson

This friend is big enough to have his own chair.

4 Staple the top closed. Add yarn for hair as you staple. Create a face and other details using construction paper and decorative trims.

More Ideas

Use markers or paint to create the face and clothes. How can you make your Nelson unique?

1 Open six double sheets of newspaper, and stack them together. Three of the sheets will form the front of Nelson, and three will form the back. Staple the sheets together around three sides. Leave the top open for stuffing and room for the arms and legs.

2 Roll a single sheet of newspaper for each arm and leg, securing the roll with staples. Insert the legs and arms into the body.

3 Stuff Nelson with balls of crumpled newspaper between the front three sheets and the back three sheets.

Stamp-Covered Paperweight

Start saving those stamps to make this beautiful paperweight.

You Will Need:

- canceled stamps
- water
- waxed paper
- rock
- paintbrush
- felt

1 Cut the stamps from envelopes. Soak them in water to remove them from the paper. Put the wet stamps on the waxed paper to dry.

2 Glue the stamps to the rock. Paint the stamps with glue to seal and protect the edges.

3 Cut a piece of felt to cover the bottom of the rock. Glue the felt in place. This will keep the paperweight from scratching your desk.

More Ideas

Glue magazine pictures to the rock instead of stamps. Seal with glue.

Ribbon Picture Holder

Display art from three favorite greeting cards.

You Will Need:

- white poster board
- three greeting cards
- clear glitter
- ribbon
- notebook ring

1 Cut three circles from white poster board.

2 Cut a picture from a greeting card to glue on each circle. Cover each circle with glue, press the picture in the center, and sprinkle the rest of the gluey circle with clear glitter.

3 Cut a long strip of ribbon. Cut a triangle shape from the bottom end to make two points.

4 Staple the top end of the ribbon into a loop. Put a notebook ring through the loop.

5 Glue the three pictures to the ribbon.

More Ideas

Make seasonal holders for spring, Thanksgiving, or Hanukkah.

Papier-mâché Hat

Your tops in this wacky hat.

You Will Need:

- large paper bag
- pencil
- poster board
- masking tape
- measuring cup
- water
- flour
- mixing bowl
- newspaper
- paint and paintbrush
- ribbon and other trims

This project is extra-messy, so use lots of newspaper to cover your work area.

1 Put the bag on your head. Roll up the opening of the bag until it's the height you want. Cut the rolled-up portion from the bag.

2 Trace around the opening of the bag on the poster board. Draw a larger circle around this one to make a brim, and cut it out. Tape the brim to the bag hat.

3 Mix 1 cup of water with 1 cup of flour to make a paste. Tear lots of newspaper strips. Dip the strips in the paste, and lay them on the hat. Cover the hat with two to three layers of strips. Let it dry completely.

4 Paint the hat, then decorate it with trims. As the hat dries, pull it out a little on the sides. Or find a bowl that is about the size of your head. Turn it upside down and cover it with plastic wrap. Slip the hat over the bowl. This hat dries very hard, so you want to be sure the bag dries in a shape that will fit over the top of your head.

More Ideas

Instead of painting the hat, use a layer of colorful magazine pictures or construction paper cut in strips for your final surface.

Greeting-Card Place Cards

Any dinner table is special when you add a set of these place cards.

You Will Need:

- ruler
- thin cardboard
- construction paper
- greeting cards
- markers

1 For each place card, cut a 3-inch square from the cardboard. Fold the square in half.

2 Cover the folded place card with construction paper.

3 Cut a small picture from a greeting card. Glue the picture to the card.

4 Use the markers to write the names of your guests.

More Ideas

Create place cards for different holidays, such as Thanksgiving, Christmas, or Passover.

Jellybean Basket

This little basket makes a great party favor.

You Will Need:

- greeting cards
- pencil
- plastic margarine-tub lid
- hole punch
- thin ribbon

1 Cut a picture from a greeting card. Trace around the lid on the card to make a circle. Cut the circle out.

2 Cut four 1½-inch slits, equal distance apart, in from the edge of the circle to make four flaps. Punch a small hole in the top edge on each side of one flap. Do the same thing to the flap directly across from the one you first punched.

3 Thread one end of a ribbon through the hole on one side of the first flap. Thread the other end of the ribbon through the hole on the opposite flap. Tie the ribbon in a bow, pulling the circle up to form one side of the basket. Do the same thing on the other side.

4 Cut a strip from another card for a handle. Glue it inside the basket. Glue decorations on the handle.

More Ideas

Fill the basket with paper grass and add goodies.

Start with a larger lid to make a larger basket.

Old Glory Collage

Make this flag to hang on your door for Independence Day.

You Will Need:

- white construction paper
- magazines
- cardboard
- twine

More Ideas

Use sticker stars instead of cutting out stars.

Make a smaller version of the flag on construction paper. Hang this outside during your Fourth of July picnic.

1 Cut a square of white construction paper to mark off the blue section on the flag. (Do not glue it to the cardboard.)

2 Glue red pictures from the magazines over the cardboard. Stop at the upper left-hand corner where the blue section will be.

3 Cover another sheet of white paper with white pictures. Cut the paper into six white strips. Glue them to the flag. If the strips are too short, cut more strips to add to them.

4 Cover the white square with blue pictures cut from the magazines. Trim the edges. Glue the blue square to the upper left-hand corner.

5 Cut thirteen stars from yellow pictures. Glue the stars in a circle on the blue square. Glue the ends of a piece of twine on the back.

Super Storage Holders

Organize your magazines, mail, and other stuff.

You Will Need:

- sturdy box with lid
- brown paper
- magazines and calendars
- pasta box
- large cardboard box
- colored plastic tape
- pencil
- construction paper
- hole punch

To Make the Storage Box

Cover a box and lid with brown paper. Once you decide what the box is to be used for, cut out pictures from magazines and calendars that remind you of the contents. Glue just a few pictures over the box, or cover the entire box with a collage of pictures. Can you guess what is stored in the box shown?

To Make the Basic Holder

1 Cut the sides of the box partway down at a slant, then cut across the front of the box to remove the top.

2 Cut pictures from magazines and calendars. Glue them to the box.

3 Give the edges a finished look by covering them with the colored plastic tape.

To Make the Mail Holder

Cut letters that spell "mail" from a magazine. Glue the letters across the front of the box. Trace around the back of the box on construction paper. Cut paper to fit in the back of the inside of the box, and glue in place. Do the same thing on the bottom of the box. Punch a hole in the back for hanging.

To Make
the Magazine Holder

Make sure your box is large enough to hold your magazines. Glue on pictures from old issues or other pictures that you like.

More Ideas

Make a picture-covered container on pages 28 and 29 to match your magazine and mail holders for a neat desk set.

Notebook House

Design a house of your very own, then use cutout figures to tell a story.

You Will Need:

- magazines and catalogs
- large notebook
- markers
- fabric, wallpaper, wrapping paper
- paper clips
- greeting cards
- masking tape

1 Cut the furniture and details for each room from old magazines and catalogs.

2 You can make the top part of each notebook page the wall and the bottom part the floor. You can cover the wall and floor by coloring with markers or gluing on pieces of fabric, wallpaper, or wrapping paper.

3 Arrange the cutouts in a way that you like, then glue them in place in the notebook.

4 Stand the notebook up. Open to the room you wish to use. If the pages do not stay open, secure them with paper clips.

To Make the Stand-Up Figures

Cut small pictures of animals and people from the greeting cards. Bend the outer loop of the paper clip down to make the clip stand. Use the masking tape to attach a figure to the front of the paper clip that sticks up. The bent part of the paper clip should be behind the figure.

More Ideas

You might want to make the storage box on page 20 to keep the notebook house and cutouts until you are ready to use them. Store your stand-up figures in there, too.

New rooms can be added to the notebook house over time.

Card Gift Tags

Select some favorite figures from your greeting card collection to make gift tags.

You Will Need:

- greeting cards
- hole punch
- embroidery thread

1 Cut a picture from the greeting card.

2 Punch a hole in the top.

3 Cut a length of thread, and knot the two ends together. Thread the loop through the hole in the picture, then thread the opposite end of the loop through itself to secure the tie to the tag.

More Ideas

A set of these tags in a plastic sandwich bag tied at the top with a pretty ribbon makes a welcome gift.

Moving-Picture Cube

Here is an unusual way to display your pictures.

You Will Need:

- construction paper
- magazines or greeting cards
- two reinforcement rings
- yarn

1 Cut six identical squares from construction paper. Fold the corners to the center, making a smaller square. Unfold the corners. Glue a favorite magazine picture or greeting card in the center of each square.

2 Glue the four squares together, side by side. Glue a square to the bottom.

3 Poke two holes in the center of the last square, about an inch apart. Put a reinforcement ring over the back of each hole. Thread a piece of yarn through the two holes, and tie the ends together for a hanger.

4 Glue the last square to the top.

More Ideas

This is a good way to display photographs, too.

Deck the Halls

Save your holiday cards to make one-of-a-kind decorations.

You Will Need:

- thin cardboard
- aluminum foil
- magazines
- ruler
- pencil and pen
- holiday greeting cards
- ribbon and other trims
- paper
- plastic wrap
- hole punch
- paper clips
- jingle bells

To Make the Twelve-Day Christmas Calendar

Cover the cardboard with aluminum foil. Tape the foil in the back. From magazines, cut out the number twelve and the letters that spell "days of Christmas." Glue them across the top of the calendar. Make a 2-inch square pattern from cardboard. Use the pattern to trace and cut twelve colorful picture squares from the greeting cards. Glue the bottom and side edges of each square to the calendar. The top should be open, like a pocket. Tape a piece of ribbon to the back of the calendar. Cut twelve 1-by-4-inch strips of paper. On each strip write your "gift" for the day, one gift for each of the twelve days of Christmas. Gifts can be words of love and support, ideas for family holiday fun, or promises to do extra chores. Fold each paper strip "gift" in half, and tuck it in one of the pockets of the calendar.

To Make the Christmas Card Wreath

Cut a 2-by-4-inch rectangle from the back of one card. Trace around the pattern on eighteen to twenty cards. Cut the traced rectangles out. Arrange the rectangles in a circle, overlapping each other, on a piece of plastic wrap. Glue the cards in place. When the glue has dried, peel the wreath from the plastic wrap. Glue a loop of ribbon to the back. Add a bow to the front.

To Make the Paper-Clip Garland

Cut small pictures from the cards. Punch a hole on both sides of each cutout. String the pictures together with paper clips slipped through the holes. When the garland is as long as you want it, slip a jingle bell on the paper clip at both ends.

More Ideas

You might want to add other decorations to your calendar, such as sequins, glitter, or curls of ribbon.

You can make the wreath for spring using flowery cards.

Try cutting smaller rectangles to make a tiny wreath to hang on a Christmas tree.

Invite your friends to help make the garland. See how long you can make it.

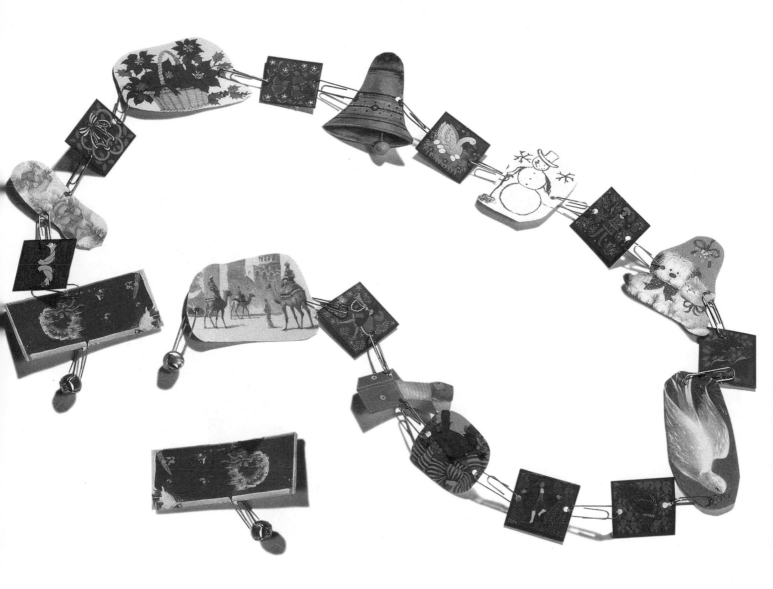

Picture Pins and Rings

Design your own jewelry.

You Will Need:
- greeting card
- jewelry pin
- clear nail polish
- chenille stick

Choose a picture from a greeting card to use for the pin or ring. Cut the picture out.

To Make the Pin

Attach the jewelry pin to the back of the picture. Cover the front with clear nail polish to protect it.

To Make the Ring

Wrap one end of the chenille stick around your finger, twisting the ends together to make a ring that fits. Trim off the extra chenille stick. Glue the picture on the ring where the two ends of the chenille stick are joined.

More Ideas

If you do not have a jewelry pin, try a small safety pin. Glue the back of the pin to the back of the picture, using masking tape to hold the pin in place while the glue dries.

Add tiny details to the pin or ring by gluing on sequins, craft jewels, and other trims.

Newspaper Ned

Roll some old newsprint into a puppet.

You Will Need:
- newspaper
- markers
- construction paper
- pompons and other trims

1 Close a double sheet of newspaper, and roll it into a puppet. Tape or staple the roll to secure it.

2 To make hair, cut slits in the paper and fluff them out.

3 Add a face and details using markers, paper, and other trims.

More Ideas

Make arms from newspaper, and staple to the sides.

Felt Travel Box

This felt board makes a long trip more fun.

You Will Need:

- felt
- shoe box
- magazines and catalogs

1 Cut a piece of felt to fit inside the lid of the shoe box, then glue it to the lid.

2 Cut pictures of people, animals, and objects from the magazines and catalogs.

3 Glue each picture to felt. Let the glue dry. Trim around the edges of each picture.

4 Use the pictures to make scenes on the felt-lined lid. When you are not playing with the pieces, store them in the box.

More Ideas

Decorate the outside of the box with cutout pictures from magazines or greeting cards. Cover with glue to seal.

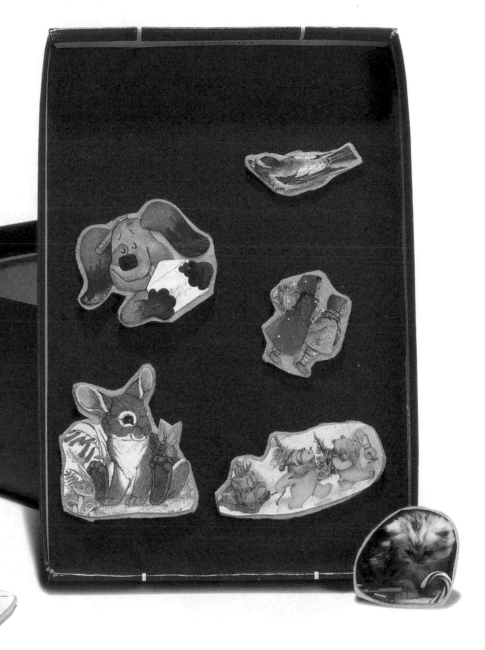

Custom Containers

Cover simple containers in different ways to hold your toys and other treasures.

You Will Need:

- magazines and catalogs
- plastic or cardboard containers
- ribbon and other trims
- pencil
- hair pins

To Make the Picture-Covered Containers

Cut out your favorite words or pictures. Glue the pictures over the container. Cover the pictures with a coating of glue to hold down the edges and protect the pictures. Decorate the top and bottom of the container with ribbon or other trims.

To Make the Rolled-Paper Holder

Tear several colorful pages from the magazines. Lay the pencil on one edge of a page.

Squeeze a thin line of glue across the opposite edge. Roll the page around the pencil toward the glued edge. Press the glued edge down to secure the roll. Slip the pencil out of the roll. If the glue is not holding the roll in place, slip a hair pin over each end of the roll until the glue dries. Cut the tubes to the same height as the container. Cover the container with glue, and stick the paper rolls on the container. Decorate with trim.

More Ideas

If the container has a lid, you might want to glue a decorated wooden bead to the center of the lid for a handle.

If you're making a container for a relative or a friend, choose pictures or words that the person would like.

You can use paper rolls to cover any straight-sided container. You can also use them to decorate flat surfaces, such as picture frames or box tops.

Story-Figure Magnets

Write a story, then use your refrigerator as a stage.

You Will Need:
- greeting cards
- magnetic strips

1 Cut figures from old greeting cards.

2 Glue a magnetic strip on the back of each figure.

3 Stick the figures on the refrigerator to use for play and storytelling.

More Ideas

You can also play with your story figures by sticking them on an old cookie sheet.

You might want to add some houses and scenery to your storytelling collection.

Keep your magnets in the storage box on page 20.

Homemade Alphabet

Collect lots of letters to play word games.

You Will Need:

- magazines and catalogs
- thin cardboard
- plastic margarine tub with lid

1 Cut words from the magazines and catalogs. You might want to cut out some punctuation marks, too, such as question marks and exclamation points.

2 Glue the words to thin cardboard.

3 Cut the letters apart.

4 Use the margarine tub to store your letters.

More Ideas

Add more letters to make more words.

Decorate your storage container with pictures or letters.

Magazine Valentine

Try this different idea for making Valentine's Day cards.

You Will Need:

- pencil
- thin cardboard
- construction paper
- magazines
- white paper
- ribbon and other trims

1 Sketch a small heart on the thin cardboard. Cut the heart out to use as a pattern.

2 Make a folded card from construction paper that is slightly larger than the heart pattern.

3 Use the pattern to trace a heart on the front of the card. Cut the traced heart out.

4 From a magazine, cut an area of red or pink color that is slightly larger than the heart. Glue the magazine picture inside the card so that the color shows through the cutout heart. Cut a liner from the white paper. Glue the liner inside the card.

5 Add some ribbon or trim to the front.

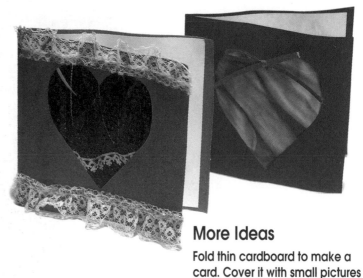

More Ideas

Fold thin cardboard to make a card. Cover it with small pictures in one color or in different colors. Then trace and cut out your heart pattern.

Thanksgiving Centerpieces

Make these impressive turkeys for your Thanksgiving table.

You Will Need:

- round balloon
- measuring cup
- water
- flour
- mixing bowl
- newspaper
- brown paint and paintbrush
- thin cardboard
- poster board
- magazines
- masking tape

This project is extra-messy, so use lots of newspaper to cover your work area.

1 Blow up the balloon and knot the end.

2 Mix 1 cup of water with 1 cup of flour to make a paste. Tear newspaper into strips. Dip the strips into the paste, and wrap them around the balloon. Let dry completely, then pop the balloon and discard.

3 Paint the body brown. When dry, tape a ring of cardboard to the bottom.

4 Cover the poster board with magazine pictures in fall colors. Then cut out a head, two feet, two wings, and lots of tail feathers. Glue the head to one end of the body. Cut eyes and a beak from poster board scraps. Glue them to the head. Cut a wattle from a red magazine page, and glue it so it hangs down from the beak.

5 Glue the two feet to the body below the head. Glue a wing on each side of the body. Secure heavy pieces with masking tape until the glue dries. Spread the tail feathers out in a fan shape, and staple them together at the bottom. Glue the tail feathers to the back of the turkey.

More Ideas

Using the body shape, try making
a swan or a duck.

Designer Envelopes

Turn colorful pictures into eye-catching envelopes.

You Will Need:

- envelope
- calendars, magazines, or catalogs
- pencil
- white paper

1 Carefully unglue the seams of the envelope, and flatten it out to use as a pattern. Place the pattern on a picture so that the picture will be on the front of the envelope.

2 Trace around the envelope, and cut it out.

3 Fold the new envelope exactly as the pattern envelope was folded. Secure the seams with glue. Glue on rectangles of white paper for the address and return address spaces.

4 Use a sticker or glue to seal the flap.

More Ideas

Collect envelope patterns in several sizes, and store them in a zipper-close bag.

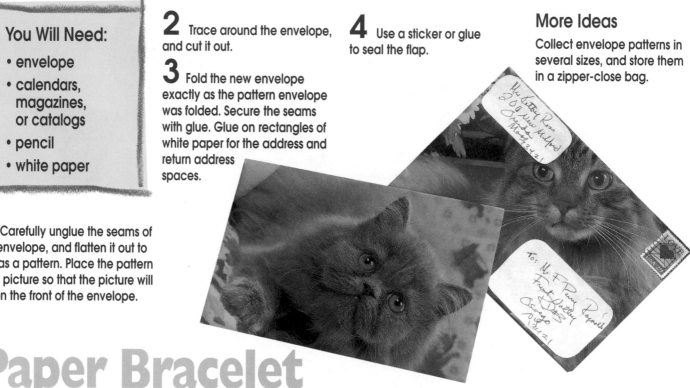

Paper Bracelet

Wear this jewelry anytime.

You Will Need:

- newspaper
- acrylic paint and paintbrush
- nail polish

1 Cut sixty-four small hearts from newspaper. Glue four together, one on top of the other, spreading glue over the entire heart. Repeat until you have sixteen sets.

2 With white glue, fasten the top of one heart over the tip of the next, curving them slightly as you work. Coat the bracelet with the glue and let dry overnight.

3 Cover with acrylic paint. When this is dry, decorate the hearts with red nail polish.

More Ideas

Create other shapes for your bracelet, such as seashells or stars.

Marble Maze

Test your skill with this maze game.

You Will Need:

- shallow box or lid
- magazine
- pencil
- plastic drinking straws
- marble or wooden bead
- marker

1 Cover the shallow box or lid with magazine pictures.

2 Tear several pages from the magazine. Roll each page around the pencil a few times. Slip the pencil out and continue rolling the page. Secure the edge of the rolled paper with glue.

3 Design your maze in the bottom of the box using pieces of straws. Make sure the paths are wide enough to allow the marble to pass through. When you are happy with the design, replace the straws with the paper rolls. Use the straws to measure the length of each roll. Glue the rolls to the bottom of the box.

4 Poke a hole in the side to drop the marble through at the beginning of the maze. Write the word "start" near the hole. At the end of the maze, poke a small hole through the bottom of the box so the marble can rest. Write the word "finish" near the hole.

More Ideas

Time yourself to see how quickly you can move the marble through the maze.

Don't forget to make some paths in the maze that lead nowhere.

Puzzling Projects

Homemade jigsaws are fun to put together.

To Make the Jigsaw Puzzle

Cut the poster board to the same size as the picture you are using. Glue the magazine or calendar picture to the poster board.

Let dry. Fold a strip of colored plastic tape over all four sides of the puzzle. Use the marker to draw the shape of each puzzle piece on the back. Divide the puzzle into about twelve pieces. Cut the puzzle apart following the lines. Store the pieces in a zipper-close bag.

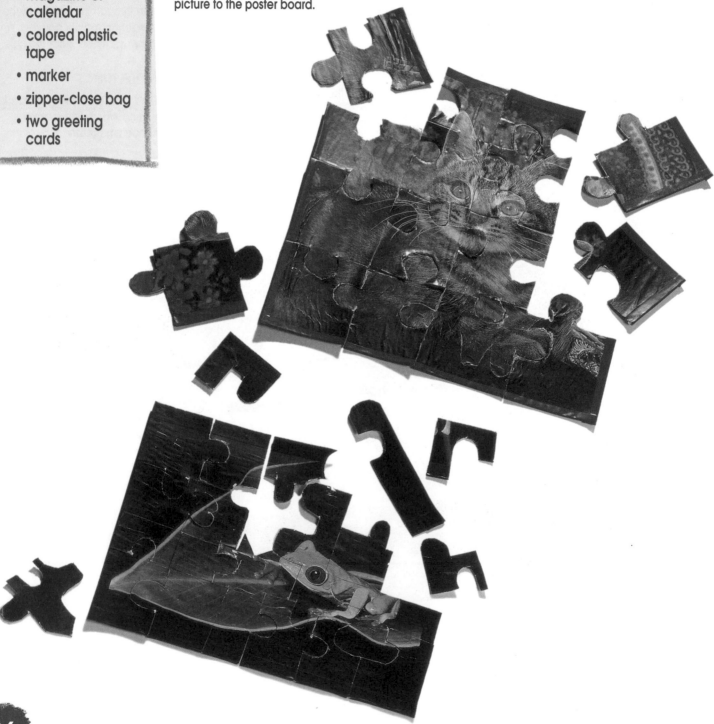

To Make the Two-Sided Puzzle

Cut the picture off the front of each greeting card. Trim the two pictures so that they are the same size. Glue the two pictures back to back so there is a picture on each side. Let the glue dry before continuing. Cut the pictures into five or six pieces to make a puzzle.

More Ideas

Glue a picture from a calendar or a magazine to a piece of thin cardboard. Cut the picture into horizontal strips. Mix up the strips. Try to put the picture back together.

Happy-Sad Flower Puppet

Turn this flower's face to suit your mood.

You Will Need:

- magazine
- pencil
- thin cardboard
- construction paper
- markers
- hole punch
- metal paper fastener

1 To make the stem, select a magazine picture with lots of green in it. Starting at one corner, roll the page around the pencil four times. Slip the pencil out, and continue rolling to the opposite corner. Glue the corner down to secure the roll.

2 Cut two identical circles from the thin cardboard. Cover them with construction paper. Cut flower petals from yellow-colored pictures. Place one circle color-side down. Glue the ends of the flower petals around the circle. Glue the second circle over the first circle, color-side up.

3 Draw a face on the flower. (Notice how the smile and frown are drawn.)

4 Punch a small hole in the center of the flower and in the top of the stem. Attach the flower to the stem using the paper fastener.

5 Cut leaves from construction paper. Glue the leaves to the stem.

More Ideas

Make four or five flowers in different heights, and put them in a vase.

Doorknob Decoration

Make your door a festive entryway.

You Will Need:

- greeting card
- 12-inch chenille stick

1 Find a greeting card with a large figure or picture that you like.

2 Close the card, and cut the figure out through both the front and back.

3 Glue the front and back of the card together with the two ends of the chenille stick between them so that the chenille stick forms a hanger.

More Ideas

Cut a piece of poster board 4 inches wide and 8 inches long. Measure down from the top of the short side about an inch and draw a 2-inch-wide circle. Cut a slit down from the top to the circle, and cut the circle out. The poster board should now slip over your doorknob. Cut pictures from old magazines to decorate the hanger.

Patchwork Stocking

Fill a paper stocking with your Christmas wishes.

You Will Need:

- construction paper
- magazines and catalogs
- yarn, ribbon, and other trims
- jingle bell
- thin cardboard

1 Cut a stocking shape from construction paper. Cut colorful squares from pictures in the magazines and catalogs.

2 Glue the squares on the stocking to make it look like patchwork. Trim around the stocking. Glue the stocking to construction paper, leaving the top of the stocking unglued.

3 Cut pictures of gifts you are wishing for from the catalogs. Tuck the pictures at the top of the stocking, and glue in place.

4 Glue trim and a loop hanger to the stocking. Glue a jingle bell to the toe.

5 Glue strips of ribbon or trim around the picture. Fold the top of the picture over a strip of cardboard. Tie a long piece of yarn together. Slip part of the loop under the fold to form a hanger. Glue the fold and yarn in place.

More Ideas

Make a two-sided stocking. Add a loop and hang it just like a real stocking.

39

Works of Art

"Draw" with paper to make your very own masterpiece.

You Will Need:

- greeting cards
- paint and paintbrush
- paper plates or construction paper
- markers
- ribbon, yarn, and other trims
- newspaper comics
- unused crossword puzzles
- cardboard

To Make the Greeting Card Picture

Cut pictures from the greeting cards, and arrange them in a picture. Glue the shapes to a painted paper plate or construction paper. Add details to the picture using markers and trims. Frame your creation by gluing it to a slightly larger plate or piece of paper. Add a ribbon hanger.

To Make the Comics Art

Cut circles, triangles, and other shapes from the comics section of the newspaper. Arrange the shapes on construction paper to make a picture. Glue the shapes to the paper. Use yarn and markers to add details.

To Make the Crossword Mosaic

Create a design in the crossword puzzle by coloring all the blank spaces in different colors. Glue the finished project to cardboard. Cut a piece of construction paper slightly bigger than the puzzle. Glue the puzzle to the center of the paper to create a frame. Glue a yarn or ribbon hanger to the back.

More Ideas

If you look closely at the daily newspaper, you will find lots of things to color. How about the comics section?

Cover both sides of the cardboard-mounted crossword puzzle with clear packing tape, and use it under a vase or as a place mat.

41

Rebus Letter

Create a picture-and-word message.

You Will Need:
- magazines
- paper

1 Cut out small pictures from the magazines that can represent either part of the word or the entire word. Do this for the whole message you want to create.

2 Cut out letters to finish the words.

3 Glue the pictures and letters to a sheet of paper to write your message.

Can you read our letter?

More Ideas

Create a rebus for your birthday party invitation.

Picture-Perfect Postcard

Here's an idea for reusing old greeting cards.

You Will Need:
- greeting cards made of thin cardboard
- pen or marker

1 Cut the picture panel from the front of the greeting card.

2 On the back of the panel, draw a line down the center to create a message section and an address section.

More Ideas

To create a note card from a greeting card, open the card so that all four sections of the folded card are showing. Cut the card in half, removing the section with the verse and the section next to it. This will leave the card blank for you to write on.

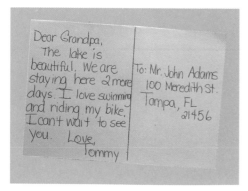

Dear Grandpa,
The lake is beautiful. We are staying here 2 more days. I love swimming and riding my bike. I can't wait to see you. Love, Tommy

To: Mr. John Adams
100 Meredith St.
Tampa, FL
21456

Papier-mâché Puppet Pal

Act out a story with this silly hand puppet.

You Will Need:

- round balloon
- cardboard tube
- masking tape
- measuring cup
- water
- flour
- mixing bowl
- newspaper
- paint and paintbrush
- yarn, buttons, and other trims
- felt

This project is extra-messy, so use lots of newspaper to cover your work area.

1 Blow up the balloon to the size of a tennis ball, and knot the end. Cut a 1½-inch ring from the cardboard tube for the neck. Tape the balloon to the cardboard ring with the knot of the balloon inside the ring.

2 Mix 1 cup of water with 1 cup of flour to make a paste. Tear lots of newspaper into strips. Cover the head and neck form with layers of strips dipped in the paste. Fold pasted strips to stick out on each side of the head for ears. Cover the folded strips with more layers of pasted paper to strengthen them. Add a nose for the puppet in the same way.

3 Let the head dry completely before painting it. Use trims for hair, eyes, and a mouth.

4 Cut a front and back body from felt. Make sure the body is large enough to put your hand in after the seams have been glued. Cut hands for the puppet from felt. Glue the front and back together, with the hands in between. (Do not glue the neck or the bottom together. These need to be left open.)

5 Glue the body to the neck. (You might want to use a rubber band to hold the body in place while the glue is drying.) Decorate the body with cut felt and other trims.

More Ideas

Make two or three puppets, and put on a puppet play with your friends.

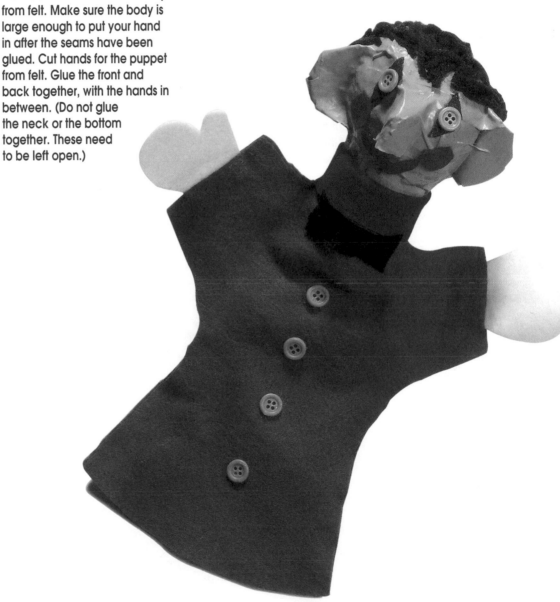

Bookmark Bonanza

Make some of these for yourself, or give as gifts.

You Will Need:

- greeting cards
- ruler
- pinking shears
- ribbon
- old envelopes
- canceled stamps
- pencil
- drinking glass

To Make the Zigzag Bookmark

Choose a sturdy greeting card, and cut a rectangle about 2 inches wide and 3½ inches long. Give the rectangle a fancy edge with the pinking shears. Cut two crosswise slits near the top of the card and two near the bottom. The slits should be just wide enough to slip a piece of ribbon through. Cut a 6-inch piece of ribbon. Thread it through the slits at the top and bottom. Cut a triangle-shaped piece out of the ends of the ribbon.

To Make the Corner Bookmark

Cut the corner from the bottom of the envelope. The edge can be straight, or you can create a fancy one. Cover the corner with postage stamps cut from old envelopes or a picture cut from a greeting card. Slip the bookmark over the corner of the page where you stopped reading.

To Make the Medallion Bookmark

Trace around a small drinking glass on two cards. Cut the two circles out. Cut a 15-inch piece of ribbon. Fold the ribbon in half, and glue the circles together back to back, with the fold of the ribbon in between them.

More Ideas

Try making other bookmark shapes, such as a triangle or a square.

Use embroidery thread instead of ribbon.

Newspaper Pumpkins

These jack-o'-lanterns will be around for many Halloweens to come.

You Will Need:

- newspaper
- string
- measuring cup
- water
- flour
- mixing bowl
- orange paint and paintbrush
- twig
- brown chenille stick
- green and black felt

This project is extra-messy, so use lots of newspaper to cover your work area.

1 Crumple two sheets of newspaper into a ball. Tie the ball with string to help keep the round shape.

2 Mix ½ cup of water with ½ cup of flour to make a paste. Tear some newspaper into strips. Dip the strips into the paste, and wrap them around the ball. Wrap the ball with three layers of pasted strips. Let dry, then paint the pumpkin.

3 Poke a small hole in the top of the pumpkin, and glue in a twig for a stem. Wrap the chenille stick around your finger to make a vine. Stick the end of the chenille-stick vine in glue, then into the hole.

4 Cut a leaf from the green felt, and glue it to the stem. Cut facial features from the black felt, and glue them in place.

More Ideas

Two or three of these pumpkins in slightly different sizes make a wonderful Halloween display.

Greeting Card Frame

Here is an easy way to frame your small works of art.

You Will Need:

- greeting card with border
- paper
- colored pencils or markers
- thin ribbon or yarn

1 Cut the picture out of the border of the card.

2 Cut a sheet of paper to fit inside the card. Draw a picture on the paper.

3 Glue the ends of a piece of ribbon to the inside of the card to make a hanger.

4 Glue the picture to the inside of the card, over the ends of the ribbon.

5 Close the card, and glue the frame over the picture.

More Ideas

Write a greeting on the back of the frame, and give your artwork as a gift.

Shaped Notepad

You can make these simple little pads in a hurry.

You Will Need:

- greeting card
- pencil
- white paper

1 Close the card, then cut out the back and front of the card you want to use for the cover.

2 Trace the shape of the cover on the white paper. Cut the paper in stacks of six to eight sheets at a time.

3 Assemble the stack with the front cover on top and the back cover on the bottom. Staple the pad together at one edge.

More Ideas

Add your name on the cover with glue and glitter.

Title Index

Subject Index

Look What You Can Make With
PLASTIC BOTTLES AND TUBS

Over 80 Pictured Crafts and Dozens of Other Ideas

Edited by Kathy Ross

Look What You Can Make With

Plastic Bottles
and Tubs

Edited by Kathy Ross
Photographs by Hank Schneider

Boyds Mills Press

Craft Coordinator:

Kathy Ross

Craft Makers:

Kerry O'Neill
Kathy Ross

Contributors:

Dorothy F. Appleton	Norah Grubmeyer	Jane K. Priewe
Katherine Corliss Bartow	Edna Harrington	Kathy Ross
Dorris Caines	Joann M. Hart	Andrew Smith
Jennifer Carling	Murley Kay Kight	Matthew Stockton
Barbara Casper	Karen Kremsreiter	Marilyn Thomason
Marie E. Cecchini	Lory MacRae	Sharon Dunn Umnik
Rosie Centrone	Judy Manchanda	S. Uslan
Mindy Cherez	Carol McCall	Jan J. Van Pelt
Kent Douglas	Donna Miers	Frances Wales
Paige Matthews Eckard	Clare Mishica	Dava Walker
Laurie Edwards	June Rose Mobly	D. A. Woodliff
JoAnn Fluegeman	Sandra J. Noll	Mildred K. Zibulka
Mary Galligan	James W. Perrin, Jr.	Patsy N. Zimmerman

Copyright © 2001 by Boyds Mills Press
All rights reserved

Published by Bell Books
Boyds Mills Press, Inc.
A Highlights Company
815 Church Street
Honesdale, Pennsylvania 18431
Printed in China

U.S. Cataloging-in-Publication Data
   (Library of Congress Standards)

Look what you can make with plastic bottles and tubs : over 80 pictured crafts
and dozens of other ideas / edited by Kathy Ross ; photographs by Hank
Schneider. — 1st ed.
[48] p. : col. photos. ; cm.
Includes index.
Summary: Toys, games, and other things to make from plastic bottles and tubs.
ISBN: 1-56397-567-X
1. Plastic bottle craft — Juvenile literature. 2. Plastics craft — Juvenile
literature . [1. Plastic bottle craft. 2. Plastics craft .] I. Schneider,
Hank. II. Title.
745.572 21 2001 AC CIP
2001091961

First edition, 2001
Books in this series originally designed by Lorianne Siomades
The text of this book is set in 10-point Avant Garde Demi, titles 43-point Gill Sans Extra Bold

Visit our Web site at www.boydsmillspress.com

10 9 8 7 6 5 4 3 2 1

Getting Started

This book is filled with fun, easy-to-make crafts, and each one begins with a plastic bottle or tub. You'll find a wide variety of things to make, including toys, games, and gifts.

Directions

Before you start each craft, read the directions and look closely at the photograph, but remember—it's up to you to make the craft your own. If we decorate a craft with markers but you want to use glitter paint and stickers, go for it. Feel free to stray from our directions and invent new crafts.

Work Area

It's a good idea to keep your work area covered. Old newspapers, brown paper (from grocery bags), or old sheets work well. Also, protect your clothes by wearing a smock. A big old shirt does the job and gives you room to move. Finally, remember to clean up when you've finished.

Materials

You'll need a lot of plastic bottles and containers, so start saving now. Ask friends and relatives to help. Keep your craft-making supplies together, and before making each craft, check the "You Will Need" list to make sure you have everything. In this list we will often specify a certain type of container. For some crafts, however, more than one kind of container will work. Look at the type of container used for the craft pictured, then see what you might have on hand that is similar in shape and size. Also, since you'll need scissors, glue, tape, or a stapler for almost every craft, we don't list these supplies.

Other Stuff

When we show several similar crafts, we'll often list numbered directions that apply to all of the crafts, then specific directions for each craft. When you start a craft, make sure the bottle or container is clean and the label has been removed, if possible. Warm, soapy water is helpful in loosening labels. Sometimes you will need adult help scraping off a label and the glue that might be left behind. Every once in a while we come across a label that will not come off. In this case we use the container for a project that allows you to cover the label, rather than remove it.

Some containers are easier to cut than others. Soaking a container in warm water will soften it and make cutting easier. If you are having trouble cutting a container, ask for adult help.

Several of the projects call for paint. Because the bottles and tubs are plastic, poster paint is not the best choice. The best paint for these projects is a non-toxic acrylic paint. This is readily available in craft stores.

That's about all. So, choose a craft and check your container stash for just the right one for the job, and have fun. Before you know it, you'll be showing everyone what you made with plastic bottles and tubs.

Bottle Town

Turn bottles into an entire neighborhood.

You Will Need:

- plastic bottles
- construction paper
- markers
- craft beads, rickrack, sequins, pompons, craft feathers, yarn
- poster board
- hole punch
- metal paper fasteners
- cotton balls
- tops from old lipstick or glue-stick tubes
- lids and caps
- small plastic pill bottles
- masking tape

To Make the Houses

Cut around each bottle about 3 to 5 inches from the bottom. The bottom of the bottle will become the house. Cut doors and windows from paper, and glue them to the house. Add details with markers, beads, and other trims. Fold a piece of poster board in half, and cut a roof for the house. Punch a hole in the back top edge of the house and in the back center of the roof. Attach the roof to the house with a paper fastener so that the roof will open. Use cut paper and other decorations to add details to the roof, such as a chimney. Glue a puff of cotton to the top of the chimney for smoke.

To Make the Tube Puppets

Snip some fuzz off the side of a pompon for colorful hair. Glue the hair to the top of the tube. Punch eyes from paper. Add pupils with a marker. Glue the eyes to the tube. Glue a tiny pompon to the tube for a nose. Add other trims. Slip the tubes over your fingers to use as fingerpuppets.

To Make the Lid People

Glue a variety of lids and caps together to create a person. Add details with ribbon, buttons, and other items.

To Make the Pill-Bottle Pals

To make people, cover the top part of the bottle with two rows of masking tape for the head. Color the tape with markers, and draw on a face. Add yarn hair. You might want to add hair ribbons to make a girl. Wrap the bottom half of the bottle in construction paper for the clothes. Trim with rickrack or other decorations.

For an animal, leave the bottle uncovered, or wrap in construction paper. Add details using markers and trims. Stuff the inside of the bottle with cotton balls to give the puppet a snug fit on your finger.

More Ideas

Use bottles of different colors and sizes to make a whole neighborhood of houses. How about an apartment building made from a tall bottle? You might want to add a fire station made from a large red detergent bottle. You really should have a library! What else?

Glue lids on the people for hats. Try using wiggle eyes, trims, tiny beads, and buttons for your tube puppets. Let your imagination take over, and make your people as varied and interesting as real people.

For animals, tip the bottles sideways and use the bottoms for the faces.

Comet Toy

Make this comet for some outdoor fun.

You Will Need:

- round plastic bottle with cap
- colored tissue paper
- colored plastic tape

1 Cut the top part off the bottle for the nose of the comet. Leave the cap on the bottle.

2 Cut long strips of colorful tissue paper for the tail.

3 Glue the ends of the tissue-paper strips around the inside of the bottle. Let the glue dry.

4 Decorate the outside of the bottle with strips of colored plastic tape. Toss the comet into the air, and watch the flowing tail follow as it falls.

More Ideas

Make one for Independence Day with red, white, and blue streamers.

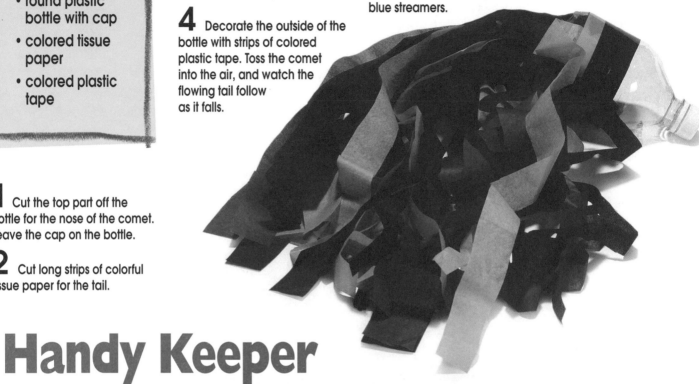

Handy Keeper

Here's a fancy container for storing tiny items.

You Will Need:

- container with plastic lid
- wallpaper scrap
- old greeting card picture
- permanent marker

1 Cover the container with wallpaper.

2 Cut a picture from an old greeting card. Glue the picture to the side of the container.

3 Label the top with the name of what you plan to store in it.

More Ideas

Make a matching set of two or three containers for your mom or dad to store nuts and bolts, sugar packets, or small treasures.

Clowning Around

Use these puppets to put on a show.

You Will Need:

- plastic dish-soap bottles
- medium-size plastic-foam ball
- foot-long stick or dowel
- fabric
- two wooden beads
- felt, pompons, yarn, ribbon, chenille sticks
- aluminum foil
- colored tissue paper
- rubber band
- cotton

More Ideas

Cut out white-felt wings to make an angel puppet.

To Make Clonker Clown

Cut the bottom from the plastic bottle. Push the plastic-foam ball onto one end of the dowel, and glue it in place. Put the end of the dowel down through the neck of the bottle. Press and twist the ball onto the bottleneck. Glue the head in place and let dry. Cut two strips of fabric for arms. Tie a wooden bead to each strip. Glue the end of each arm on each side of the top of the bottle. Use the felt and other trims to give the clown a face, hair, and clothes. When you hold the clown puppet by the dowel and twirl it back and forth, the hands will "clonk" against the bottle.

To Make the Clown Stick Puppet

Turn the bottle upside down so that the bottom of the bottle becomes the top of the clown head. Cover foil with a thin layer of glue, then with a sheet of tissue paper. Shape the foil, tissue-side out, over the head. Secure the hat with a rubber band at the bottom where you wish the brim to be. Turn the foil out below the rubber band to make the brim. Trim off the excess foil. Decorate the hat. Add details for a face. Glue a funny fabric bow at the neck. To make the handle, soak a wad of cotton in a mixture of glue and water. Wrap enough cotton around the stick so that it will fit snugly in the spout.

Vases and Planters with Pizzazz

Hold your flowers and houseplants in these unique containers.

You Will Need:

- various plastic bottles and tubs
- fabric
- pencil
- ruler
- ribbon, yarn, and trims
- paper plate
- rubber band
- chenille sticks
- food coloring
- toothpicks

To Make the Fabric-Covered Planter

Place a tub on the wrong side of a large piece of fabric. Trace around the tub. Measure the height of the tub and add 2 inches. Enlarge the circle by that amount all the way around, and cut the circle out. Rub glue around the inside rim of the tub. Set the tub on the center of the circle, and fold the fabric up, pressing the edges into the glue. Place another tub inside the first tub. Tie a ribbon around the rim.

To Make the Yarn-Covered Planter

Cover the outside of a plastic container with glue. Starting at the bottom, wrap the container with bands of different-colored yarns. Glue a simple shape made from yarn onto the planter.

To Make the Fluted Flower Basket

Glue the bottom of a small round tub to the center of a paper plate. Let the glue dry. Cut flaps every 2 to 3 inches from the outer edge of the plate to the bottom of the container. Glue the flaps in place around the container. A rubber band will help secure them while the glue dries. Remove the rubber band when the glue has dried, and tie a pretty ribbon around the container. Punch a hole on either side of the container. Twist two chenille sticks together to make a handle. Insert each end into a hole, and twist the ends to secure.

To Make the Painted Vase

In separate containers, mix a tiny drop of food coloring with a small amount of white glue. Use a different toothpick as a paintbrush for each color. Dot around the top and bottom of a clear plastic jar with the colored glues. (Use tiny amounts of colored glue, or it will run down the side.) Draw a simple design around the vase. Tie a pretty ribbon around the rim.

More Ideas

Instead of painting the vase, cover it with glue, then sprinkle with glitter.

9

Shipshape Vessels

Launch these boats in your sink or bathtub.

You Will Need:

- plastic detergent bottle
- white construction paper
- clear packing tape
- plastic drinking straw
- modeling clay
- permanent markers
- white dish-soap bottle
- hole punch
- toothpaste cap
- paint and paintbrush
- plastic berry basket
- plastic scraps
- dowel

More Ideas

Make passengers for the ships by drawing faces with a permanent marker on something that floats, like cork or plastic foam.

To Make the Sailboat

Cut the top part off the bottle about 2 to 3 inches from the bottom. The bottom part will become the boat. Cut the neck ring from the top of the bottle. Glue the ring in the center of the bottom of the boat. Let dry. Cut a sail from white paper. Cover both sides of the sail with clear packing tape to make it waterproof. Glue the sail to the straw. Let dry. Press some clay into the neck ring. Press the bottom end of the straw into the clay to mount the sail. Add decorations using permanent markers.

To Make Columbus's Ship

Cut the top part off the white dish-soap bottle, leaving the base about 4 inches tall. Cut around the edge of the bottle as shown. Use the hole punch to make portholes. Glue the toothpaste cap inside the bottom center of the ship. Paint the outside of the ship. Cut a tiny rail from the side of the berry basket. Glue the rail to the back of the ship. Cut a sail from bottle scraps and decorate with permanent markers. Glue the sail to a piece of dowel. Glue the end of the dowel inside the toothpaste cap. If it is not snug, wrap the end of the dowel in glue-soaked cotton to create a tight fit.

Windmill

Set this on your windowsill to welcome spring.

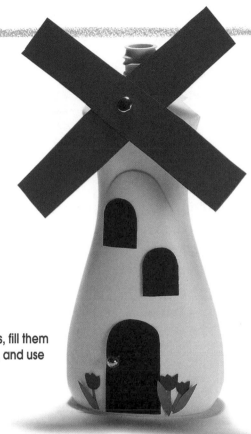

1 Punch a hole in the top front of the bottle.

2 Cut doors, windows, and tulips from paper scraps, and glue them on the bottle.

3 Glue a small bead on the door for a doorknob.

4 Cut two strips from another bottle or lid to make the paddles. Punch a hole in the center of each paddle. Attach the two paddles to the windmill with the paper fastener.

More Ideas

Make two windmills, fill them with small pebbles, and use as bookends.

"Let's Party" Hat

A hat like this will put anyone in a party mood.

1 Set the paper plate right-side up. Place the bowl in the center, and trace around it with the pencil. Draw a second circle about 3/4 inches in from the first circle. Cut out the smaller circle. Turn the plate over.

2 Spread glue around the edge of the opening. Set the bowl over the opening. Let the glue dry.

3 Decorate the hat with sticker stars. Blow a little air into the balloons, and knot them. Make chenille-stick coils by wrapping them around the pencil. Tie the balloons and coils with ribbon. Staple the decorations around the brim.

4 Cut long pieces of ribbons for ties. Punch a hole in the brim on each side of the hat. Attach the ribbons.

More Ideas

Use different-size containers for larger or smaller hats.

Use bottle caps to make hats for dolls. Glue paper circles underneath for the brims.

Teapot Tea-Bag Holder

It's teatime. This teapot is really a storage container for tea bags.

You Will Need:

- round container with plastic lid
- self-adhesive paper
- bottle cap
- construction paper
- fabric trim

1 Cover the outside of the container and lid with the self-adhesive paper.

2 Glue the bottle cap to the center of the lid. Cover the top of the cap with construction paper. Add trims.

3 Cut a strip of construction paper. Glue the two ends of the strip to the container to make the handle.

4 Roll a square of paper into a spout. Secure the rolled spout with tape. Cut four 1-inch slits around one end of the spout. Spread the tabs out, and glue the spout to the container. Use tape to help hold the spout in place while the glue dries. Trim the spout.

More Ideas

Cover the container with fabric scraps instead of paper for a textured design.

Berry-Basket Frame

Show off your latest school picture in this neat frame.

You Will Need:

- plastic berry basket
- pencil
- construction paper
- ribbon
- thin cardboard

1 Cut the bottom off the berry basket. Cut the center out, leaving a border.

2 Trace around the outside and the inside of the frame on construction paper. Cut the tracing out.

3 Weave ribbon into each side of the frame, if you wish. Glue the edges down on each end to secure the ribbon. Glue the basket frame to the construction-paper frame.

4 Trace around the outside of the frame on cardboard. Cut the cardboard tracing out. Glue the two sides and the bottom edge of the frame to the cardboard.

5 Cut a triangle shape from the cardboard, slightly shorter than the height of the frame. Bend the two sides of the triangle. Glue the flat part of the triangle to the back of the frame to make a stand. Slip your picture inside the frame through the opening at the top.

More Ideas

Add other decorations to your frame, such as sticker stars or tiny seashells.

Great Games

These hand-held games don't need batteries.

You Will Need:

- small margarine tubs with lids
- corrugated cardboard
- markers
- hole punch
- red craft beads
- plastic wrap
- bottle cap, round stickers, reinforcement rings
- small pompon
- clear packing tape
- thin ribbon

To Make the Apple Tree Game

Cut a 1½-inch band from the top of the tub. Trace around the bottom of the band on the corrugated cardboard twice. Cut out both circles. Trim the edges of one of the circles until it fits snugly inside the band. Remove the circle, and draw an apple tree with markers. Punch holes in the branches where apples should be. Press the other cardboard circle inside the plastic band, and glue in place. Put glue underneath the apple-tree circle, and press it to the bottom of the puzzle. Let dry. Add a red bead for each hole in the picture. Cut out the center of the lid so that you are left with only the rim. Cover the top of the puzzle with clear plastic wrap. Snap on the lid rim. Trim the excess wrap. See if you can shake all the "apples" in place.

To Make the Lion Skill Game

Glue the cap, open-side up, to the center bottom of the tub. Let the glue dry. Use the stickers to make a lion face. Drop the pompon into the container. Cut out the center portion from the lid, leaving an inch-wide rim. Cover the opening on both sides with clear packing tape. Punch holes three-quarters of the way around the rim. Tie ribbon through each hole to make a mane. Punch two holes, side by side, in the bottom edge of the lid. Thread a piece of ribbon through the holes and tie in a bow. Trim the edge of two round stickers. Stick one on each side of the mane for the ears. Snap the lid on over the face. Help the lion get a nose by getting the pompon into the cap.

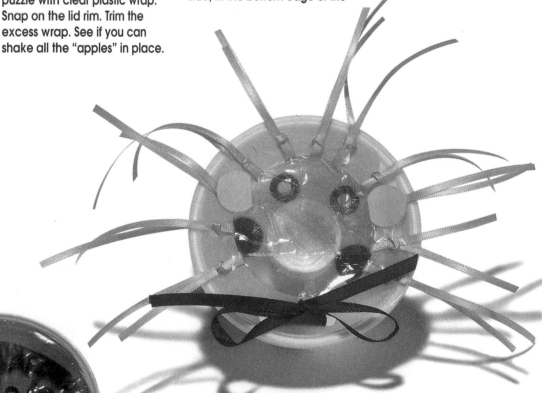

More Ideas

You might have another idea for a puzzle picture. You could make a face with holes for the eyes, nose, and mouth. How about a row of candles with holes for the flames?

Simplify the games by including only holes or a cap and a pompon, rather than drawing a picture.

...And More Games

Make these games, then challenge your skills.

You Will Need:

- milk jug
- hole punch
- chenille sticks
- paint and paintbrush
- string
- sponge
- medium-size plastic-foam balls
- pencil
- large plastic lids
- small pebbles
- plastic soda bottle
- round stickers or construction paper
- bottle cap
- pompon
- yarn
- plastic wiggle eyes

To Make the Toss-and-Catch Jug Game

Cut the top section off the milk jug. Punch holes around the cut edge of the catcher. Weave chenille sticks in and out of the holes all the way around the edge. Paint designs on the bottle. Let the paint dry. Cut a 2- to 3-foot length of string. Tie one end of the string around the neck of the bottle. Tie the sponge to the other end of the string. Hold onto the handle and try to catch the sponge in the catcher.

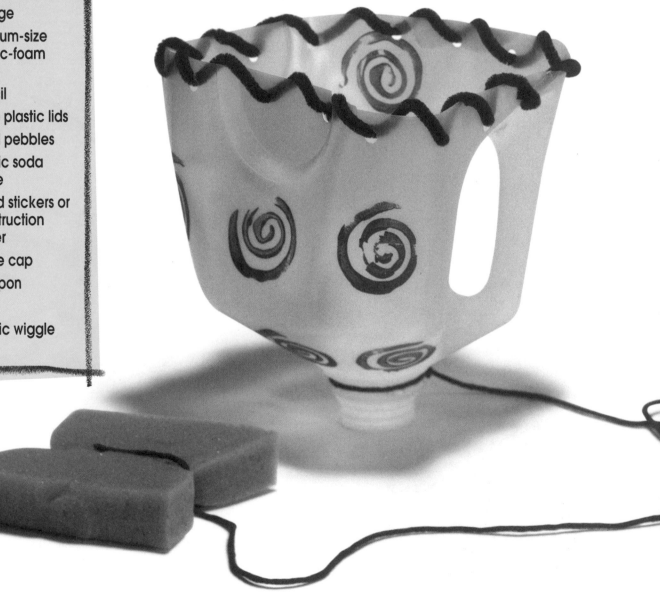

To Make the Wraparound Game

Paint the plastic-foam ball and let it dry. Cut a 2-foot piece of string. Poke a small hole in the ball with the point of the pencil. Fill the hole with glue, then use the pencil to push one end of the string into the ball. Let the glue dry. Cut the center from a large lid to make a ring. Tie the end of the string to the ring. Toss the ball into the air and try to get it through the ring. Keep going until the string is wrapped around the edge of the ring.

To Make the Bottle Clown Hoopla

Put some small pebbles in the bottom of the soda bottle to keep it from tipping over. Decorate the bottle with round stickers or construction paper. Firmly push and twist the plastic-foam ball onto the neck of the bottle. Press the cap into the head for a hat. Remove the cap, dip the edges in glue, then put it back on the head. Glue a pompon to the top. Add a yarn chin strap. Use stickers and the wiggle eyes to give the clown a face. Cut the center out of each lid so that you are left with the rims to use as hoops. Try to throw the rings over the clown.

More Ideas

Make the Toss-and-Catch Jug Game more challenging: the longer the string, the harder it is to play.

Have a friend make a Wraparound Game, too, and have a wraparound race.

15

Finger Soccer

This game goes anywhere.

You Will Need:

- green paint and paintbrush
- corrugated cardboard
- white correction pen
- plastic berry basket
- chenille sticks
- aluminum foil

1 Paint a rectangle of corrugated cardboard green. Use the white correction pen to add lines to the field.

2 Cut the berry basket in half to make the two goals. Place them at each end of the field.

3 Poke two holes in the cardboard on each side of the goals. Thread chenille sticks up through one hole, through the side of the goal, and down through the second hole. Twist the ends of the chenille sticks together to secure them.

4 Make a ball from aluminum foil. Your hand will be the soccer player for this game, using the middle finger and pointer for legs to kick the ball.

More Ideas

Take this in the car when you travel with a friend, brother, or sister.

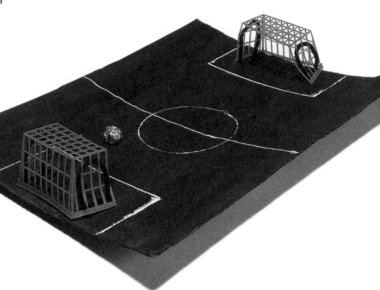

Disc Flyer

Play catch outside with this easy-to-make flyer.

You Will Need:

- large round bleach bottle
- construction paper

1 Cut the bottom from the bottle.

2 Cut small shapes from construction paper. Glue the shapes on the flyer to decorate it.

3 Hold the disc flyer between your thumb and index finger, and toss it to a friend.

More Ideas

Take this and the Sand Pail and Scoop on page 17 to the beach.

Sand Pail and Scoop

Build your sand castles with these handy beach toys.

You Will Need:

- two plastic milk jugs or large bleach bottles, one with a cap
- hole punch
- twine
- paint and paintbrush

1 To make the sand pail, cut the top off the milk jug. The bottom will become the pail.

2 Punch two holes on two opposite sides. Thread a length of twine through the holes. Knot them together to form a handle.

3 To make the scoop, leave the cap on the jug. Cut away the bottom of the jug and the two sides below the handle to form a giant scoop.

4 Decorate the pail and scoop with paints.

More Ideas

When you're heading to the beach, bring along clean plastic tubs of all sizes to make different sand shapes.

Garden-Variety Fun

Attract birds to your yard with an easy-to-make feeder and birdhouse.

You Will Need:

- gallon and half-gallon jugs
- colored plastic tape
- acrylic paints and paintbrush
- foam paint stamps
- self-adhesive paper
- aluminum pie pan
- metal paper fastener
- string
- empty seed packets
- hole punch
- clear packing tape
- sticks

To Make the Bottle Bird Feeder

Cut a large rectangle from the front of a gallon-size jug. Tape the edges. Use paint to decorate your feeder.

To Make the Plastic Watering Jug

Use the foam stampers to stamp a pretty design with paint on a milk jug. Add details using the paintbrush.

Then create the handy plant markers and watering jug for a cheerful garden.

To Make the Jug Birdhouse

Cut a hole on one side of a jug about 2 inches up from the bottom. The hole should be large enough to put your fist through. Cut shapes from the self-adhesive paper, and stick them on the side. Poke a small hole through the bottom of the jug and the center of the pie pan. Add more holes on the bottom of the pan, near the sides. Glue the bottom of the jug to the inside of the pan. Push a fastener through the holes in the center of the jug and pie pan. Tie a piece of string around the neck of the jug for a hanger. Put the cap on the jug.

To Make the Milk Jug Plant Markers

Cut a rectangular shape from the side of a milk jug. Cut the front from the packet of seeds you wish to mark, and glue the picture on the plastic rectangle. Punch a hole in the top and bottom of the marker. (This is easiest to do before the glue dries.) Cover the front and back with clear packing tape. Punch through the tape in the holes you've already made. Insert the stick through the holes.

More Ideas

Use permanent markers or self-adhesive paper to decorate the watering jug.

Make your own paint stampers by cutting simple shapes from a plastic-foam tray and gluing each shape to an empty thread spool.

Patchwork Purse and Hat

Wear your own designer accessories.

You Will Need:

- fabric scraps
- gallon-size plastic bleach bottle
- colored plastic tape
- ribbon
- large pompon

To Make the Purse

Cut lots of 2-inch squares from different fabrics. Cut the bottom part off the bleach bottle, just below the handle. Cover the bottom with glued fabric patches. Cover the top edge with plastic tape. Poke a hole on each side of the purse. Cut long pieces of ribbon. Thread the ends through the holes, and knot the ends to make a handle.

To Make the Hat

Cut the handle from the top of the bottle. Glue a patch of fabric over the two holes where the handle was removed. Cover the hat with glued fabric patches. Cover the cut edge with plastic tape. Glue the pompon in the spout. Poke a hole on each side of the hat. Cut four long pieces of ribbon. Tie the ends through each hole to make ties.

More Ideas

Use the hat design on page 11, and cover the hat with the same fabric scraps to match your purse.

Cardholder

This will come in hand-y when playing card games.

You Will Need:

- two lids from small margarine tubs
- metal paper fastener
- stickers

1 Poke a hole in the center of each lid.

2 Hold them together, print sides in, with the paper fastener.

3 Decorate the outsides with stickers.

4 Slip your playing cards in between the two lids.

More Ideas

Glue your favorite playing card from an old deck to your cardholder.

Nature Paperweight

Bring a bit of the outdoors to your desk.

You Will Need:

- small plastic soda bottle
- pencil
- cardboard
- green paint and paintbrush
- small pebbles
- dried flowers and leaves
- green yarn

1 Cut a dome from the bottom of the bottle.

2 Trace around the opening of the bottle on the cardboard. Cut the circle out, making it slightly larger.

3 Paint the circle green.

4 Glue pebbles, flowers, and leaves on the cardboard.

5 Glue the plastic bottle dome over the arrangement. Tie green yarn around the base of the paperweight.

More Ideas

Add tiny figures, such as deer or birds, to your scene.

Make several paperweights and give as gifts.

Mess Masters

This trash eater and toy tamer will help keep your room tidy.

You Will Need:

- gallon-size plastic bleach bottle
- yarn
- rickrack and other trims
- large plastic wiggle eyes
- pompon
- permanent marker
- milk jug or laundry detergent bottle
- construction paper

To Make the Garbage Gobbler

Cut the top part of the bleach bottle almost all the way off, leaving a hinge near the handle. (By pulling on the handle, the bottle should open and shut.) Glue tufts of yarn inside the spout for hair. Glue rickrack around the top and bottom of the opening to look like teeth. Glue on the wiggle eyes and a pompon nose. Add face details with permanent marker. Decorate the bottle with fabric trims.

To Make the Toy Stasher

Cut the top off the milk jug or detergent bottle, leaving the handle. Paint the bottle, or leave it the original color. Glue on a face made from cut paper.

More Ideas

Create other animal faces, such as a bear or a mouse. Use yarn to make fur.

Bottle Sculpture

Express yourself with this free-form work of art.

You Will Need:

- 2-liter plastic soda bottle
- old compact disc (CD)

1 Cut the spout from the bottle and save for another project.

2 Start cutting around the side of the bottle, going around and around so that you have a continuous strip of plastic.

3 Twist and bend the plastic strip into a sculpture, weaving the strip through itself to secure the loops of plastic.

4 Glue your work to the shiny side of the CD to display.

More Ideas

Set the sculpture near a window so the light will shine through the plastic and reflect off the CD.

Use two bottles of different colors to make a sculpture.

Cut geometric shapes from different-color containers, and glue them on the sculpture.

Mosaic Masterpiece

Arrange plastic squares to make a colorful creation.

You Will Need:

- plastic container scraps in different colors
- paper plate
- thin ribbon

1 Cut the plastic scraps into ½-inch squares.

2 Arrange the squares on the paper plate in a design or a picture. Glue the squares in place.

3 Cut a piece of thin ribbon to use as a hanger. Glue the ends to the back of the mosaic.

More Ideas

Use the squares to make a picture on a scrap of wood.

Use a colored paper plate for the base, or paint or color a plate with markers.

Wrap the plate in plastic wrap and use it to serve cookies. To clean it, just change the plastic-wrap covering.

Drum Set

Keep the beat while you keep secret stuff inside.

You Will Need:

- small, medium, and large plastic tubs with lids
- aluminum foil
- construction paper
- two metal paper fasteners
- chenille stick
- extra lid
- old compact disc (CD)

1 Cover the three tubs with aluminum foil. Cover their lids with glue and construction paper.

2 Poke a hole in one side of the two smaller tubs. Poke a hole through each side of the large tub at the top. Attach a smaller tub to each side of the large tub using a paper fastener.

3 Poke two holes through the side of the large tub. Thread the chenille stick through the two holes.

4 Cut two plastic circles from the extra lid to make the cymbals. Cover each cymbal with construction paper. Poke a hole in the center of each cymbal. Slide the cymbals onto the ends of the chenille stick. Trim off any excess. Fold the ends down and secure them with glue.

5 Snap the lids on all three drums. Glue the shiny side of the CD to the large drum to steady the set.

More Ideas

Write the name of your favorite music group on the large drum, or make up a name for your own group.

Desk Mates

Deck out your desk with these holders and helpers.

You Will Need:

- plastic dish-soap bottles
- plaster of Paris (follow the directions on the package)
- paint and paintbrush
- felt scraps
- sponge
- gallon-size plastic container
- yarn

To Make the Basic Holder

1 Cut off as much as necessary from the bottle to make the holder you want.

2 Fill the holder with plaster of Paris for a base. Let the plaster dry for an hour.

3 Paint the holder, and decorate with felt scraps. Glue felt underneath.

To Make the Letter Holder

Cut a ½-inch-wide slit out of each side of a bottle. Leave about 1 inch below each slit so there is a base at the bottom of the letter slit. Fill the bottom with plaster of Paris up to the slits.

To Make the Pencil Holder

Add about 1 inch of plaster of Paris to the bottom.

To Make the Stamp Sponge

Add about 1½ inches of plaster of Paris to the bottom. Cut a piece of sponge to fit in the top. Moisten the sponge as needed to wet your stamps.

To Make the Scrap Basket

Cut off the top portion of the gallon-size container. Decorate with felt and yarn.

More Ideas

Decorate the holders with photographs, pictures cut from greeting cards or wallpaper, or your own drawings.

Create more holders as you need them. How about a paper clip holder? Or one for pushpins?

Bottle Banks

Keep the lid on your savings.

You Will Need:

- 3-liter clear soda bottle with cap
- pink and black construction paper
- black chenille stick
- four film canisters
- large clear plastic bottle with wide neck and cap
- aluminum foil
- nuts, bolts, lids, bottle caps, and other items
- felt

To Make the Piggy Bank

Cover the end of the cap with a circle of pink paper. Glue two small black dots for the nostrils. Make eyes from the black construction paper. Glue them near the nose. Cut triangle-shaped ears from the pink paper. Pleat the bottoms. Glue the bottom of each ear to the head. Cut spots from the black and pink paper, and glue them on the body. Poke a hole in the bottom of the bottle. Wrap the black chenille stick around your finger to make a curly tail. Dip one end of the tail in glue and stick it in the hole. Cut a coin slot in the top of the pig. Glue paper to the bottom of the pig. Then glue the film canisters toward the front and back to create legs. Keep the pig upside down and undisturbed until the glue has dried.

To Make the Robot Money Guard

Cover the the cap of a large clear plastic bottle with aluminum foil. Make sure you can still screw the cap on and off the bottle. Give the robot facial features using nuts, bolts, and other items. Glue square panels of felt to the front and the back. Give the robot an array of buttons and switches using your caps and other objects.

More Ideas

Use other materials to make your favorite animals or characters. You could use craft feathers to make a bird or cotton balls to make a rabbit.

Jingle Ghosts

Are those ghosts ringing?

You Will Need:
- plastic milk jug
- hole punch
- thread
- jingle bells

1 Cut ghost shapes from the sides of the milk jug.

2 Punch eyeholes in the head of each ghost.

3 Poke a small hole in the top of each ghost. Tie a loop of thread through each hole to make a hanger. Poke a small hole in the bottom of each ghost. Thread a jingle bell onto a piece of thread, and tie the thread to the ghost.

More Ideas

Hang the ghosts in a breezy place to hear the bells jingle.

Make shapes for other holidays, such as Christmas or Independence Day.

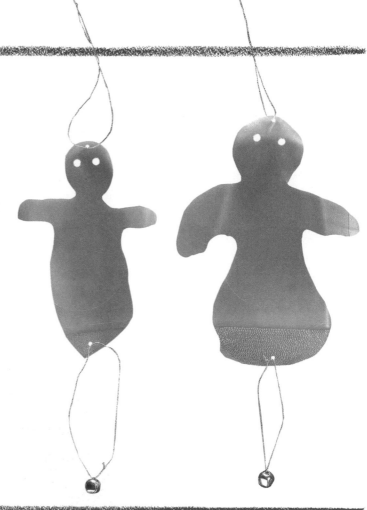

Pincushion

This is just what a sewer needs.

You Will Need:
- margarine tub with lid
- cotton balls
- fabric
- rickrack, ribbon, and other trims

1 Cut the center from the lid, leaving the narrow rim around the outside.

2 Stuff the tub with cotton balls.

3 Squeeze glue around the top edge of the tub. Lay a piece of fabric over the top of the tub, and snap the lid rim over the fabric to secure it. Trim off the excess fabric around the outside.

4 Decorate with rickrack and other trims.

More Ideas

Pincushions don't have to be square. Look for rectangular tubs with lids.

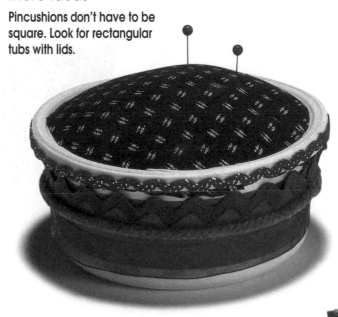

29

Bathroom Basketries

Scrub-a-dub-dub! Someone you know would like these baskets to store soap and such.

You Will Need:

- round plastic food containers
- fabric
- ruler
- pencil
- ribbon
- plastic dish-soap bottle
- paper
- sponge
- permanent marker
- hole punch
- two long shoelaces

To Make the Soap Basket

Place a plastic container in the center of the fabric. Measure the height of the container. Add about 1½ inches to this measurement. Measure the fabric starting from the bottom of the container until you reach the total measurement you want. Make small marks on the fabric with the pencil, going all the way around the container. (You should see a circle forming.) Cut the circle out. Squeeze glue around the inside rim of the container. Place the container in the center of the fabric. Pull the fabric up around the container and press the edges into the glue. Work the fabric evenly around the rim. Let the glue dry. Tie a ribbon around the outside.

To Make the Toothy Toothbrush Holder

Cut the top part off the dish-soap bottle. Cut rounded sections out of the front and the back of the bottle so that the sides look like the roots of a tooth. Poke a few holes in the bottom for drainage. Press a piece of scrap paper into the bottom of the bottle to make a pattern. Trim off the excess paper from the pattern so that it fits in the bottom. Use the pattern to cut a piece of sponge. Place the sponge in the bottom of the holder. Write a name with permanent marker on the front.

To Make the Shower Caddy

Poke three holes in the bottom of each container. Poke or punch a hole on the top and bottom of opposite sides of each container. Knot the end of one shoelace. Thread the other end in the bottom hole of one container and out the top hole on the same side. Pull the lace tight, then add the second container, and then the third. Do the same thing with the other shoelace on the opposite sides. Arrange the containers so they are evenly spaced and hang straight. Tie the two loose ends of the laces together at the top to create a hanger. Hang this caddy over the shower fixture to hold bath and shower supplies.

More Ideas

Turn the soap basket into a planter by lining it with an identical container. It could also make a terrific dresser catchall for coins, jewelry, or small toys.

Tom

Money-Holder Necklace

This necklace is perfect for keeping track of your lunch money.

You Will Need:

- film canister
- yarn
- pencil with a point
- craft beads
- rickrack or other trims

1 Poke a tiny hole in the center of the lid.

2 Cut a 2-foot piece of yarn. Thread the two ends of the yarn down from the top through the hole in the lid. (You may need a pencil to help push the ends through.) Knot the two ends together, and pull the knot up tight against the inside of the lid.

3 Thread craft beads onto the double strand of yarn outside the lid. Slide the beads down.

4 Decorate the outside of the canister with rickrack or other trims. Wear the necklace around your neck so your money is there when you need it.

More Ideas

Make the holder without the yarn necklace. Store paper clips inside.

Raggedy Crayon Doll

This little helper can hold an armful.

You Will Need:

- plastic dish-soap bottle
- hole punch
- yarn
- felt
- two small buttons
- rickrack and other trims

1 Cut off the top half of the bottle, leaving an oval-shaped piece attached to the back.

2 Punch holes around the head. Cut pieces of yarn. Tie two pieces through each hole to make the hair.

3 Cut a triangle nose from felt. Glue the nose, two button eyes, and a yarn smile to the head.

4 Cut two arms from felt. Cut two hands, and glue one to the end of each arm. Glue an arm on each side.

5 Decorate with rickrack and other trims.

More Ideas

Use curling ribbon to make hair or plastic wiggle eyes instead of buttons.

Desk Aquarium

Keep these carefree fish on your desk or shelf.

You Will Need:

- 3-liter soda bottle
- masking tape
- colored plastic tape
- 42-ounce oatmeal container
- black poster paint and paintbrush
- light-colored construction paper
- markers
- string
- pencil
- corrugated cardboard
- felt
- green chenille sticks

1 Cut the bottle in half. Fold masking tape over the bottom edge to create a better gluing surface. Wrap colored plastic tape around the outside edge to cover the masking tape.

2 Cut a 2½-inch-tall piece from the bottom of the oatmeal container. Paint it black. Turn the bottom half of the bottle upside down to form the aquarium. Put some strips of masking tape over the dome to create a better gluing surface. Glue the black box over the top of the dome.

3 Fold the construction paper in half. Draw some fish. Cut them out so that you have two sides for each fish. Color the fish on both sides.

4 Cut pieces of string. Glue the two sides of each fish together with the end of a string in between. Use masking tape to tape the other end of each string inside the dome so the fish hang down.

5 Trace around the open end of the aquarium on the cardboard. Cut the circle out, and cover it with felt. Shape some seaweed plants out of the chenille sticks. Glue the seaweed to the felt-covered cardboard. Glue the bottle in place over the cardboard with the fish hanging down.

More Ideas

Make smaller aquariums from smaller bottles.

Add old aquarium decorations, such as a diver or a treasure chest. Glue small pebbles on the bottom.

Bookend Friends

Turn a pair of bottles into some very unusual bookends.

You Will Need:

- two identical laundry detergent bottles with handles
- felt
- plastic wiggle eyes
- white sequins
- ribbons and trims
- craft feathers
- large pompons

To Make the Elephants

The handle will form the trunk. Cover the bottle with felt. Glue two wiggle eyes above each trunk. Glue on sequins for toe nails. Cut ears from felt, and glue in place. Decorate the cap of each bottle to look like a hat.

To Make the Birds

Glue a long triangle of felt over each handle for a beak. Glue two wiggle eyes on the handle. Glue lots of feathers on each side of the bottles for wings. Glue a large pompon in the spout along with three or four feathers.

More Ideas

Put stones in the bookends to give them extra weight.

What other animal could you make? A lion with a yarn mane? A peacock with construction-paper feathers?

COLOR ME A RHYME

YOLEN ~ STEMPLE

WORDSONG ~ BOYDS MILLS PRESS

LIGHT, SHADOWS, AND MIRRORS

Highlights

FASCINATING FOOD

Highlights

Jane Yolen's Mother Goose Songbook

Yolen / Stemple / Hoffman
Caroline House • Boyds Mills Press

TO THE MOON AND BACK

LARRICK / O'NEILL

"What a Doll" Telephone Pal

Stand this friend next to the phone, and those important numbers will always be handy.

You Will Need:

- plastic dish-soap bottle
- 3-inch plastic-foam ball
- colored map pins
- yarn
- ribbon and trims
- felt scraps
- black permanent marker

4 Cut arms and hands from the felt scraps. Glue a hand to each arm. Decorate with trim. Glue an arm on each side of the body, then glue the two hands together.

5 Use the black marker to write important phone numbers on the dress.

More Ideas

Add a loop of colored tape to hold a pen or a pencil to the doll.

1 Remove the cap from the bottle. Firmly push and twist the plastic-foam ball over the neck of the bottle.

2 Push the map pins into the front of the ball to create a face. Glue yarn bits to the head. Attach a bow to the hair with a map pin.

3 Glue on rows of trim and ribbon to decorate the dress. Glue a bow at the neck.

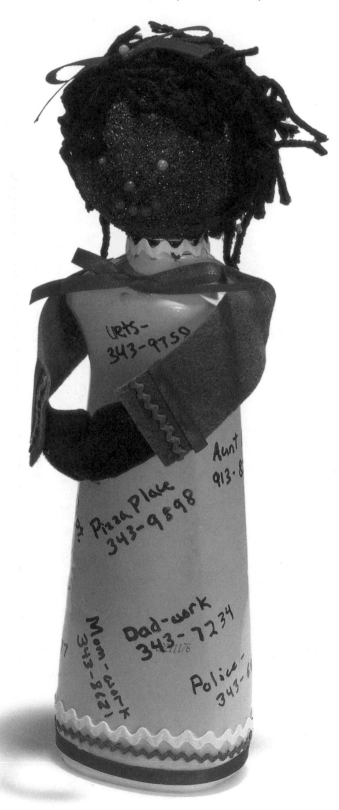

Hanging Planter

Here's a simple hanging basket to hold a favorite plant.

You Will Need:

- large plastic bottle
- paint and paintbrush
- hole punch
- twine

1 Cut off the bottom half of the plastic bottle.

2 Decorate the planter with paint.

3 Punch three evenly spaced holes around the rim.

4 Cut three 18-inch pieces of twine. Knot the three pieces together at one end.

5 Thread one length of twine through each of the three holes. Tie the ends of the twine together underneath the planter.

More Ideas

Decorate your planter with flower stickers instead of paint.

Add small pebbles to the bottom of your planter if you're planting seeds or transplanting a plant.

Bottle Bracelets

Wear this jewelry with your favorite outfit, or give as a gift.

You Will Need:

- small plastic soda bottle
- rickrack or other fabric trims
- small beads

1 Cut the spout off the bottle. Cut around the bottle to make 1-inch bands. Use scissors to even out the edges.

2 Glue trims and beads around each band.

More Ideas

Try covering a bracelet with yarn, either by wrapping yarn around the bracelet or gluing pieces of yarn across the band lengthwise.

Use old jewelry pieces to trim a bracelet.

How about decorating with nail polish?

Holiday Candy Cups

Make these delightful candy-cup favors for your holiday party.

You Will Need:

- small plastic bottles and containers
- pen
- white and green tissue paper
- plastic wiggle eyes
- pompons
- chenille stick
- ribbons and trims
- red nail polish
- yarn
- craft beads, glitter, sequins, sticker stars, sparkle stems
- felt
- cotton swab
- hole punch
- marker

To Make the Basic Candy Container

1 Cut off the top of the container. Cut away part of the back and sides, leaving the front and a cup, about 1½ to 3 inches tall, at the bottom.

2 Use the pen to sketch the shape you want. Cut around the shape so that it sticks up from the candy cup.

To Make the Shamrock Candy Cup

Cover the shamrock shape with glued-on bits of crumpled green tissue paper. Glue on wiggle eyes, a pompon nose, and a chenille-stick smile. Glue a bow on the stem.

To Make the Valentine Candy Cup

Use a pink or white container. Paint the heart with red nail polish. Decorate the heart with glued-on bits of white tissue paper. Glue trims around the container. Tie pink and red ribbons around the container in a bow.

To Make the Chocolate Bunny Candy Cup

Use a brown container. Glue wiggle eyes and a pink pompon nose on the bunny head. Knot two pieces of pink ribbon or yarn together in the center, and glue them under the nose for whiskers. Glue trims around the container. Glue a big bow at the neck.

To Make the Christmas Tree Candy Cup

Cover the tree shape with glued-on bits of green yarn. Decorate the tree with beads, sequins, sparkle stems, and sticker stars. Cut a stand from felt. Glue a piece of trim across the felt. Glue the stand under the tree.

To Make the Dreidel Candy Cup

Cover the dreidel shape with glue, then blue glitter. Add one of the four Hebrew letters found on a dreidel using pieces of silver sparkle stem. Cut off one end of a cotton swab. Dip the cotton in glue, then in silver glitter to make a handle. Tape the handle to the back of the dreidel shape.

To Make the Ghost Candy Cup

Use a white or opaque container. Punch two small holes for eyes. Punch several small overlapping holes to make a larger hole for the mouth. Punch a hole in one hand. Use a marker to color a wooden bead for a pumpkin. Draw on a jack-o'-lantern face. Glue a piece of green chenille stick in the hole in the bead for a stem. Attach the stem to the ghost's hand.

More Ideas

Line the cups with small squares of tissue paper in holiday colors.

Tillie the Turkey Centerpiece

This turkey will be the talk of your Thanksgiving table.

You Will Need:

- gallon milk jug
- construction paper
- red plastic cup
- red chenille stick

1 Cut around the handle portion of the milk jug to remove it. (Do not cut off the neck of the jug.)

2 Glue cut-paper eyes and a beak to the cup. Twist the chenille stick around your finger to make the turkey's wattle. Glue the wattle to one side of the beak. Glue the head over the neck of the jug.

3 Cut lots of paper feathers, and glue them on the jug.

4 Make a fan of large, colorful paper feathers for the tail. Staple the feathers together. Glue the tail to the back.

More Ideas
Fill the jug with dried or artificial flowers.

Holiday Noisemaker

Give this a shake and celebrate the new year or Purim.

You Will Need:

- hole punch
- two identical margarine tubs
- small pebbles
- ribbon or yarn
- sticker stars

1 Punch eight holes, evenly spaced, around the rims of both tubs.

2 Put some pebbles in one of the tubs.

3 Turn the second tub over so that the rim of the first tub touches the rim of the second and the holes are lined up across from each other as close as possible. Thread yarn or ribbon through each set of holes, and tie in a knot. Let the ends hang loose for a festive look.

4 Decorate the outside with some sticker stars or other decorations.

More Ideas
Poke a hole in the bottom of the noisemaker, and add a dowel handle.

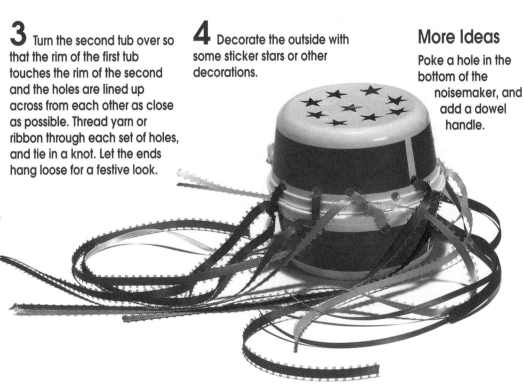

Clown Note Holder

This little friend holds messages that you can change in a snap.

You Will Need:

- construction paper
- 16-ounce clear plastic bottle
- paint and paintbrush
- felt, fabric, yarn, ribbon, and other trims
- medium-size plastic-foam ball
- pompons
- old sock
- old compact disc (CD)
- spring-type clothespin
- string
- markers

3 Twist the plastic-foam ball onto the bottleneck. Use yarn and trims to give the clown a face and hair.

4 Cut the cuff from the sock to use as a hat. Tie off the open end of the hat with yarn or ribbon. Glue the bottom of the clown to a CD.

5 Tie the clothespin to one end of a piece of string. Color the clothespin with markers. Attach a note to the clothespin. Lower the clothespin and note down inside the body so that you can read the note through the heart. Secure the string by twisting the head over it, leaving the excess string hanging down in back of the clown.

More Ideas

You can create other characters, such as a witch with a felt cape or a rabbit with floppy felt ears.

1 Cut a heart shape from paper. Tape it to the bottom of the bottle. Paint the bottle around the heart. Let the paint dry. Remove the paper to reveal the unpainted heart shape.

2 Cut arms, feet, and a collar from felt or paper. Glue them in place. Decorate the body using felt, ribbon, and other trims.

A Bunch of Baskets

A tiskit, a tasket, you'll love these springtime baskets.

You Will Need:

- construction paper
- pencil
- large and small plastic bottles and tubs
- thin cardboard
- hole punch
- metal paper fasteners
- pompons
- plastic scraps
- pen
- felt
- plastic wiggle eyes
- chenille sticks
- ribbons and trims

To Make the Confetti Basket

Cut narrow 2-inch strips of construction paper. Curl each strip around a pencil. Cover a margarine tub with the curled strips. Cut a handle from thin cardboard. Cover both sides with construction paper. Glue the two ends of the handle in place. Decorate the handle with pretty ribbons.

To Make the Jumbo Basket

Cut a bleach bottle in half. Cut a 1-inch strip from around the top of the bottle to use as a handle. Scallop the edges of the strip. Cut slits around the edge of the basket. Bend the tabs outward. Punch a hole in each end of the handle and on each side of the basket. Use paper fasteners to attach the handle. Decorate the basket with glued-on cut-paper flowers with tiny pompon centers.

To Make the Mini Basket

Use a small margarine tub with a pattern on the outside. Cut a handle from around another container. Punch a hole on each side of the basket and in each end of the handle. Attach the handle to the basket using paper fasteners. Cut a flower and leaves from plastic scraps. Punch a hole in the center of the flower and in the end of each leaf. Punch a hole in the handle, and attach the flower and leaves with a paper fastener.

To Make the Bunny Basket

Use the pen to sketch the head of a rabbit in the top portion of one corner of a milk jug. Cut around the head. Cut ear liners from pink felt or paper, and glue them in place. Glue on wiggle eyes, a pompon nose, and chenille-stick whiskers. Glue a big bow at the neck. Add trim around the edge of the basket.

More Ideas

Fill the baskets with paper grass or squares of colorful tissue paper and some Easter goodies.

Pedestal Snack Bowls

When you're ready for a party, fill these dishes with your favorite treats.

You Will Need:

- round plastic bottles or containers
- metal paper fasteners
- plastic cup or margarine tub
- permanent markers
- colored plastic tape

To Make the Basic Bowl

Choose the size bowl you want to make. Poke a hole in the bottom of the bowl and the base. Join them together, bottom to bottom, using a paper fastener.

More Ideas

For your party, decorate your balloons in the same color as your bowls. Use streamers that match.

To Make the Small Bowl

Use a margarine tub or other container for the bowl. Cut a plastic cup in half, and use the bottom part for your pedestal. Color with markers.

To Make the Large Bowl

Cut off the top portion of a bottle, and use the bottom for the bowl. Cut a scalloped edge around the bowl. Use a margarine tub for your base. Decorate the pedestal using strips of colored plastic tape or permanent markers.

Jack-o'-Lantern Party Favor

Fill this funny face with Halloween goodies.

You Will Need:

- pencil
- margarine tub with lid
- orange, green, and black construction paper
- hole punch
- green chenille stick

1 Trace around the lid of the container on the orange paper. Cut the circle out. Glue the circle to the lid. Stand the container on edge.

2 Cut a face and stem for the pumpkin, and glue them in place.

3 Poke two holes through the top edge of the pumpkin. Push the ends of the chenille stick through the holes to form a handle. Twist the two ends of the chenille stick together inside the pumpkin.

More Ideas

Make a bunch of these jack-o'-lanterns, and fasten them to fishing line. Hang in a window or a doorway.

Tea-Bag Caddy

This little teapot is perfect for a wet tea bag.

You Will Need:

- plastic dish-soap bottle
- pencil
- nontoxic permanent markers

1 Cut away the top part of the bottle.

2 Sketch the handle of the teapot on one side of the bottle and the spout on the other. Sketch the lid between the spout and the handle. Cut away the sides of the bottle, leaving the lid, spout, and handle.

3 Fold the parts of the teapot out and down on each side.

4 Use the markers to decorate the caddy.

More Ideas

If you're giving this to someone as a gift, you might want to write the person's name on the bottom of the caddy.

Hanging Creatures

These wacky animals will brighten your home.

You Will Need:

- plastic dish-soap bottle
- hole punch
- twine
- paint and paintbrush
- plastic scraps
- metal paper fasteners
- plastic wiggle eyes

To Make the Basic Planter

1 Cut an opening large enough to put a plant in one side of the bottle.

2 Punch a hole on each side of the opening. Thread twine through each hole. Tie a knot in each end to make a hanger. Decorate the bottle with paint.

To Make the Bird

Cut wings and a tail from the plastic scraps. Punch a hole in the wings, tail, and body. Attach the wings and tail to the body with paper fasteners. Glue wiggle eyes near the spout.

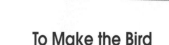

o Make the Fish

Cut fins and a tail from the plastic scraps. Punch a hole in the fins, tail, and body. Attach the fins and tail to the body with fasteners. Glue wiggle eyes to the sides of the bottle.

More Ideas

Add gravel to the bottom of the planters for drainage, then add dirt and some seeds or a plant.

Make a school of fish or a flock of birds to hang outside.

Make smaller creatures using travel-size bottles.

Title Index

Subject Index